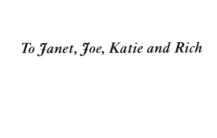

To Janet, Joe, Katie and Rich

And so, though Hannibal's claims to be reckoned a great general are manifold, there is none more conspicuous than this, that though engaged for a great length of time in an enemy's country, and though he experienced a great variety of fortune, he again and again inflicted a disaster on his opponents in minor encounters, but never suffered one himself, in spite of the number and severity of the contests which he conducted: and the reason, we may suppose, was that he took great care of his personal safety. And very properly so: for if the leader escapes uninjured and safe, though a decisive defeat may have been sustained, fortune offers many opportunities for retrieving disasters; but if he has fallen, the pilot as it were of the ship, even should fortune give the victory to the army, no real advantage is gained; because all the hopes of the soldiers depend upon their leaders. So much for those who fall into such errors from foolish vanity, childish parade, ignorance, or contempt.

Polybius, Histories, Book 10.33.

Put Hannibal into the scales; how many pounds' weight will you find in that greatest of commanders? This is the man for whom Africa was all too small – a land beaten by the Moorish sea and stretching to the steaming Nile, an then, again, to the tribes of Aethiopia and a new race of Elephants! Spain added to his dominions: he overleaps the Pyrenees; Nature throws in his Alps and snow: he splits the rocks asunder, and breaks up the mountain with vinegar! And now Italy is in his grasp, but still on he presses: 'N is accomplished,' he cries, 'until my Punic host breaks down the cit and I plant my standard in the midst of the Subura!' O what a sight What a picture it would make, the one-eyed General riding on the monster! What then was his end? Alas for glory! A conquered m headlong into exile, and there he sits, a mighty and marvellov in the King's antechamber, until it please his Bithynian Maje No sword, no stone, no javelin shall end the life which once throughout the world: that little ring shall avenge Cannae a of blood. On! on! thou madman, and race over the wintr mayest be the delight of schoolboys and supply declaimer

Hannibal's Road

The Second Punic War in Italy
213–203 BC

Mike Roberts

Pen & Sword
MILITARY

First published in Great Britain in 2017 by
Pen & Sword Military
an imprint of
Pen & Sword Books Ltd
47 Church Street
Barnsley
South Yorkshire
S70 2AS

ISBN 978 1 47385 595 3

A CIP catalogue record for this book is available from the British
Library

Typeset in Ehrhardt by
Mac Style Ltd, Bridlington, East Yorkshire
Printed and bound in England by TJ International,
Padstow, PL28 8RW

Pen & Sword Books Limited incorporates the imprints of Atlas,
Archaeology, Aviation, Discovery, Family History, Fiction, History,
Maritime, Military, Military Classics, Politics, Select, Transport,
True Crime, Air World, Frontline Publishing, Leo Cooper,
Remember When, Seaforth Publishing, The Praetorian Press,
Wharncliffe Local History, Wharncliffe Transport,
Wharncliffe True Crime and White Owl.

For a complete list of Pen & Sword titles please contact
PEN & SWORD BOOKS LIMITED
47 Church Street, Barnsley, South Yorkshire, S70 2AS, England
E-mail: enquiries@pen-and-sword.co.uk
Website: www.pen-and-sword.co.uk

Contents

Introduction

No toil could exhaust his body or overcome his spirit. Of heat and cold he was equally tolerant. His consumption of meat and drink was determined by natural desire, not by pleasure. His times of waking and sleeping were not marked off by day or night: what time remained when his work was done he gave to sleep, which he did not court with a soft bed or stillness, but was seen repeatedly by many lying on the ground wrapped in a common soldier's cloak amongst the sentinels and out guards. His dress was in no way superior to that of his fellows, but his arms and horses were conspicuous. Both of horsemen and of foot-soldiers he was undoubtedly the first – foremost to enter battle, and last to leave it when the fighting had begun.

Livy, *The History of Rome*, Books 21.4.

Late in the year 216, Lucius Postumius Albinus led two Roman legions and their attendant allies, amounting to perhaps 25,000 men, along a road in the Po River Valley in northern Italy. He was a patrician, a member of one of the ancient aristocratic families of the city of Rome, and a veteran of real reputation, who was first elected consul in 234. In this term of office, as one of the city's two chief magistrates and army commanders, he fought against tough Ligurian peoples, who inhabited the rugged country along the coast and into the Apennines west of Genoa. It seems in the next year he was for the first time elected praetor, one of four officers who frequently held independent command and possessed legal and military powers only exceeded by that of the consul. An unusual sequence as normally the praetorship was a step on the way to the highest office of consul. He was again returned to the consulship in 229 and on this occasion he took charge alongside Gnaeus Fulvius Centumalus in the war against the Illyrian queen, Teuta. Holding high command and doing well, Apollonia fell to his efforts and he drove off the Illyrian aggressors attacking Rome's allies at Epidamnos and Issa, even taking the war into the interior and imposing

Roman authority on a number of local tribes, while in 228 his command was prolonged so he could see events out to a satisfactory conclusion. Far more than just a military man, he knew the value of making friends in the new world the Romans were entering, sending articulate representatives to put a spin on their intervention over the Adriatic, at both the convocations of the Aetolian and the Achaean leagues, important powers in mainland and Peloponnesian Greece. Though his political hand may have been less sure at home, where he was not awarded the ultimate accolade of a triumph, despite one being given to colleagues who had not obviously achieved more than him and perhaps done less.

Postumius was not heard much of for twelve years after these events, though this should not be seen as curious and far from indicates his career was in some kind of eclipse. In fact, this man who had been consul twice and led armies in at least two significant wars would have almost certainly remained a senior figure of great prestige and authority in republican politics. Many members of the Senate would never become consuls at all and to gain the honour more than once was pretty uncommon in this period until the strains brought on by the second great war against Carthage.[1] Up until then, despite that Rome was repeatedly at war throughout its existence, apart from a few periods of extreme civic peril it was not customary for candidates, however glorious their antecedents, to repeatedly hold high office and lead great Roman armies. So that Postumius had achieved this in the High Republic certainly suggests his past good service would not have been forgotten, that his peers considered he had great qualities and needed to be brought back to the fore in the desperate times brought on by the invasion of Hannibal. So this was a veteran who had been recalled to the colours after a decade and sent north to Cisalpine Gaul by 216 at the latest and in fact was probably already there when he was elected a praetor, *in absentia*, to command the army on that northern front. An experienced and previously clearly a very competent officer called on to face one of Rome's oldest enemies who, now allied to Carthage, threatened to do even more damage to her cause in the north of Italy, while Hannibal made hay in the middle of the Peninsula. There is even a suggestion that many hoped that if Postumius had sufficient success it might incline Gallic warriors fighting in Hannibal's army to return to defend their own hearth and home.

Clearly this general, about to make an unfortunate name for himself at the time and who has almost been forgotten to history was no tyro. He was there to fight an enemy who had inhabited the region for centuries. These Gauls had, since first descending on Italy in the 500s, been long settled in the Po Valley and indeed a war band from a tribe called the Senones had captured Rome itself in 390. On occasions they bent the knee to the Republic but it had always been a frangible authority and in 218 many of these people had sickened of the thrall of tedious Latins, whose planting of colonies at Placentia, Cremona and Mutina had caused deep resentment. Postumius' early efforts against this enemy surely must have been satisfactory, as while still in the field with his soldiers he was given even greater responsibility, when elected consul for the year 215 despite suffering from the disadvantage of not being present in the capital to canvass for support. In fact it was a post he would never occupy, but again indicates the extent of his stature; not many had achieved the feat of winning the highest honour in Roman political life three times before.

The consul in waiting directed his march towards the homeland of the Boii, a tribe who inhabited the eastern section of the territory, north of the Apennines, watered by the Po. His army marched through country not far from modern Bologna, moving towards the foothills past Mutina where open land began to give way to a deep dark forest called the Litana Silva where pigs snuffled for acorns that had fallen from mighty oaks. But while they marched on an invasion road the Boii warriors had seized up the narrow body shields and long swords hanging on the walls of their houses to take up the way of war. These men and their leaders knew the country and had planned a devastating ruse. Correctly predicting the Roman route they cut through the trunks of the trees to the point where they were still standing, but the slightest push would bring them crashing down.

> The Boii cut into the trees at the base, leaving them only a slender support by which to stand, until they should be pushed over. Then the Boii hid at the further edge of the woods and by toppling over the nearest trees caused the fall of those more distant, as soon as our men entered the forest.[2]

Soon it was only possible for the marching soldiers to see a narrow road through the foliage, that would allow passage for the heavily armed legionaries. And the fight to come would be like no other, few of the men could have even seen their leader and less knew what was happening. Postumius had led his troops into the edge of the wood completely unprepared for the awful fate awaiting them. Let down by their scouting it was impossible for the men to know what was happening up ahead in the shadows of the dark forest. There were worrying sounds as the wind drifted through the foliage, whether it was natural or something more ominous was difficult for them to know. The creaking of the trees was not something many were used to, but equally it might signify nothing at all, and their line of sight was hardly more than a tunnel directly in front of them, which when the road veered, as it frequently did, scarcely allowed vision more than a few score yards ahead. This was not some ambush, with details filtering rearward of the front men being in trouble, but it seems all along the line the men were struck simultaneously in this terrible trap the Boii had laid. There was no hope, with hardly a moment's warning or cautionary shout the legionaries, allies, transports and cavalry animals all were crushed under the weight of falling timber, each tree bringing to earth its tottering neighbour.[3]

The terror must have been palpable as so many were struck and those who escaped death by crushing finding the Gauls roaring their war cries and weighing in 'sword in hand' to finish them off or to take the survivors prisoner. After the dust of calamity had begun to clear the final drama played out, when a few of the remaining troops, no longer in organized maniples but just collected in bands of survivors, with the consul elect at their head, hounded all the way, attempted to cut a path out of the trees towards a bridge over a river, on the other side of which they hoped to find safety. But on nearing what they trusted was an escape hatch they found it flung shut in their faces. The Gauls had already taken the grounds and formed to cut them off. Down by the sloping bank the last stand occurred, as the Boii warriors closed in. Postumius was cut down by men with long slashing broadswords who hated Rome, paying with his life for a lack of attention in reconnoitring the army's line of march. Leaving behind him a column of death, with many legionaries still in place in marching order, utterly crushed under the weight of the falling trees or hacked down as they tried in vain to build an effective defensive perimeter.

It is claimed that hardly ten men survived of those thousands frozen by fear as they marched under the dark canopy of threatening trees, but this is surely hyperbole. The killing power of falling trunks and branches was unlikely to be quite that efficient. Still the high command was wiped out and most of the men with them while the general's body was stripped and his head hacked off; a trophy that was then taken to the most sacred place to be cleaned out and gilded, in preparation to act as a sanctified drinking cup for their holy men.

The barbarians cut off his head, scooped out the interior, and after gilding it used it for a bowl in their sacred rites.[4]

But this was only the most extravagant example of looting. For the rest it was the routine, but vastly important task, of stripping off war gear from the broken bodies of men who had little real chance from the beginning. In the Shadow of Cannae this careless commander had constructed his own calamity and when word of it reached the capital the effect was similarly calamitous. Shutters came down on shopfronts, while the streets were practically deserted, as people quaked in fear at home. It took official cajoling to get the traders up and going again and something like a return to normal life, to 'stop the unofficial public mourning' while the regime back home decided upon a replacement consul for the year to come.

Dark woods filled with awful barbarians this time in northern Germany would bring calamity to a much later Rome. But if that disaster at the Teutoburger Wald brought the first of the emperors to demand that Varus give him back his legions,[5] at least that defeat had stood alone and in the grand scheme of things did not represent a major depletion of the imperial military establishment of AD 9. This bloodletting in peninsular forests was different, it came as just the latest military disaster that was draining the lifeblood from a republic that had experienced nothing like it before. Certainly in the First Punic War there had been catastrophes but largely they had been the result of huge losses of military shipping to the vagaries of weather, not to the sharp blades of enemy weapons. The numbers lost may have been terrific, but the psychological impact was not as great as so many of those who died were from allied coastal towns or if Roman, from the poorer classes who provided the city's oarsmen and sailors. Now it was not just cold figures, Romans of the propertied classes, including wealthy knights and even the senatorial elite had been dying in their thousands. There is a story that the sister of Publius Claudius Pulcher who had lost a naval battle in the First Punic War at Drepana in Sicily declared, when her palanquin was held up by crowds in the streets of Rome, that she wished her brother would suffer another such reverse so the casualties might thin out the populace a bit. This is not something that anybody would have said after Cannae, however appallingly snobbish they were, when every family from the highest to lowest was agonizing over the loss of their military age men.

It would be difficult to overestimate what a multiplier this latest disaster was in the bloody arithmetic that Rome was forced to face in the early years of her second great war with Carthage. The numbers of casualties that she had suffered in two years of fighting with Hannibal and his allies were just extraordinary, the sort of bloodletting that would have completely eliminated Sparta and Athens and even wrecked the prospects of a larger national entity, like Philip II's Macedonia. But by the end of the third century Rome was a place with expedientially more assets. Polybius, a Greek historian of great standing, made no bones about the military potential of the people Hannibal had taken on, claiming the Romans and Campanians alone could call on 250,000 infantry and 23,000 cavalry. While others listed for potential service were 80,000 Latin foot and 5,000 horse, 70,000 and 7,000 of each from the Samnites. The Iapygians and Messapians, who lived in Italy's heel near Tarentum, were claimed to be able to provide 50,000 and 16,000, and the Lucanians 30,000 and 3,000. Even the Marsi, Marrucini, Frentani, and Vestini from the hills east of Rome in the modern Abruzzo could at a push raise 20,000 infantry and 4,000 horse. Altogether when Hannibal arrived in Italy the men mentioned as able to bear arms against him – Romans, Latins, colonists and allies – probably amounted to over 700,000 foot and 70,000 horse. And even these numbers did not take into account some few north Italians like the Picentes and the Paeligni and also Bruttium allies from way down in the toe of the peninsular boot.

Though it must be remembered that the supporting evidence for some of these numbers is difficult and esoteric, if not actual flummery around high and low points in the census figures.[6] Yet we do have real evidence to go on. Roman sources dating from the first century to the fourth century AD, drawing on earlier records, report citizen head counts for twenty-five different occasions, beginning in the third century and ending in the second. Un-amended, these totals range from 137,000 to 395,000 registered individuals, with the lowest count being in the year 203. Though the numbers do have to be treated carefully, because it is not absolutely clear what the censuses they were based on were actually recording. Were they registering those citizens the military might draw on for levies or were they about information collected on who were due to pay taxes? Factors that might bring very different results, as all citizens of military age would be logged for the first, while heads of households alone would be recorded as responsible for paying up the required monies. Still though the distribution of the data suggests a measure of corruption in the reading of the original censuses, some kind of median around 300,000 can be accepted and however they are cooked these calculations don't take us far from the ballpark figures given by Polybius as he stacked up the odds against Hannibal when he took on the Peninsula Behemoth that was the Roman Republic.[7]

Of course the Greek historian's original total included Samnites, Lucanians, Campanians and others, many of whom were soon to be no longer dependable as a source of allied soldiery and in many cases even took up arms against the Roman alliance. These deductees must have reduced the Republic's potential military pool by at least 200,000, leaving after subtraction something between 500–600,000 available to be called to the colours to fight not only Hannibal's army of invasion but to contest those other fronts where there were enemies to confront. On the face of it these seem Xerxes-like figures, reminiscent of the vast and unreliable numbers described by Herodotus, that crossed the bridge of boats over the Hellespont on the invasion road to Greece. But the evidence is that there was no great exaggeration, after all the Samnites alone had had the military strength to overrun Campania, an act that triggered generations of war with Rome in the fourth and early third centuries. On one occasion during the wars of the 320s it is reported that Rome had mobilized ten legions, over 40,000 men in her field army so if this onetime enemy had faced such numbers on occasions with plenty of success, it is not unreasonable to assume that her own manpower reserve then had approached 80,000, of which half could have been mobilized to make something like an equal contest of it in the field. And this potential would have remained considerable even after Rome had despoiled her of a draconian amount of real estate as was the norm after defeat in so many wars.

But the sequence of Hannibal's triumphs had cut and blasted at the body of the stalwart Republic. The calculation of numbers of Roman and allied losses in the years up to and including Cannae can only be guesstimates. Indeed all figures in this period are suspect, casualties especially, due to bias in our sources and to failures in copying and translation over the centuries. Yet accepting this, it would be tedious to repeat this truism every time those facts and figures are cited. Or even to point up when a writer shows the particular axe he is grinding, though some of the more notable examples might need to be noticed. Yet now we must marshal the figures we are given if only to get a feel for how massive the blows had been in the time since Hannibal's army descended weary and half starved from the Alpine passes. The defeats on the Ticinus and Trebbia rivers could have together cost the Republic 25,000 men and not much less for the combination of those fallen at the Battle of Trasimene and the further losses in Umbria, when 4,000 cavalry from the other consular army were snapped up, half killed and half captured by Hannibal's celebrated cavalry commander Maharbal, surprised as they marched to help the already dead Flaminius. After that came the defeat of Minucius, when he had to be rescued by Fabius Maximus, that must have cost several thousand men and of course Cannae where even at the lowest calculation of losses overtopped 40,000 and at the highest reaching an improbable 70,000. So when the 25,000 lost in the forest to the Boii was accounted it only came as the latest stroke against what was a weakened corporation. Yet it was another crippling blow, this time at the hands of peoples who in the generations before the Romans had become very used to besting.

All these men fallen in battle would have brought the total butcher's bill to near 130,000 and even if this is high, because allied prisoners were loosed back home or just the consequence of typical exaggeration, much of any shortfall would have been covered by those dropping out through normal attrition, accident or illness. So if we assume the casualties of these awful early years amounted to approximately this figure, and Livy says more, having Mago reporting to the Carthaginians that 200,000 enemies had been killed and 50,000 taken prisoner, then the Roman alliance would have found itself with something between 400,000 and 500,000 men left to draw on, after these battlefield deductions and the defections in Campania, Samnium and many other parts of southern Italy. As we know that at its most extreme effort of mobilization the Republic put twenty-five legions and their allied auxiliaries under arms, well over 200,000 soldiers would have been in the field facing the foe. So when the men needed to man the fleets where included, who came from those citizens who fell below the property qualification for filling the ranks of the army but where still accounted in the potential fighting population, this must raise the total to near a quarter of a million. It takes no great expertise in mathematics to understand that at the height of her efforts the Republic was fielding at least half of its potential military manpower. These are numbers it is difficult to imagine in modern times and indeed are the kind of quantities that would be very difficult to see as sustainable for any people for any length of time, particularly in a society where there were large numbers of slaves, in industrial, agricultural and domestic situations, a total bound to include a good few fit young people, who might turn against their masters if there were not able bodied men around to control them.

It is only this haemorrhaging of manpower, with one Roman citizen in five over seventeen years of age lost in the first three years of the war, that makes believable that apart from lowering the age of recruitment to seventeen and the adjustment down of the property qualification for joining the ranks of the legions, that the state also turned to two sources of soldiery that would have been utterly incredible at any other time. Fit and able slaves were offered freedom if they signed up to fight and clearly a considerable number were tempted, as soon a commander called Tiberius Sempronius Gracchus is reported at the head of an army made up largely of such recruits. The second new stock of fighters came from convicted criminals, who were given the chance to redeem their lives by serving the state on the front line of battle. We get no mention of these men in action but certainly at least 6,000 criminals and debtors were recruited and armed with Gallic weapons captured after the victories of 223. Nor was it just a massive manpower endeavour: to fund these efforts of financial reforms and manipulation of the specie needed to be essayed; that would include draconian tax hikes and end with coinage, specifically the bronze As, being reduced in value by more than 80 per cent.

Not that this would be the only time the Republic would bleed so, after body blows registered by foreign foes. In only another hundred years other enemies would kill her people on almost as great a scale. A combination of Germans and Celts would deal Rome a series of defeats that certainly compare with the disastrous trouncings suffered by the Republic between 218 and 216. Indeed at the Battle of Arausio in 105 the losses suffered are claimed as exceeding those of Cannae with tales of 80,000 main line troops falling and 120,000 casualties if auxiliaries and camp followers are counted in. And if the terrible bloody arithmetic registered at the disasters of Noreia, Burdigala and Arausio can be seen to match up to those Hannibal inflicted equally the terror brought to both the corridors of power and the common streets of the Tiber city was comparable, before Marius crushed the Teutones at Aquae Sextiae and Cimbri at Vercellae. Yet in fact the reality was not comparable, because these barbarian hordes were never a threat like Hannibal. Firstly there was no real direction to their wrecking path; after their great victories the hordes split moving east, north and west but showing no joint intent to descend on the Italian Peninsula. And even if they had Rome's allies and subjects in Italy would never have been tempted to throw in with these giant intruders from the frozen north however dissatisfied they were with Roman rule. The Hannibal test would stand out as the most uniquely dangerous the Republic would face from a foreign power in all the years since the fourth century, when by besting and co-opting her neighbours in central Italy the city had made itself a Mediterranean power.

The final effect of the great Carthaginian's efforts would cause sea changes in the social and economic make-up of the Roman Republic and have ramifications for the rest of its existence, particularly as in the decades after the defeat of Carthage, the life of many Roman citizens remained deeply militarized and if the wars they were involved in were no longer a struggle for actual survival, more foreign adventures in Greece and Asia and police actions in Iberia, still up to 10–25 per cent of Roman adult male population would remain serving in the legions every year. Encouraging a march to empire the impact of which would be a key trigger for political and military developments, which played such a part in the replacement in just over 150 years' time of the republican system with an imperial Caesarean version.

This book is first a journey, a peregrination, but it is not the one that Hannibal is famous for. It is no part of my plan to reargue where the site of the 'Island' at which point his army veered off from the Rhone Valley, really was, or if fire and vinegar could have prefigured dynamite as a rock clearer on the descent from the Alps. Secondly it is a military chronicle but not the one many are familiar with that climaxed with the extraordinary triumph at Cannae. The expedition that the Carthaginian general led from the sun-kissed coast of the Iberian Levant, over the Pyrenees, through southern Gaul, across the wide flowing Rhone and into the horrors of a late autumn crossing of the snow-covered crags of the Alps is familiar enough for a famous English cricketer leading circus elephants to follow it over a generation or so ago, to a more recent televised 'in their footsteps' experience, by three Australian brothers on pushbikes. But not so well known is the ten years of footsore marching when Hannibal and his army traversed the beautiful green and brown hills of southern Italy facing the massed armies of Rome. This country planted by Oscan peoples, Samnites, Lucanians and Bruttians with Greek metropolises dotting the coast was where he contested with an enemy that called on all its military resources to hold him in check. He and his men marched along well travelled Roman roads or through trackless glens and vales but always with enemy armies not far away threatening to surround and crush him. An itinerary that the author was able to follow over several months when he was based not far from the putative site of the capitulation of Roman Legions to the Samnites in 321 at the Caudine Forks. Always outnumbered in this period Hannibal kept his mixed army of mercenary warriors, allied war bands and enemy deserters together with never a suggestion of sedition or mass absconding however dark things looked. Concerns about mutiny and betrayal amongst the army was never a perennial theme in the discussions in Hannibal's command tent and if some individuals did run, leaving his army and even ended up fighting for Rome, this was the nature of warfare in any age.

The defeat of Postumius in 216 is one of the least noticed of Rome's disasters in the Second Punic War, in the many accounts that litter the libraries of the world. The rest of the campaigning by the Carthaginian army that invaded Italy in 218 however has never lacked chroniclers. The great victories of the Trebbia, Trasimene, Cannae and the campaigns in the couple of years after, are an epic that has been told many times by many writers in many languages, from academic historians to enthusiastic amateurs. But most of these authors, while describing Hannibal's extraordinary successes and the equally incredible response of the Romans, who refused to cave in and mobilized the resources of central Italy to keep up the fight, tend to give the decade between 213 and 203 only the most perfunctory notice. Instead they concentrate in those years on the rise of the younger Scipio, his success in Spain and the preparations and execution of the invasion of Africa.

This is understandable, partly because Polybius, the source most respected for coming hot on the heel of events and considered very credible on military affairs, is only very fragmentary for what happened in peninsular Italy in those years. Also there have always been other problems in dealing with this topic, the informants who do detail the incidents of this place and time come much later and are much less reputed. Livy particularly with a tendency to play fast and loose with causality, leaving a picture where the Roman soldiers' ability to face any trick or trauma leaves little room for explanation of their failures.[8] Also the difficulty of making sense of this last decade in Italy is bound to make these events less attractive for those looking for a ready-made structure to hang their story around. But it is not reasonable, leaving such an extended phase of this extraordinary man's life hardly discussed. And the desire to know in detail what happened to him during this period has always been what I have come away with, after reading most authors who have chronicled the career of the great Carthaginian.

It is the achievement of Hannibal, staying loose in southern Italy and Magna Graecia for ten years in the face of the massively deployed resources of Rome and her allies that is the inspiration for this book, the one achievement of the man that seems insufficiently celebrated. So the motivation behind this volume is to look closely at this least covered, but deeply fascinating aspect of his life, when he seemed to traverse and retraverse the country at will, tangling with some of Rome's most important men. And certainly the ancient historians who provide substantial information for the period contain enough of colour and detail to allow an attempt to understand and tell the story of both him and his opponents in the later stages of the Great Italian War. Indeed if Roman literature began a generation before the Carthaginian invasion, aping Greek drama they discovered in contact with the cities of Magna Graecia, the birth of Roman history coincided almost exactly with Hannibal's Italian years when Quintus Fabius Pictor, a member of the Scipio clan, wrote the first real history of Rome in Greek, again showing exactly where the inspiration for the new discipline came. Though soon enough it would be disseminated in Latin while the likes of Cato the elder, a veteran of the Hannibal war, early the next century would produce the earliest Roman history originally written in that language. Livy, a provincial from Padua and the main ancient chronicler of these events to survive in detail, whatever his own shortcomings, is at least refreshingly honest on the failings of his sources, accepting not only the inadequacies of the histories of Rome first appearing in the very years under discussion, but also understanding that the family annals and funeral orations that many consulted, came from people quite prepared to massage or even fabricate achievements for their ancestors.

This is a narrative that hopefully does justice to a fascinating time when a people with a genius for war met the greatest genius of war. In the history of the western world, before the age of Caesar, there were many great commanders whose qualities can be appreciated even within an acceptance of Clausewitzian 'friction', that ensures so much warfare is subject to the vagaries of chance. An understanding that in conflict and particularly in battle the idea of the directing commander's hand always being the key factor is far from the whole truth, that it would frequently be the combination of individual soldiers and their officers, their motivation and actions, that might make the difference. Yet still enough can be gleaned from the sources we have to suggest the qualities of the leaders in this war could give the edge to one side or the other. That such a thing as a real general existed even if the decisiveness of their contributions was moot and that their talents should be noted in amongst the rest of the factors that led to a decision. And amongst these who are generally accorded a place in the 'palace of martial renown' the likes of Pyrrhus, Eumenes of Cardia, Epaminondas, Scipio Africanus, Marius, Sulla and Lucullus sit in the antechamber while in the throne room fighting it out, like smoking Joe Frazier and Mohammed Ali, for the title of the 'Greatest' are without doubt Hannibal and Alexander the Great. Of the latter it might be said that he did little more than burst a balloon, when he brought the vast Persian Empire down, that his triumphs were over nature and distance rather than stalwart opponents. It is perhaps not inappropriate that he had his toughest fight; his closest encounter was not against men but against animals when he had to deal with Porus' elephants at the River Hydaspes in 326. While Hannibal was triumphant so often against the odds, over one of the very best armies of the ancient world, showing tactical talent, unmatched in recorded millennia.

Nor is it just because of the intrinsic interest of the story of Hannibal and his key lieutenants, but also that of his enemies that makes the effort of covering the era of conflict that came after the extraordinary victories of 218–216 well worth making. This period was when Hannibal had successes in bringing over many of Rome's subject allies, great cities like Capua and Tarentum, important peoples like the Samnites, Apulians, Lucanians and Bruttians. While the rulers of Syracuse, the most important place on Sicily, also turned from firm friends of Rome into enemies after the death of their long lived King Hiero II and Philip V, the king of Macedonia, allied himself to an unstoppable looking Carthaginian juggernaut and promised to involve the Republic in Adriatic troubles that would bound to divert resources and energy they would have liked to have had available to fight fires nearer home. To make an attempt to understand the motivation and doings of both the great names and where the extreme paucity of evidence allows to even try and get a feel for the human history. Through archaeology and probability to feel what the conflict was like for those involved in the ranks, marching with the elephants or riding warhorse both into fierce battle and wrecking the farms, fields and homes of their enemies.

The aim will be to try and understand the events from 213 until Hannibal left peninsular Italy in 203. So the years between 218 to 213 will receive only the most cursory retelling in these pages, to give some context to readers coming new to the topic. It is a story that must consider how the divided, fractious ruling elite that led the Roman Republic combined sufficiently to face the avalanche of disasters orchestrated by their great enemy. A time when after having weathered the storm and by mobilizing sometimes over a quarter of a million men Rome had pushed the pendulum so hard it had come swinging back against the Carthaginians. But also a time when, despite the odds, Hannibal retained such a psychological hold over his normally hugely aggressive enemies that they allowed him to march at will, loose throughout territories they had controlled for at least two generations despite being virtually surrounded by numerous, hostile and often veteran armies. An epoch during which, though almost always outnumbered, he and his officers conducted successful campaigns in Campania, Samnium and Lucania around towns like Capua and Tarentum and down round the Italian toe in Bruttium as well. Remaining for much of the time a constant menace in their opponent's own backyard, even threatening the walls of Rome itself on one occasion and showing in numerous encounters that he and his followers had lost nothing of the abilities displayed in the earlier more famous victories. And indeed, when it seemed his brother Hasdrubal was bringing him the kind of reinforcements he had previously not received, looking like he might even finally bring the Republic to its knees.

It is impossible not to agree with Robin Lane Fox in the preface to his wonderful book on Alexander, 'Augustin, Cicero and perhaps the emperor Julian are the only figures from antiquity whose biography can be attempted' and Hannibal is not among them. Little enough is established even of his appearance, only that while crossing the Arno marshes a dose of ophthalmia permanently cost him the sight in one of his eyes. Yet it is still possible to know something of this complex man, after all contemporary accounts of his life were written, one by a man named Sosylus the Lacedaemonian who also taught him Greek, and fragments survive in quotations and as sources for later writers. It is no doubt finally from these we learn scraps of personal detail: that he left behind a Spanish wife called Imilce and an infant son when he departed New Carthage in 218 and that he had at least one dalliance with a local woman when wintering in Salapia in Apulia. Also character traits are discussed by Polybius who claims that his African informants stressed Hannibal's avarice while his Roman ones emphasized how cruel and merciless their great opponent was.[9]

Of course his cunning in dealing with both his own men and his enemies is recounted by many. A Greek writer could report almost with admiration that Hannibal would deck himself in wigs and other disguises so he could move unrecognized amongst friends and enemies, to learn what they were really thinking. While others report that he persuaded his men that those who died bravely in battle would be reborn, by finding a man who looked just like a particularly valiant casualty and convincingly presenting him as the deceased to his followers.[10] And there was his battlefield trickiness, illustrated so often by his successes in the early years as well as in the victories in the period on which we are concentrating. This had been demonstrated first in his Spanish campaigns when he ensnared a Carpetani army while they tried to cross the River Tagus to get at him and at the Siege of Saguntum in 219 when by a feigned retreat he managed to trap and dispatch a large number of the defenders outside the walls.[11] Then while fighting in Campania he defeated one army by making the Romans stand to arms by pretending to attack them, while his own men slept. So when the signal was given to wake and prepare a real attack, the exhausted enemy, themselves then asleep, were overrun and killed. Or near Casilinum when on a stormy night he divided his troops, attacked in relays and so vanquished another enemy force. A common touch can also be recognized in accounts that have the great general dressing just like his men, sleeping in the open with the private soldiers and claiming that his only indulgence was the magnificence of his horses and their accoutrements. Also he is shown as very accessible, no paranoid tyrant surrounded by his bodyguard, such that the son of a leader who had introduced the Carthaginians into Capua could without let or hindrance bring a sword into a party thrown in Hannibal's honour with the intention, though later persuaded out of it by his father, of assassinating the city's new ally.

Still many of the accounts that are left must be treated with caution, because it is largely Roman voices we hear who often feel strongly the need to denigrate their country's greatest ever adversary. But even viewed through an enemy prism it was impossible to not perceive Hannibal's talents and the charisma that could keep such a disparate coalition of peoples firm in Carthage's cause for so long in the Italian years. And as time passed and wounds healed it became possible for Romans of later generations to appreciate their most dangerous enemy, not least because their own greatness grew with his, as after all they did finally beat him in battle and win the war. Though it is not my intention to essay a criticism of Livy, Plutarch, Appian or any of the other main sources there will inevitably be some discussion of their claims because the nature of the evidence pertaining to this period is well characterized by Tom Holland in his preface to *Rubicon*, 'the reader should take it as a rule of thumb that many statements of fact in this book could plausibly be contradicted by an opposite interpretation'. An acceptance of which should be accompanied by another realization of the partialities in one's own writing to which I no more than anybody can be immune. Suffering a not uncommon sympathy with this classic case of the underdog achieving amazing things before finally losing out to the big battalions, that is almost bound to surface in this story of the fear and terror of war. Particularly as most can find something extremely human as they follow the young man leading armies across Spain, France, Italy and Africa who morphs into an ageing exile still eager and intelligent, but ultimately frustrated at the courts of kings who, in the egotism of unfettered power, fail to utilize a man whose qualities might have made a difference. If Alexander is touched with madness, Scipio somehow contrived, while Caesar lacks something of the human then Hannibal comes down to us with qualities of talent and humanity in a war against a lifetime enemy who is less able to secure our affections. As these Romans begin a trajectory that will see them dominate so much of our own occidental world though remaining always more extraordinary than congenial, despite the fact that so much of what we in Western Europe are, from codified rights and laws, to dreams of universal citizenship, derives from a past for which they were the crucial engine.

Maps

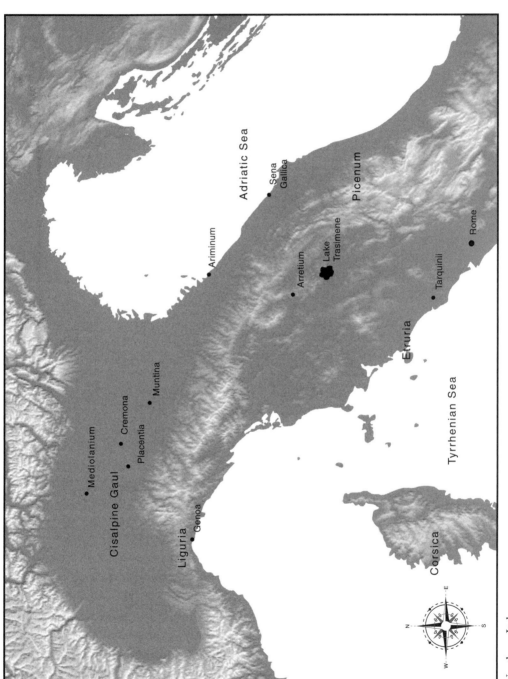

Northern Italy.

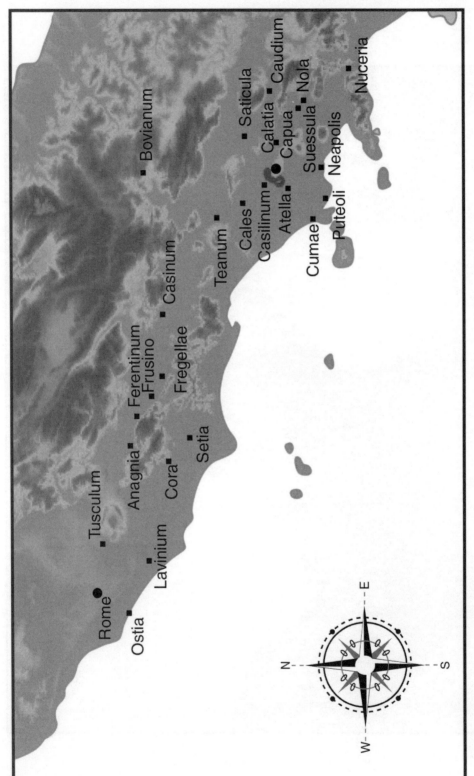

Central Italy.

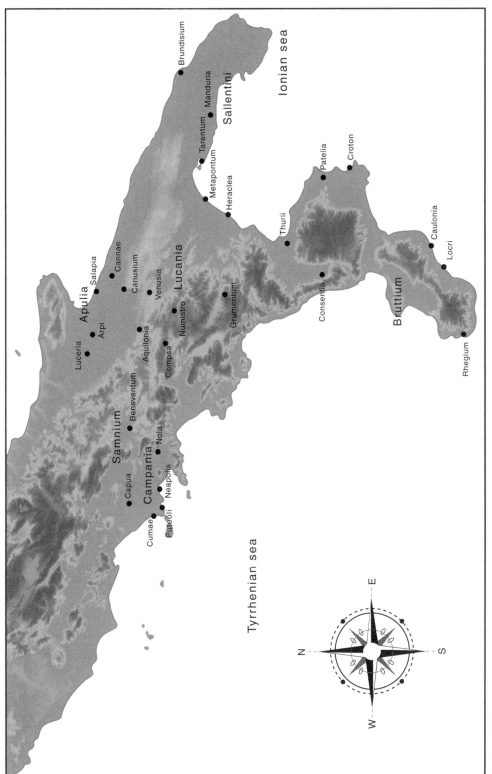

Southern Italy.

Chapter 1

A Second Round

One man, by delaying, restored the state to us. He valued safety more
than the mob's applause; Hence now his glory more resplendent grows.

Cicero referring to Fabius, in *on Old Age*

Rome seems like a prodigy, a city that won by the sword an empire
the like of which the western world had and would never again see.
A political entity of phenomenal longevity that no other imperial
competitor even came near to matching, yet that grew from a small
community that may have been something like Romulus and Remus' bandit
camp, nestling in its famous seven hills, on the banks of the Tiber. Having
thrown out their last king in 509 the aristocratic revolutionaries involved
found themselves caught up in social convulsions that threatened the very
privileges they had just acquired. These patricians, rich, old established
families had intended to monopolize the high offices of state, but they
found the commons unprepared to be permanently excluded from power,
and these citizens made their point effectively on a number of occasions
by downing tools and proceeding to secede. Climbing the Aventine Hill
and apparently preparing to establish a new and different Rome of non-
patricians, whether these were affluent nouveau riche, tradesmen or the
small farmers who represented the great bulk of the community who
produced the necessities of life and fought the city's wars. These occasional
bouts of self-assertion squeezed concessions from an elite whose snootiness
could never quite conceal the reality that their lifestyle was dependent on
these people threatening to leave them to it. These dynamics of permanent
class rivalry drove developments for many centuries after the fall of the last
Tarquin, enabling the development of a ruling Senate that embraced both
patrician and plebeian nobles, working with some popular representation,
all of whom contrived to believe that the revolutions that created them had
somehow followed hallowed Roman tradition.

Yet when the secession movement triumphed in the fourth century it was in no sense some dawn of an egalitarian Republic. As so often in such movements the benefits were only really felt by those who had the money to join the club that had so reluctantly granted conditional entry. Plebeians could now even reach for the consulship and indeed soon practice directed that in each year one consul must come from a patrician and one from a plebeian family, but the differentiation was only of lineage, never of wealth, though the entrenched snobbery of patrician bluebloods would always remain. And access to the great Roman magistracies if not denied by rule to the impecunious they certainly were by practicality. The process of climbing the political career ladder, the '*cursus honorum*', was only open to those with coin in their pocket. Though there was an element of meritocracy, after all the ruling class did refresh itself very occasionally with new blood. Over the ages there were changes in personnel at the top, families with impeccable pedigrees who claimed descent from the gods might fall on hard times and newcomers sometimes entered the Senate and won high office. And if all the citizens had some say in things, the reality was of a largely self-contained ruling class who made sure they took most of the good stuff going. There was no involvement on the model of Greek democracy, no pattern of lottery balls choosing amongst all the citizenry who should administer the city. The details may be hugely contested but the feeling is much more of a modern western democracy, a mixed system of government where the man in the street has the most limited and distant voice while a rich and powerful, almost hereditary ruling class, rule the roost. Yet still the citizenry could not be utterly disregarded because like our modern leaders these Romans also require their votes to win the highest offices of state, needing to work within the electoral approval of the citizen body, though it is hardly a surprise that the centurial assembly that elected most of the officials was heavily rigged towards the richer voters.

There were hints, particularly when the pressure was put on their pockets that the common people might get uppity, despite the Roman in the street being as much a sucker for the 'great con' as his contemporary counterpart, that what was good for the rich was somehow good for them too and one of the great nonsenses that with bread and circuses has so often kept the lid on many a real boiling cauldron of discontent. They could vote, they had to fight and pay taxes; these were the lot and the entitlement of the ruled classes. They also could find a voice, if a magistrate would coordinate it and the assemblies where the people met might make policy decisions that were clearly against the wishes of the Senate. This did not happen often but it did occur nonetheless and during the stresses of a war that seemed not to be being won, where the Senate could on occasions be traduced as both incompetent and corrupt, it certainly seemed on the increase.

Conservative, pragmatic and pious; the senatorial nobility was not absolutely exclusive, money and talent could purchase entry but only very occasionally; and its *raison d'etre* remained competition for the elected magistracies that brought power and reputation. Any who failed to at least try and compete to win eminence were an aberration and Romans denigrated aberrations even more than most people. The '*cursus honorum*' may not have been compulsory but a man who did not climb the greasy pole, to try and grab some of the prizes of power and fame in politics and warfare was certainly considered an oddity, sometimes facing censorious looks from peers and populace for not just himself, but family and dependants as well. Despite a history of dramatic change the Roman psyche remained somehow antipathetic when it came to constitutional changes; to mess with tradition was to risk the anger of the gods, who demanded an absolute adherence to ancient custom. A mixed constitution that, within an adherence to tradition and articulated love of the old ways, was strong and sufficiently successful that after the years of secession it kept the Tiber polity at least for some centuries from fracturing. By apparently defending everything they had behind them the Romans had transformed themselves into one of the most convention bound political entities in the ancient world. But in the years of crisis, when Hannibal rampaged through the Peninsula, a preparedness to bend the rules became manifest. Though innovation was always best if it could be clothed in hallowed tradition or given a pious overlay, if a man was to be allowed to stand for a position well before the proper age, he would do well to claim divine sanction or point to a precedent from centuries before. It might be chintz and reproduction, but the style the Roman favoured reminded him of the days of the regicide Brutus or the plough boy and military hero Cincinnatus, not the newfangled decor he felt was overtaking in his own lifetime.

Compromising in the shadows of gods and ancestors, these superstitious people had muddled through for centuries despite a grossly selfish, uncooperative ruling elite whose concerns were very clearly family above everything, despite sanctimonious claims of being prepared to sacrifice all for the fatherland. But party leaders indulging in sectional fights, were the common currency of any polity, just as contradictions and paradoxes are equally the norm in any human organization. The defining purpose of the lives of Rome's privileged was to win competitive elections to the highest offices, most particularly the consulship, the two magistrates who embodied for a year the power, glory and prestige that had belonged to the old kings. So not unlike their modern counterparts however counterfeit, a common touch had to be striven for. But unlike our own times the engine of election had nothing of party, what organization there was resolved around clan connection and clientage, faction and cabal. Nor was it just competition with one's rivals; in all the great families there was a perceived need to surpass or at least reach the heights of the generations before. Acceptance of just doing a decent job was not a principle that many of these characters could live with and this attitude seemed to have served them well in dealing with the nations around them. The Romans had risen to be top dog in the centre of the Peninsula they inhabited and believed they had been able to do so because of the unique qualities encapsulated in their constitution.

They were not a deeply self-aware people, introspection did not come easily. This population who prided themselves on the sanctity of their word were the same who after the defeat at the Caudine Forks in 321 found a loophole to renege on their god-sworn agreement as soon as their soldiers were safe back home. The venerable Samnite leader knew his Romans when he advised that his compatriots should either unconditionally free or alternately slaughter all their Roman prisoners, realizing as he did, that if they did the former there was a chance of their enemy appreciating the gesture and the latter would at least disable their military for a generation. But that any other course would lead to the worst of both worlds, as any conditions made to free them would not be kept and the released prisoners would soon be back under arms facing their own men in battle again. The ancients made comparisons with Sparta when trying to understand Rome, seeing two peoples whose identity was bound up with military achievement and who both showed desperation to avoid losing face in their dealings with outsiders. They were also both communities who had persuaded themselves that they were implacable, who only negotiated when the enemy were on their knees with a sword at their throat; a self image that turned out very useful when they moved to dominate and exploit those parts of Europe, Africa and Asia that they would soon find themselves in contact with. It was a reputation worth a couple of legions to bumptious Roman envoys who circulated the courts of the Hellenistic kings and the people's assemblies in Asia and Greece. But this character if not a complete fabrication had largely been self constructed in the years of the Hannibal war; before that they had not been so different. It had been no truceless war against Latins, Volsci, Aequi, Etruscans or Samnites. The centuries of conflict with these peoples had been peppered with negotiated peace treaties and armistices that the Romans were happy to keep or break as it suited them. Some cessations were indeed accepted as a result of defeat in battle, in an effort to save the city's precious soldiery. Even the vaunted refusal to deal with Pyrrhus, king of Epirus was hardly so exceptional, as that enemy hardly represented an immediate mortal danger. The Epirote had certainly hammered a Roman army at Heraclea in 280, but the next battle at Asculum in 279, so near to Herdonia and Canusium where Hannibal would take on Roman foes, was the archetype of the Pyrrhic victory where the winner was almost as crippled by their losses as the defeated side. So by definition not in a condition to attack a well-defended city like Rome, with plenty of unspent resources to bring to her defence. But the Second Punic War had perhaps justified the smug conceit of folk who claimed they would never deal with an enemy who was still in arms against them. Who would only dictate terms to either an opponent whose army was crushed in battle or who came begging cap in hand to the Tiber power.

It was as if they had been built for the struggle *à outrance* and that was what the war with Hannibal would be. And after the grim years of loss, of crawling back from the brink, had been finally topped with success, then it was possible to believe in the picture of themselves so carefully constructed from little but a blind old man rejecting the blandishments of a Hellenistic king with a broken army. A facade of confidence that would stand high and steady for well over a century after the defeat of Hannibal, and would later only be occasionally and briefly punctured as when hordes of giant Germans stormed into Gaul and the Po Valley at the end of the second century, when a tenacious king from Asia caused decades of trouble early in the first century or perhaps when a Thracian gladiator led a slave army that tore up southern Italy for a few years in the same period.

The ancient history of the Occidental world is shot through with epic rivalries. Hittites against Egyptians, Greeks against Persians, Athenians against Spartans, Syracuse against Carthage in Sicily, and later Rome against Parthians and Sassanian Persians. But certainly one of the most significant and dramatic contests was that between Carthage and Rome in the third and second centuries, particularly as this rivalry ended with the extirpation of the losing side and legend has it that the city of Carthage was ploughed under and the land it had stood upon, sown with salt, so it could never again sustain a major population. A contest forever associated with the epic of Hannibal, when for years Carthaginian arms were triumphant and the great man himself at loose in Italy for not very far short of a generation. These two peoples who had locked in mortal combat for the second time in this war had been familiar with each other for centuries and just because Italian, and before them Sicilian Greeks, portrayed Carthaginians as the dangerous other, should not make us forget this. Human interaction was sundered on occasions by ethnic tension, but the norm was surely contact, association and accommodation, even if enlivened by family, class and local rivalries at every level. There had certainly been colonies of Punic traders and perhaps even settlers in Rome and many other Italian cities for centuries and we know of at least three treaties between the two powers between the sixth and third centuries; Polybius had seen the bronze tablets on which the articles were inscribed. And if the accusations of child sacrifice flung at the Carthaginians has been subject to some substantiation when Punic sites have been excavated it should not be forgotten the Romans themselves carried out human sacrifices at the most harrowing moments of their history. Two Gauls and two Greeks, one man and one woman, were buried alive in the cattle market to appease the deities after the trauma of Cannae and this was not the first or last occasion on which it happened.

Even in terms of miles between, the chasm was not so great. In the lead-up to the final war, Cato the elder used the example of a fig grown near Carthage that had taken only a few days to get to Rome to show how proximate the Punic city was. Though his contention was neither very accurate, and that she posed any threat at that time was dishonest, the neutered African polity could never have ever challenged Rome after her disastrous defeat during the Second Punic War. Not exactly neighbours but they were very much part of the same world. Nor was it just a central Mediterranean world, the west too was very much 'Terra Cognita'. Phoenician and Carthaginian influence had been felt in north-west Africa, Iberia and the Balearic Islands for centuries and Rome's relations with a city in the Iberian Levant had even been ostensibly what ignited the Second Punic War. Even the south of Spain, if more of a stretch for the Italian lubbers, was not an unknown land and they would soon be sending armies, fleets and all the paraphernalia of power there, almost immediately after the Second Punic War began. Hannibal himself was very much a man of this interconnected west Mediterranean community. If he was born at Carthage, his formative years were spent in Spain; princelings from local Iberian tribes would have been his playfellows just as much as the sons of the Carthaginian blue bloods who had accompanied Hamilcar Barca to Spain. His formative years had included the very best Greek education could offer. Culturally like many of Carthage's elite he was the product of a syncretism that included African, Greek and Iberian dimensions. A real man of the 'middle sea' that had become interconnected over the previous few thousand years in terms of culture, lifestyle and Pantheon and soon after his lifetime was becoming advertised as a politically unitary place by Polybius, a near contemporary chronicler of the age. And finally Hannibal would find the winds of chance and his own ambition would take him from the far west in Iberia to the far east of the Mediterranean Basin, to spend his last years in the Hellenistic world of Alexander the Great's successors.

But as with the Greeks in Sicily, when Carthage and Rome's spheres of influence rubbed up against each other around the straits of Messene in the middle of the third century their relationship had swiftly changed from cooperation to rivalry and then brutal contest. A situation where earlier histories of amicable contacts required reinterpretation, to justify a war to the knife with people who not long before had stood surety for each other in the face of a threat from King Pyrrhus. In the telling of this story we seem to receive everything through a Tiber town prism, any possibility of a direct Carthaginian contribution was lost when the archives and libraries of Carthage were given as loot to Rome's Numidian allies after 146 and subsequently lost. Though within this tradition we can still hear echoes from the other side, as Roman analysts and historians happily mined the works of such as Sosylus and Silenus, Greeks who lived through and recorded Hannibal's campaigns just as Alexander the Great's tame intellectuals had chronicled the Macedonians' conquests of the Persian Empire and beyond. These Carthaginian headquarters' correspondents were quarried for details that could not be found in Roman archives and so can be dimly heard in the output of Livy, Polybius and the rest. A Roman tradition of research that went back at least to the referencing of Cineas, the friend and secretary of Pyrrhus, who wrote a much cited life of that warrior king.

A common cultural context remained, within which both sides played a propaganda game. The Carthaginian invader tried to legitimate his eruption into the Italian Peninsula by associating himself with Hercules, a demigod who approximated to the Punic Melqart, who had passed, with herds of cattle taken from the giant Geryon, from Spain through Italy overthrowing ogres along the Tiber on his way. Now it was Hannibal who had come to overthrow the tyranny of Rome and allow a revival for subject Italians and Greeks, if a convincing work by Richard Miles is to be believed.[1] This could be important in pushing his plan as Italian allies, Greek townsmen and even Latin colonists would be required to jump the Roman ship if the Carthaginians were to win real success. This idea in itself would not be decisive, but it could be important mood music that might allow deeply traditional peoples to justify their actions in dumping their commitment to the Republic and join what in 216 must have looked very like the winning side.

There were other factors that mattered too; class was of course always there and there were plenty amongst the Italian allies and Greek cities who were discontented, feeling exploited by local aristocracies who with the backing of their peers at Rome, ensured their own local power base. At both Nola and at Tarentum this seems to have been the governing factor, but this was never the whole story as often as not it was an aristocratic faction opposed to Roman hegemony that led the way into Carthaginian arms, backed by a common people feeling again their own potential. But that it was aristos who we hear of sending feelers to the Carthaginians should not blind us to the truth attested by the histories, that for most, the move to an anti-Roman stance reflected a desire for at least some form of social change in places where the Roman inclination was to set the status quo in aspic. Differences in political culture could be important too. There was always tension between a Roman political tradition, where the power of popular assemblies was more potential than actual, against places in Magna Graecia where the direct rule of an assembled citizenry was the order of the day. Foreign emissaries on arriving at Rome went straight to the Senate, but as often as not when Romans arrived to peddle their line in Italian Greek communities it would be the citizen body itself that would hear what they had to say. The stories of rough handling of Roman envoys by rowdy characters from the Tarentine streets, with a local drunk even defecating on one of the delegate's togas, in the run-up to an old war with that city are telling and reveal fault lines that would make a real difference once Roman power seemed shaken to its foundations.

Carthage, the city that would provide the High Republic with by far its greatest test, was traditionally founded in 814, though archaeology suggests early in the next century, by colonists from the great Levantine trading city of Tyre, over the centuries had become the greatest power in the western Mediterranean and this nation of shopkeepers waxed in wealth and power on the basis of their trading fleets. This state founded by refugees from

Phoenicia had found a way to dominate her patch of the middle sea that was almost the opposite of the road travelled by Rome, constructing a loose confederation of places essentially tied together by commercial self-interest, while at the same time suppressing most of the indigenous powers of the Maghreb and contesting for control of Sicily with local people and Greek colonists. An inconclusive contest that was interrupted for a few years early in the third century by the eruption of Pyrrhus, a stormy petrel tested in the disintegrating world of Alexander the Great's successors.

The Punic metropolis like Rome also prospered under a mixed constitution which Aristotle compares with that of Sparta and Crete. Claiming the council of elders with its twenty-eight members plus the two annually elected chief magistrates, the suffets, was equivalent to the Gerousia that comprised the same number and including Sparta's two kings. The tribunal of Hundred and Four was matched with the five ephors in functioning to oversee the actions of the city's generals and as a powerful court of last resort, and with presumably the citizen assembly of Sparta matching the popular assemblies in the Punic city. Though really there was very little similarity with this city of merchant princes, these inhabitants of North Africa were commercially and intellectually adventurous in a way that was the very opposite of Sparta's xenophobia, philistinism and contempt for commerce. It is very difficult to imagine Sparta producing the great agriculturalist Mago whose scientific expertise and reputation was sufficient for the Roman conquerors to make sure at least his written output wasn't lost when they obliterated the city at the end of the Third Punic War.

In the very middle of the third century an expanding Rome, now in control of much of mainland Italy, fought its first war with the Carthaginian Empire. In what initially seemed a contest of whale against elephant, it turned out the land monster was versatile enough to duke it out on the waves as well. Great sea battles, disastrous losses in storm-tossed seas, grand sieges in Sicily and an ultimately vanquished Roman invasion of Africa all ended in a defeat for Carthage in 242. Ejected from Sicily, and soon from Sardinia too, financially hampered by reparations laid on her in the peace treaty, the great African city immediately after the war was almost brought to its knees by the combination of a rebellion by her unpaid mercenary army and revolution amongst her Libyan tributaries.

The man whose expertise was essential in Carthage weathering this storm was Hamilcar Barca, a young general who cut his teeth in charge of the army in the last years of the war in Sicily. But having saved his homeland from destruction was but a prelude to his greatest achievement, creating a new Punic empire in Iberia. Phoenician and then Carthaginian colonists with their trading muscle had long been important in the very south of the Peninsula, rich with minerals mined in the hills and panned in its rivers, but Hamilcar starting from 237 transformed this loose hegemony into a direct rule, over most of what is now Andalusia and the Spanish Levant. In the process gaining control of a country that rapidly produced the money required to both pay off Carthage's war indemnity, and by drawing on numerous warlike Iberian peoples, could mobilize an army that might serve not only in Spain, but could further any other aims a Carthaginian warlord might contemplate. Hasdrubal 'the handsome', Hamilcar's son-in-law, took over for eight years after Hamilcar was drowned on campaign. This potentate established a new capital at Carthago Nova, present day Cartagena, as he kept the power seat warm for Hamilcar's eldest son Hannibal. This young man took command at the age of 26, on the assassination of Hasdrubal, and after a short period of military consolidation, embarked on the conquest of the city of Saguntum. That either advertised or instigated, opinions differ markedly on chronology and intention, another conflict between Carthage and Rome that would not be long in coming.

With Carthage hardly a sea power at all since the first war when she had been forced to destroy most of her navy, Hannibal had to travel overland to take the fight to Italy, something he must have intended for some time. The road through Gaul across the Rhone, bamboozling local opponents and skirmishing with some Roman cavalry on the way, and then over the Alps at a hard time of year took its toll. The 50,000 infantry and 9,000 horse that had left Spain may have been reduced to 20,000 foot and 6,000 cavalry but once descended into the Po Valley there followed a military tour de force that can only be compared to Alexander's conquest of the whole of the Persian Empire in a handful of years. We are so familiar with the series of triumphs that Hannibal won between 218 and 216, that it is sometimes easy to underestimate just what he did achieve. First bullying a mixed force under Consul Scipio at the Ticinus River, drawing a full consular force under an experienced general through a frozen river, while simultaneously laying an ambush, brought him his first full battlefield victory in Italy. Then after destroying this enemy he passed down through the Apennines, the limestone spine of Italy, through an awful swamp in the Arno Valley, before ambushing another belligerent consul, absolutely destroying his army, killing the man himself before sending his lieutenant to eliminate the cavalry of the other major force the Romans had deployed against him.

By 217 it was a changed world the Roman leadership had to face, and one gestated in a series of military disasters the like of which the Republic had hardly experienced before. They had known plenty of defeats in their time, the city had even been sacked by Celtic marauders in the early fourth century and three quarters of a century later her legions had gone under the yoke at the Claudine Forks, previous calamities that at least had allowed the Republic to germinate institutional responses to the emergency she now faced. The Romans had also evolved new governmental roles once the city's power had spread out from the limits of its original Latin environs, like the four praetors who could deputize both judicially and militarily if the consuls were absent and administer far away provinces like Sicily and Sardinia. Even the limited fighting far from home they had experienced before the Second Punic War had ensured that proroguing army commands (allowing a magistrate elected for a year to continue in his military role into the following campaigning season) had been experimented with, even if it was not yet the norm. It is claimed that this first occurred in a war around the Greek city of Neapolis in the 320s. Also importantly the constitution had long countenanced the appointment of a dictator in time of crisis, a common expedient in a number of Latin cities, which allowed the streamlining of normal partisan political practice; where the usual dynamic that demanded a sharing of the governmental spoils amongst a good proportion of the elite families was overridden in an effort to ensure both competence and coherence in the army command.

This most desperate hour now brought a man, whose coming seemed to offer a spark of hope to the battered Republic. Plutarch offers us two choices for the genesis of the Fabius clan; that they were descended from Heracles coupling with a nymph who lived near the River Tiber or a more prosaic derivation from the occupation of ditch digger.[2] But whatever the reality they were an old patrician family, well used to the reins of power and the feel of the consular seat on their buttocks. The warty but congenial man from this family, who would now step up to lead the state in its hour of danger, was an experienced old campaigner who had won his first consulship in the year 233. Born around 280 he surely took an active part in the First Punic War though nothing is known of it. The nobility of his birth and the fame of his ancestors must have meant he was early in distinction even if his biographer suggests he was something of a laggard in learning, particularly so in respect of public speaking, a fact that is perhaps corroborated by his being near 50 when he first became consul. But during this stint he was awarded a triumph for his victory over the Ligurians, a Gallic people whom he had defeated and then driven into the Alps and after that fame and recognition came hard and fast, making him the pilot to which the people looked when buffeted by one of the greatest tempests in their history and meaning his earlier accomplishment turned out to be only a preamble to the greatest achievement of all, the saving of the Republic.

Named dictator, as sole commander-in-chief he duelled for part of 217 with Hannibal earning himself the nickname 'Cunctator', the delayer. Becoming the first to realize what had happened was not just a pattern of hard luck and finally smelt the coffee, understanding the only chance for Roman arms was to refuse to face the invader in battle and instead to try and wear him down by dogging his trail, while keeping to high defensible ground. Yet not everyone could stomach this policy, even the disasters they had so recently suffered at the hands of Hannibal could not contain the bloody belligerence of a Roman elite, who believed the only true way to fight was to take the enemy head-on. This was an attitude that ended creating a very unusual, indeed almost unique, restructuring of the Republic's high command. The dictatorship was a special, but not that unusual, arrangement whereby one man took full powers, rather than the normal two consuls, for a maximum of six months. The justification might be to have one directing head in a military emergency, but it could be more mundane, to name someone to arrange elections or carry out ceremonial when a consul was not present in the city. But if this rule of one man for a few months when Fabius took over was the result of military emergency, even the terrors of the Trebbia and Trasimene could not suppress the whispers of discontent as the old general trailed after Hannibal in Campania refusing to lock horns. The people's patience was paper-thin for any strategy that did not involve a head-on assault on the enemy so this policy of keeping on Hannibal's heels but refusing battle became deeply unpalatable; a sentiment that found a focus in the figure of Fabius' master of horse Marcus Minucius Rufus. The master of horse was the dictator's deputy, but on this occasion he did not support his superior's strategy at all. A considerable figure himself, having been a consul in the year 221, he saw no reason to blindly follow his leader's orders, indeed when Fabius was absent from camp, off his own bat he instigated an attack against Hannibal near Geronium in modern Abruzzo which turned out quite well.

Ambitious Roman grandees were not going to forgo competing for the prizes of politics even for Hannibal. They could subdue their urges for the public good when absolutely necessary but not for ever, as would soon become clear. Fabius' master of horse did not just represent men who disliked the 'delayers' strategy; they were also aspirants who wanted a share of the prizes at the top table that this man and his people seemed to be monopolizing. So on the basis of a very small success his supporters managed to get Minucius given equal authority as Fabius himself and the two of them ended camping separately but nearby with the different sections of the army they commanded. This was an almost unique and fairly pointless outcome as all it did was replicate the normal situation of having two consuls, invalidating the very idea of appointing a dictator in the first place. As it turned out this eccentric arrangement did not last, because when Hannibal trailed a bait Minucius swallowed it whole and found his army half destroyed after confronting the Carthaginian again, only to have his bacon saved by his colleagues' army riding timely to the rescue from their neighbouring encampment. This embarrassing reverse involved considerable bloodletting and was enough to convince Minucius finally to follow where Fabius led. But if this man had an admirable ability to learn from his mistakes there were still plenty of enthusiasts back home, who, confident in Rome's vast resources, determined to raise an army large enough that it could not fail in battle even against Hannibal.

So when Fabius' six month stint as dictator was over, the newly elected consuls mobilized the largest army the Republic had ever sent out. They raised 80,000 troops or more for the field army, a number of men and animals, made even greater by a trail of servants and camp followers, that would have needed 100 tons of wheat per day to sustain themselves. So despite a beefed up commissariat still the whole must have seemed like a swarm of locusts as they cut a swathe through a friendly country of cornfields, vineyards and olive trees. One of its commanders was a fighting fool called Varro, a man denigrated as a demagogue and snobbishly dismissed as the son of a butcher, who, it is claimed, was swept to power on the votes of the common man rather than the proper support of the rich and respectable. This upstart ensured the enormous army he led with his colleague Lucius Aemilius Paullus came face-to-face with Hannibal at Cannae in Apulia, a place near the Adriatic coast, where he had gone to resupply his army, and where he was able to choose a fine, flat, open battleground, to maximize the effect of his superiority in cavalry. The upshot was probably one of the most famous military encounters in all history, the classic example of double envelopment, which enshrines the Carthaginian general as the most consummate tactician of all time. A victory won by a Carthaginian force little more than half the size of the Romans and that cut a bloody path through the ranks of the Roman ruling class. Varro's fellow consul, over a quarter of Senate, several previous consuls, an ex master of horse and twenty or so military Tribunes were left dead on the field of battle.

There had never been a sequence like Trebbia, Trasimene and Cannae. Hannibal had cut and blasted at the body of the stalwart Republic and that even before the weakened corporation had suffered another crippling blow from Gallic peoples who they had become used to besting in recent years. They were stupefied by the magnitude of their defeats and overawed by an exaggerated but still possibly immediate threat to Rome itself. No one in the Senate or anywhere else could absolutely know what the way out might be in these extreme circumstances and how the wounds might be healed and any kind of face shown to a world that seemed to be tumbling around them. There may be arguments about the efficacy of Hannibal's grand strategy, whether he really ever had a chance of prising away enough of Rome's support to reduce her to a local Italian power again, but few can convincingly put up a competitor to Cannae as the finest battlefield success in ancient or modern times. Nor could its immediate results be denied that saw great cracks emerging in Rome's hegemony, as most of southern Italy deserted the Roman cause. Subjects, allies and even old friends in Sicily jumped ship and this would become the background of an epic struggle that would consume the powers of the Peninsula for another thirteen years.

The man from Africa who was the cause of this churning furore had had much to do after his great triumph. It took time to strip the dead, but it was crucial if only to provide the best arms for the men not re-equipped after Trasimene and to have a store ready for future recruits. And though he had not lost many men in comparison with the defeated army still they had either be taken care of, in the hope that they may rejoin the ranks or their bodies given appropriate funerary rites. Celebrations took time too, to reward, promote and decorate the many men who had done so well on the wide fields by the banks of the Aufidus River. With this done the issue was how to exploit the victory beyond securing the captives and the loot from the two great Roman army camps. Hannibal's policy remained the same with the prisoners, that the non-Romans were set free to go home and hopefully win the favour of their compatriots, while envoys were sent to Rome offering the rest back for ransoms and to see if the enemy might now be in the mood to listen to terms of peace after being so utterly crushed in battle.

Hannibal had a man called Cathalo take his proposals to Rome, but he found no takers there. While the story here is part theatre, to glorify the Roman self-image of absolute defiance in the face of defeat, that disaster brought out their world conquering qualities, still the facts remain. Cathalo was shown the door by a lictor, not even received by the Senate and an offer to ransom Roman prisoners rejected, though undoubtedly this refusal to do what was required to free their men was part realism. Finding the money would have been very difficult, after they had just paid out a wedge to compensate owners for slaves who had volunteered to fight, on top of the normal expense of raising the new legions and warships they required to survive. The state that had absolutely refused to countenance negotiations with Hannibal after Cannae was virtually broke. They needed financial help from their old friend, King Hiero of Syracuse, just to sustain their efforts in places like Sicily and Sardinia while digging deep at home was required as well. A finance commission took on itself to double domestic taxation, and coins that survive show telltale signs of devaluation; desperate endeavours to bridge a fiscal chasm brought on by the three years of disaster handed to them by Hannibal. The many tens of thousands of Roman citizens lost since 218 were not just warriors, they were taxpayers as well.

Yet whatever the attitude of the principals at Rome, like the tremors of an earthquake the effects of Cannae spread out from its epicentre, threatening to overturn the hegemony that Rome had established in southern Italy in the past seventy years. First in Apulia where the battle had been fought, Arpi, Herdonia, Salapia and Aecae defected and probably many more places too, just leaving loyal those few posts where the remnant of the butchered legions found boltholes. Then as Hannibal passed into Samnium, his triumphs advertised by the train of thousands of prisoners and herds of plundered cattle that followed him, almost the whole of that nation came over except for those people in the quarter called the Pentri. There was no misoneism here, it was expected. The Carthaginians had been confident of a welcome amongst peoples who had been in life or death conflict with Rome only a couple of generations before. The subjection that these and other folk had come within living memory and its duration had been considerably less than had been the decades' long struggle with the city on the Tiber and if some of the local elite had Romanized to preserve their wealth and position, not all had. Many clung to old independent ways and would inevitably see the advent of Rome's nemesis as a portal back to an earlier and a better time. In the lands of the Hirpini too, the locals joined the Punic cause while those loyal to Rome fled, as Hannibal found a convenient base at Compsa, an ancient city sitting on a 1,200ft ridge, on the boundary of Lucania near enough to the source of the Aufidus River.

There he left his heavy baggage and loot, moving light shod west towards Campania while his brother Mago took an independent command south through Lucania and another officer called Hanno pushed on further to Bruttium. All of them encouraging and facilitating the people on the way to throw over their Roman allegiance and join with the party who had shown in three decisive battles that the gods were fighting on their side. But for Hannibal and his main force the prize was elsewhere. Once descending from the hills of Samnium into Campania he took a thrash at Napoli; control of a local seaport was always likely to be very handy, making communications with Carthage, Spain and indeed Sicily much easier. But he was never going to catch this place unprepared with the breathtaking view of the Campanian plain from its high citadel, where Fort St Elmo now stands. So despite a cavalry skirmish, where a number of Neapolitan blue bloods were killed or captured, the authorities kept faith with Rome and their defences were too strong to be easily assailed. But disappointment here was soon banished when the plum fell into Hannibal's lap. When his agents had approached the people of Capua they had found men eager to join the victorious side and capable of persuading their compatriots too; believing assurances that they would not find Roman control replaced by Carthaginian; that no tribute in men or money would be demanded and Hannibal should only provide a garrison if requested, and convinced that Punic support would allow the city to take her rightful place as the leading community in Italy; with Capua adhering other places came over too, Atella on the Napoli road and Calatia on the Appian Way leading into Samnium. But if these core Campanian communities defected, those on the coast like Cumae, Puteoli and Napoli and others to the south, Nola, Acerrae and Nuceria did not. But with such a good start the putative liberators from Africa had high hopes that judicious pressure might bring a change of mind even amongst these intransigent loyalists.

Capua's adherence had really been something, but Hannibal hoped for much more. Another coup was tried against Napoli but when these steadfast Roman allies again refused to defect he marched on Nola where he had reason to believe there were people willing to desert the ranks of the Republic's friends. But before he could take advantage of this, he found his enemy had, if not recovered from the knockout blow at Cannae, at least been making considerable efforts to patch up their wounds. The Romans discovered there were still men they had confidence in, leaders who had shown they could cope before and again might find a way. An ageing but celebrated conqueror of the Gauls called Marcellus, much will be heard of him later, who had been with a squadron of warships at Ostia when news of defeat arrived, had acted. He dispatched a legion of marines to Taenum, capital of the Oscan Sidicini. They were to defend the road to Rome from Campania while he botched together some Home Guards out of soldiers from the fleet and recently raised levies, before being sent to organize the 15,000 Cannae survivors gathering traumatized at Canusium in central Apulia, upriver from the site of the battlefield. Also a dictator had again been named, and this Marcus Junius Pera was joined by Gracchus as his master of horse, mobilizing a scratch army including new city legions, volunteer slaves and 6,000 condemned criminals and debtors armed with Gallic spoils. These were marched south through Taenum to Cales a few miles further along the Capua road.

Something like a Nola war was the story of the next few years in the fat and prosperous lands of Campania. This place, near where the first Emperor Augustus would breathe his last in AD 14, was not the size of Capua but still was central, a strategic hub on the west coast route south. One road went both down towards Lucania, Bruttium, Rhegium and the Sicily crossing and another east along to the Aufidus Valley then into Apulia, rich and fertile, producing the grains, oil and wine that any army needed to survive. The population was in two minds about their response to the arrival of Hannibal and the defection of Capua. Part of it was local rivalry, an inclination to take the opposite course to that of its grander neighbour, and it was part class, with the poorer folk eager for a change in the status quo, while an oligarch elite stuck hard to Roman friends with whom they had so much in common. This well defended strongpoint was so important that when the call came, for help from a looming Carthaginian presence, it needed answering. Marcellus had been relieved on the Apulian front and had taken his men to Casilinum, on the Volturnus River just up from Capua, when these Nolans came asking for assistance to defend their walls. From there, he sent word for the authorities to stay firm, then drove his men hard across the Volturnus up through the hills round Saticula past Suessula to get to Nola just in time to forestall the enemy.

Anticipated, the invaders turned to have yet another go at Napoli, but found the Romans there too, so left and marched briskly for Nuceria, about fifteen miles down the Lucania road. Even Marcellus would not risk leaving the vicinity of Nola to bring help so the defenders eventually surrendered and left on terms, as the town was sacked and burned before the Carthaginians turned again to deal with Nola. Now that town became the epicentre, with both parties camped outside trying to get the inhabitants on to their side. The Romans, when they received confirmation that many inside the town were in contact with Hannibal, moved into the city from their camp to ensure the people stayed loyal, they were prepared to risk getting bottled up behind its walls. A battle was in fact fought to a draw outside the town, with the defenders attacking out from the gates and despite one tradition lauding it as a great achievement, in that Marcellus was not annihilated by Hannibal, the encounter was not much more than a skirmish. Still this place was continuing to be a very tough nut to crack for Hannibal who soon changed tack and moved against Acerrae on the Napoli road, and when the people refused to submit began to surround the place with siege lines. But most of the defenders slipped away allowing the town to be taken and burned. During this activity Marcellus moved to his fortified camp 'Castra Claudiana' (Claudian camp) just above nearby Suessula to keep his forces secure, while keeping an eye on what his enemy was up to. The endgame in this year's manoeuvring saw Hannibal back on the road, pushing his men hard to reach Casilinum where control would allow him to block the path of the dictator Pera whose army was known to be pushing down from the north.

With elephants trumpeting round the field and against Saharan nomads, the garrison of Casilinum held their own, even to the extent of sallying out to interrupt the enemy siege lines and countermining where the attackers tried to tunnel under the towers and undermine the walls. There were only 1,000 defenders, levied just too late to fight at Cannae and defending a small stronghold in the town, after having massacred most of the inhabitants who they thought no longer trustworthy after what had happened at Capua. But their efforts were sufficient for the moment to forestall the Carthaginians, who left a siege fort to blockade this crucial post while the main army withdrew to winter quarters in Capua. The year that had begun with the Republic making its greatest effort to win the war had ended with them digging in just to survive. But the Romans had thought in fortress terms before; her colonies outside Latium had always largely fulfilled this function, as both forward bases and defensive boltholes and now she pursued the same policy in her resistance to Hannibal. Not that it was a great stroke of strategic genius; the choice was forced on her, all she could do when it turned out her generals and soldiers in the open field were nothing but fodder for the enemy's mincing machine. To defend from a system of fortified towns and camps was the desperate remedy of the frightened, but it made complete sense to try and hold on to key stations on a road system that might allow her, once regrouped, to come back again at the enemy.

Taenum, Cales and Casilinum on the Via Latium defended the road to Rome, Nola, Cumae, Napoli; holding on in Campania and on the coast. Beneventum and Venusia situated on the main road through Samnium and in Apulia it was Larinum and Luceria. Hold hard and hold out was the only way against Hannibal and while they pursued this as the main policy they were also fortunate in the north. The Gallic tribes despite their success did not follow up on victory over Postumius, apparently not even snapping up Rome's advanced bases on the middle Po at Placentia or Cremona. Despite this it was not for over a year that forces were sent north to oppose them. It maybe that many of the Gauls' best warriors were with Hannibal's army but still the failure to comprehensively dig out their enemies from where they had only recently arrived is extraordinary. And it gave a crucial breathing space, meaning the Republic's strength did not have to be dissipated by sending another consular army to face the Gallic threat. They would reinforce as soon as they could; two legions went to Ariminum in 215, but with this northern front largely untroubled soon magistrates could circulate amongst the colonies and allies in Etruria, rich and populous in their gentle hills, vineyards and olive groves and at Picenum, raising levies for legions that would fight in Campania, Sicily or Spain rather than having to guard the walls of their communities from hordes of raging Gauls.

With a winter respite there was a rejigging of command. Fabius, stepping in to the consular vacancy left by Postumius, took over the dictator's army, 35,000 strong at Taenum before moving to Cales to cover the road to Rome from Capua, while Marcellus took two new legions raised in the city to Suessula. Gracchus was moved too, leaving Sinuessa to cover the coastal cities west of Capua that were bound to be threatened now that city had gone over. Then the proprietor Laevinus, a consul back in 220, with two legions from Sicily, which were replaced by the Cannae survivors, was given command of Apulia, Lucania and Calabria. While the forces there were dispatched to Tarentum Varro went to Picenum to drum up more conscripts after reporting back to the Senate on his conduct on the campaign just passed. In fact the man who courted and captured disaster at Cannae found his peers remarkably forgiving and was hardly censured at all. Indeed he was repeatedly given command in the north in the years to come, apparently having been considered to have shown great courage in not despairing of Rome after the bloodbath he had brought on himself. A very different disposition than that arranged for those Cannae veterans who by fighting their way out or being left to guard the army camps somehow survived the encounter. They found themselves exiled in penal regiments, destined to fight for Rome in Sicily until all the Carthaginians had been finally driven from Italy and the whole war won.

It was the loyalty of the inner core of central Italian supporters that made everything possible and it was because of this that Rome could sustain what was probably an eighteen legion effort that year, of which seven were deployed in Campania and the south. This looked like a serious attempt to stabilize the Italian front, but when the fighting season began in early spring 215 the effort to defend the road to Rome took a real hit as Casilinum, guarding the vital Volturnus crossing, fell to the army besieging it. The Romans had tried hard to keep a hold on the place; Gracchus had made every effort, first with his slave legions, then in overall command as master of horse when Pera was called back to Rome, to succour the defenders, even trying to float wheat in barrels down the river for the garrison to pick up. Marcellus acted too and was only stopped from coming to their relief when torrential rain ensured any movement was difficult and flooding made crossing the river to approach the town impossible. So when Hannibal came down with his whole army nothing could stop Casilinum from falling. Now with the river line safe and after putting in a combined Carthaginian and Campanian garrison of 2,700 men and raising useful cash from the inhabitants ransoming their lives, Hannibal returned to his camp at Tifata high above Capua.

His intention was to be on hand to assist his allies but found they had already been trying to help themselves. While he had been securing Casilinum the Capuans had attempted something on their own behalf. These ambitious folk, newly released from Roman tutelage and hoping to establish their own hegemony in the region, decided to deal with a neighbour who had stayed loyal to Rome. They tried a coup against Cumae, a port north of Napoli, their feelings against this people may have been enflamed by the fact that 300 Campanian knights who returned from serving in Sicily had stayed faithful to Rome and been given citizenship at Cumae as compensation.

Intending to trick these Greeks, long established on the Campanian coast, the Capuans suggested the leaders from both places meet at Hamae, a local shrine, to talk over their relations, while really intending that their army, 14,000 strong encamped nearby, should be there ready to snap the attendees up. The Cumans agreed, but they too had their own agenda, as they contacted Gracchus who with his slave legions and 25,000 allies had marched down Via Sinuessa to camp at Liternum, on the dunes by the sea between Cumae and the River Volturnus. Here he had drilled his slaves and worked hard on the morale of an army, some of whom resented the presence of servile troops within their ranks, and when he got word from the agents sent from Cumae, he made his preparations. Telling the citizens to get all their movables in behind their walls where he could defend them he prepared to follow the magistrates to Hamae. It was three miles from the town and the Romans shadowed, in secret and at night, the delegates who had travelled to the meeting proposed by the Capuans. On arrival all the Campanians they could find were massacred, 2,000 fell including their commander and thirty-four military standards were taken to boot. Though the claim that the Campanians had initially tried to draw the Cumans into a trap may have been a blind to make palatable what might otherwise have seemed the polluting by the Romans of the shrine at Hanae with innocent blood.

On learning that his protégés had failed at Cumae, Hannibal tried himself but it soon became clear that no fifth column existed to let him in and by the time he got his siege equipment up, Gracchus was there to hold the walls. A failed outcome here would come as no surprise to anybody who has climbed the temple-topped acropolis at Cumae, which itself is only one of many very defensible places in a region where a white fringe of surf emerging from a beautiful blue sea contains a country full of difficult, lumpy terrain punctuated by volcanic lakes and the fiery sulphurous Campi Flegrei. So the year had started with a win and a loss but Hannibal still had much to be satisfied with as he faded back to Mount Tifata to rest his men. If Cannae had not proved the end game in the Roman war, to a considerable degree the Carthaginian strategy had seemed to be succeeding, prising so many allies and Greek cities away from Roman control had been what Hannibal had intended as his trump hand and now much had been achieved in that direction. Huge swathes of southern Italy were now either in his camp or at least no longer offering anything in the way of support to the old Peninsula hegemon. Though there was a downside to this achievement, these new friends would have high expectations of their fresh relationship. Inevitably when Roman armies took up a counteroffensive Hannibal would find envoys arriving at his camp squealing for assistance. The responsibility to try and defend these mint new friends was bound to mean his leeway in terms of strategy would become considerably constrained.

These demands for protection were first engendered by the actions of a familiar figure. All the while events had been unfolding near Cumae, Fabius took up command of the army at Cales. This man had shown determination at the start of the year, ordering that everybody in the war zones should get their crops in behind their city walls by the first of June, or their fields and farms would be burned and their slaves sold in auction. But after this he had dawdled, either discouraged by bad auspices or more likely reluctant to leave his post defending the road to Rome. Yet eventually not only did he march, ranging north of modern Caserta and capturing the towns and their Carthaginian garrisons at Compulteria, Trebula and Austicula while ending at the Claudian camp above Suessula, from where he dispatched Marcellus to go to the assistance of the authorities at Nola and ensure against pro Carthaginian 'populars' who remained determined to betray the city to Hannibal if they could. That active man also sent parties of his own men and local allies to wreck the lands of renegade Hipirni and Samnites, particularly concentrating on the region around the town of Caudium.

Hannibal had marched from Mount Tifata to Nola at the invitation of his well-wishers not long before and once there found Hanno had arrived to join him, with both his own army and with reinforcements from home as well. While Hannibal had been barrelling around Campania the authorities at Carthage had been doing their bit, although at this time the city fathers might have been expected to look to homeland security, as the African coast was already suffering from raids out of Roman Sicily. The Iberian picture had been difficult too with Hasdrubal defeated in Spain and old Spanish friends making overtures to the Romans. Meaning not only that he would not be coming to join his brother in Italy, but that the large army raised for Mago would now have to go to shore things up there rather than reinforce Hannibal's success. But despite all this, real efforts were made to help. First there had been an attempt on Sardinia, to reinforce a local rebellion there; that it resulted in a Carthaginian expeditionary force being massacred in battle and its leaders and principal Sardinian rebels killed, captured or committing suicide was unfortunate, but the home town administration had at least shown willing. And more than that a general called Bomilcar had been sent with direct reinforcements for the Italian War with Numidians infantry and elephants being landed at Locri in the deep south of Italy.

Yet even with Hanno's assistance Hannibal was unable to make progress at Nola. There are even claims of another victory for Marcellus, with that hard man rushing into battle only to be forestalled by a thunderstorm before then exiting from Nola's walls to again give the Carthaginians something of a hiding. But this, like many claimed Roman successes is improbable, no doubt there was some skirmishing but they clearly inflicted no significant reverses, though if the loss of six elephants, four dead and two captured, and the desertion of 272 Numidian and Spanish horse happened, it would have been a worry. Indeed this is a campaigning season when the ancient gentleman from Padua was intent on reporting doubtful success all round. Not only contending that three towns in Hirpini were retaken by the army based at Luceria, with rebels executed and 5,000 prisoners sold at auction. But even more improbably claiming that at about the same time as the siege of Cumae was underway, Sempronius 'Longus', the man trounced on the Trebbia three years before, killed 2,000 and captured 280 of Hanno's men and forty-one of his battle standards at Grumentum before chivvying him out of Lucania back to Bruttium, something that is difficult to assimilate with the safe arrival of that general at Hannibal's camp in Campania.

Again the best part of the fighting season had passed in stalemate outside Nola when Hannibal realized neither a fifth column nor a direct assault would get him in. So cutting his losses and sending Hanno back to Bruttium, the main army took the hilly road through Samnium into rolling Apulia, settling down for their winter in camp at Arpi, no distance from modern Foggia. With the Carthaginians now out of Campania, Fabius did some necessary housekeeping and stocked the granaries at the Claudian camp, leaving a winter garrison both there and at Nola. Nor was that it, taking a thrash at Capua he collected what crops he could for his own men, forcing the Campanians to stay mobilized in considerable numbers to protect their fields. All this as the home town authorities looked to save money, the last few years had been cripplingly expensive, sending Marcellus orders to demob his men back to Rome as Gracchus was directed east to Luceria, with two legions, to relieve Laevinus who himself was redeployed south to organize the defence of Brundisium and the Adriatic coast.

In the following year the Republic turned again to grey hair and wrinkled faces in difficult times, though not without an intervention in the voting and even a little intimidation by Fabius. The Romans might on occasions make life difficult for themselves by their dedication to contentious rivalry and inconvenient but hallowed custom, still when the chips were down they agreed that their most tried and tested men took the helm. Those who would now get down to business against Hannibal were Fabius himself, back at Rome and made consul for a fourth time, while Marcellus, out of town with his army, was elected for the third occasion. These two would lead in what would be another eighteen-legion effort across all fronts, with up to six new regiments being raised to attain this total. On top of this, orders were given to ensure 150 warships would be made available for the coming year, the latter requiring special taxes, just to pay the sailors required to man these vessels. The new fighting season did not see a great change in the arena of action as the Campanians worried that the enemy presence solid at their base at Cales on the road to Rome and still holding on at Nola, would make them vulnerable to pressure from north and south. Plenty of their leaders still had contacts in the enemy capital and knew that new legions were being raised 'for the express purpose of attacking them'. These people knew how important they were to Hannibal, Capua's defection just after Cannae had been the jewel in his triumph and to keep them firm in his cause was always going to be a priority.

The great man had been wintering in Arpi where his proximity to Gracchus in Luceria ensured some active sparring in which it is claimed 'the Romans' efficiency improved in consequence; they became progressively more cautious and less liable to be caught off their guard'.[3] And when flustered men from Capua came begging for assistance against what they believed was to be a major Roman offensive, he knew he must act. His whole army was soon trailing through the Hills of Samnium to take up their old post at Tifata, high up, overlooking both Capua and the Volturnus, a river that the enemy would have to cross to get within reach of the Campanian city. But Hannibal had not come just to wait on events and leaving his Numidians and Spaniards to garrison the defended camp and town, he now turned in a direction he had taken many times before. He still wanted a port on the coast hereabouts and had his eye on Puteoli, a Greek colony near the volcanic caldera of the Campi Flegrei, a place of boiling mud and steaming fissures. He hoped to keep his intentions obscure by leading his army down to the lake of Avernus, apparently just intent on making sacrifices at this portal to the underworld. But he soon dropped the mask of piety and after devastating territory near Cumae and cape Misenum made his 'sudden dash' for Puteoli, a place so important that Fabius had personally reinforced the place at the end of the previous year. To his chagrin Hannibal found it guarded by a Roman garrison of 6,000 men well positioned in a naturally defensible town and reconnaissance over three days revealed no weak points. So with little choice he departed, looking out for what else might be on offer and unleashed his men upon the countryside, despoiling all around the fields of his enemies, Neapolis included. The people on the coast seemed determined to cleave to Rome despite how many hidings Hannibal gave the legionaries in the field and how often he made it clear that Rome was unable to protect their productive hinterland.

This activity stirred up Fabius who had travelled day and night from Rome to reach his own army while messengers were sent to Gracchus to call him over to cover Beneventum while Fabius' son was directed to that general's old post at Luceria. By the time these rearrangements had been accomplished, Hannibal unsurprisingly already had other projects in hand. These were the years after Trasimene and Cannae when anybody looking for a change was going to make a play for Carthaginian support. There had already been hints of this at Nola, and now some of the less affluent elements, in cahoots with dissident aristocrats, intended an end to rule by the established oligarchy and had been sending out invitations for help. But before Hannibal could do anything the other consul Marcellus came from his winter quarters at Cales to Suessula and from there threw 6,000 foot and 300 horse into the town, all in just one day, despite the enemy holding the easiest crossing of the Volturnus at Casilinum. This celerity was required as more than just one enemy was on their way; apart from the main army Hanno again had been called up from Bruttium to meet his commander-in-chief at Nola.

Beaten to the punch again, Hannibal was nonetheless determined to try and get hold of this crucial post where he had twice failed before. He wrecked the country round Neapolis on his way but this was just a sideshow, he knew it would be once he got near the Romans at Suessula that the real contest would commence. Marcellus had moved down to Nola by the time he arrived and more than just waiting on the defensive, he had sent a subordinate called Claudius Nero, who would gain everlasting fame in a few years' time, with a large force of his best cavalry out after dark, to probe for the rear of the enemy's army. A battle is claimed that had the Romans pushing their opponents back but was not decisive because the horsemen had got lost in the night and failed to arrive on the field of combat in time. The small casualty list of 400 on the Roman side and 2,000 on the other suggests that this, another battle of Nola, was no epic encounter, though it is reported that Hannibal now refused to leave his camp when Marcellus again offered battle and soon after left off the siege and headed down south to Tarentum. But the reason for this behaviour is probably much more to do with both the failure of the pro Carthaginian party in the town to make a move and because news had arrived about a setback near Beneventum. Hanno had been marching up the leg of Italy from Bruttium with a good-sized army hoping to join his commander-in-chief in some decisive activity, but unfortunately bumped into another one of those competent commanders Rome was beginning to find at this time. This man was Gracchus, consul the previous year and master of horse before that, just arrived from Luceria, and he now defeated Hanno, driving him back south to ensure no junction with the main Carthaginian army would occur. Balked in one enterprise Hannibal was always prepared to try another, this time it was Tarentum where the Carthaginians had high hopes because some local contacts had ridden all the way to Lake Avernus to invite him to take over the town. This, the major town in Magna Graecia, was of even greater significance now the south was about to explode, with Syracuse preparing to sever a fifty-year friendship with Rome.

The other old head Fabius had been active too. Moving on Casilinum he intended to gain control of the crossing of the Volturnus and open up the road to Capua, but he found the enemy there prepared; a garrison of 700 of Hannibal's men and 2,000 Campanians. And more than this: from the Capua side of the Volturnus the local high command was arming anybody who would fight, slaves included, to harass the attackers as they tried to both defend their camp and set up siege lines round the river post. To cope the old man had no option but to call for help from his colleague defending Nola, suggesting that Gracchus could be brought from Beneventum to replace him, if there was still a threat to the town. Fortunately for them the Carthaginians had withdrawn and Marcellus was free to respond. Leaving only 2,000 men to hold Nola's walls, he joined Fabius in attacking Casilinum from the south side of the river, cutting the defenders off from Capua and enabling the two consuls to both drive off the enemy attacking their camp and complete the cordon round the town. It had been touch and go and Fabius might have been forced to withdraw if succour had not reached him but with the two armies united they were able to press the attack. Yet even now the older general was unsure of success and was happy to talk terms that would allow the defenders to retire to Capua; he in fact was in the middle of negotiating just this outcome when Marcellus intervened. The latter was determined that these enemies they had trapped in the riverine fortress would not live to fight another day and ordered his men to slaughter the defenders as they trudged unarmed out of town thinking they had been guaranteed safe conduct.

With this success behind them and sure that Hannibal had left the region on his way south, the two consuls moved to try and do more. Marcellus took his legions back to Nola, to secure the produce of the rich country around for his own men and deny it to the enemy. While it was probably illness that denied him the opportunity to achieve much more in that fighting season, Fabius was more determined and marched his troops past Capua up the Appian Way, into the heart of Samnium, with the aim of reasserting control where the Roman presence had been seen little in the last three years. Caudium, always the centre of resistance, was his main target while burning and wrecking at will, fertile valleys were pillaged and cattle driven off. We hear that a number of towns, Cupulteria, Telesia, Fugifulae, Orbitanium and even Compsa, were assaulted and taken, though the truth of this is difficult. The tide of success is claimed even to have reached into Lucania and Apulia where Blandae and Aecae are reported as retaken, while an extravagant 25,000 were maintained as captured or killed and 370 deserters from the Roman army returned to Rome to be thrown from the Tarpeian Rock. This is suggested as having been only the work of a few days for Fabius, which just seems improbable particularly as there is a hint that some of the achievements asserted in Apulia were the work of his son who, as proprietor at Luceria, both campaigned successfully against the town of Acuca and constructed a strong defensive camp at Ardoneae.

A confederacy had been ruined in five years, but could it rise again? The Republic that had planted the Po Valley in the north, that had established its first overseas province in Sicily and dominated treaty states and allies between might not have been completely wrecked but it still nonetheless had been fundamentally altered. In terms of territory alone nearly a third of the lands the Romans had claimed to rule had fallen away. In terms of the population of Roman-controlled Italy, after Hannibal's victories, perhaps one or one and half million or getting on for five million were no longer subject to the Tiber town, whether declared friends of the Carthaginian power or not. Few could have denied the significance of these changes but still as Hannibal took stock after half a decade in his enemy's backyard he could not have been sure what the future would bring. Had the blows he had struck been fatal? Was his enemy bleeding out and her activities the death throes of an expiring corpse? Or would the events of the next few years point in a very different direction?

Chapter 2

High-Water Mark

For the eastern quarter of Tarentum is full of monuments, because those who die there are to this day all buried within the walls, in obedience to an ancient oracle. For it is said that the god delivered this answer to the Tarentines, 'That it were better and more profitable for them if they made their dwelling with the majority'; and they thought therefore that they would be living in accordance with the oracle if they kept the departed within the walls. That is why to this day they bury inside the gates.

Polybius, *Histories*, Book, 8.28.

The whole father and son trope was very familiar to the Romans, though normally it had the father as consul and commander and son, as undisciplined but heroic subordinate, who must be chastised, sometimes even to death, to indicate that in service to the state, obeying orders must always trump any family feelings. But 213 would see a different, less familiar version involving Fabius Maximus and his son, though their family did have something of a tradition of the offspring as consul and father as lieutenant. Three generations before another venerable multiple consular happily rode behind his son's chariot when he entered Rome in a triumph over the Samnites in 292.[1] On this latest occasion the older Fabius as sitting consul had carried out the elections in autumn 214 for the following year in which his son and Gracchus were elected, both in their absence on campaign. There is no evidence to suggest that there was anything untoward in this family sequence but in the last few years Fabius had shown himself well capable of massaging access to the highest office. For the first three years after Cannae Fabius' family and supporters had almost monopolized the highest offices and we have evidence for at least two occasions when this old grandee engineered the electoral process to either place himself or one of his cohorts into a consular chair. First, after the death of Postumius he scuppered Marcellus' chances of filling the casual vacancy by either

fixing or at least utilizing some convenient thunderclaps and playing on
the tradition that both consuls should not come from plebeian families
to ensure the elected man had little option but to stand down. And a year
later he threatened to hand over his own relative by marriage, Crassus Titus
Otacilius, to the axes of his lictors when he questioned his manipulating that
year's consular elections.[2]

After young Fabius and his colleague entered their consulship, other
offices were filled too, while city contingents were raised, receiving their
arms as tradition demanded only when outside the city precincts, and fresh
drafts mobilized to flesh out the standing units, all backed by 20,000 men
enrolled from the allies. As the campaigning season opened the intention
was to position a cordon of armies to cover the enemy who were quartered
in Salapia in Apulia on a seaside lagoon not far north of the battlefield of
Cannae. To man a series of pinch points, Gracchus set out for Venusia in
south Samnium to defend along the central road where the Appian Way
would soon be extended, while a praetor with another army held Luceria in
northern Apulia. Fabius junior, collecting his father's old legions, took them
to the camp above Suessula taking over there from a man named Gnaeus
Fulvius Centumalus, who would win the consulship in 211 before dying
at Hannibal's hands the following year. This place near the Samnium hills,
west of the Caudine Pass and off the Appian Way near where it met the road
from Napoli, had been a real home from home for Marcellus campaigning
around Nola in the past few years, and the standing camp that had been
established there was named after him.

Once settled there at this Claudian camp, where a square set Norman
castle now dominates the hill and blocked off roadways make access up a steep
incline almost impossible, Fabius Maximus senior joined his son. Giving
rise to a famous story where his twelve lictors stood with rods and axes in
front of young Fabius in single file and as his father rode past the first eleven
evinced their respect for the old man by remaining silent. Then the consul
told the last lictor to order his father to dismount who swiftly obeyed and,
though many bystanders were shocked by this seeming discourtesy to such
a venerable figure, he however made it clear he totally approved this action.
He 'sprang quickly from his horse, almost ran to his son, and embraced
him affectionately'. 'My son,' he said, 'you are right in thought and act. You
understand what a people has made you its officer, and what a high office
you have received from them. It was in this spirit that our fathers and we
ourselves have exalted Rome, a spirit which makes parents and children ever

secondary to our country's good.'[3] Another tradition claims he exclaimed 'I wanted to find out, my son, whether you sufficiently realised that you are consul.'[4] But whatever we believe of this po-faced family interchange the presence of Fabius, father and son in the same camp would to many surely have presaged significant activity.

As it turned out it was not just the old ex consul that entered the army camp around this time. Another character sloped in soon after, who had come from Arpi in Apulia. This, Dasius Altinius, who arrived with an entourage of three slaves, had come in search of profit, claiming he could betray his home town to the Romans if they made it worth his while. There was a dispute amongst the command council on how to respond, as some wanted to have the man killed, as after Cannae he had taken Arpi over to the Carthaginians. But Fabius senior, though subordinate, still had the kudos and persuaded the rest that they must think of the effect on other communities in the future and welcome anyone who wanted to return to the fold. However, he still did not quite trust this particular man and suggested he be interred for the duration of the war and his fate decided when it was all over. This was done and Dasius was packed off to Cales where, though kept confined at night, he was able to live high on the hog with the money he had brought with him out of Arpi.

Arpi, defended by extensive city walls, on a byroad from Luceria to Sipontum, had long been an important ally of Rome, once sending 4,000 foot and 400 horse to help in the war against Pyrrhus, but was now functioning as an excellent base for Hannibal in north Apulia. Much had been happening there, after it was discovered Dasius had left town. When this local bigwig was missed the news got through to the Carthaginians that this important post might be at risk. Arpi, dangerously near crucial Luceria, had been an early adherent for Hannibal, but if a bloody tale is believed he was not surprised at what had occurred, as he had always had little faith in Dasius as a real Punic partisan. And now he took the opportunity of his absconding to pocket the movable wealth that very rich man had left behind. The contention that he also had his wife and children burnt alive is surely just part of the usual attempt to batten on Hannibal a reputation for horrible cruelty, but for which there is no deal of good evidence. Yet if his enemy saw more of a chance to make money than a real threat to their Apulian position, Fabius the younger saw an opportunity to count coup. Route marching his army hard from the camp above Suessula through the hills of Samnium over the Apennine spine along the monotonous tree-lined roads cutting through the green plains and gentle hills of Apulia to within only half a mile of Arpi itself. From there he reconnoitred its formidable defences, noting where it seemed poorly guarded. Once the place to strike was decided upon, great care was taken with the preparations. An assault group was outfitted, led by the bravest of the six tribunes who commanded in each of his legions and made up by the elite of the centurions. This tungsten tip was backed by 600 legionaries equipped with scaling ladders, ready to be carried straight to the walls. When the fourth watch of the night was sounded by the garrison bugles heralding the dawn it was taken as the call to start the attack. The ladders were brought to the lowest part of the wall where all seemed quiet and where a narrow gate had been noticed during Fabius' inspection. And once on the battlements the attackers, still unnoticed, slipped down and broke open the door to let the rest of the forlorn hope in.

The attackers had been fortunate that all this movement had been covered by a shattering rainstorm that from midnight drove most of the defenders indoors for shelter and drowned out the noise made by the entering men. Also there is an extraordinary report that, 'Then when the sound of the rain fell upon the ear more gently and regularly, it soothed most of the defenders to sleep.'[5] However improbable this sounds, what is clear is that once in, the attackers blew their trumpets to alert the consul, who ordered the whole of the army in through the gate. With the rain letting up and the light of dawn beginning to show, the 5,000 men of the Carthaginian garrison and 3,000 local defenders at last began to react. The Punic commander clearly had concerns about the loyalty of the citizenry, so placed them in the front of the battle line with his own men behind, to ensure they could not run away. These forces had deployed down towards the gate where the Romans entered and soon bloody street fighting began with the shadows cast by high-walled buildings keeping the scene dark even after dawn had broken. This country near modern Foggia was dead flat, but fighting street by street was always difficult and some Romans even had to enter the houses in this quarter and occupy the roofs, to stop the populace from attacking them from above. It was a tense and difficult time with squads of soldiers going from house-to-house and troops crossing from rooftop to rooftop on planks laid across, with any terrified inhabitants who had not already fled, jumping from windows or scurrying outdoors. Anything to try and escape the terrifying armoured warriors who were rampaging through their homes.

When the sun rose high enough the situation gradually became clearer as in the now illuminated thoroughfares the attackers began to recognize old acquaintances amongst the local troops, who only a year or two before had been their allies. In these circumstances shouted discussions took place, over why erstwhile Italian friends were aiding foreign African invaders. Some locals claimed they had been led astray by the oligarchy in charge and indeed in this strange phase of phoney war, it is even suggested the senior officer of the citizen troops slipped between the lines to meet with the consul Fabius himself. Who, on getting assurances that his people would not be punished for their adherence to Hannibal, returned and called on his men to turn against the Carthaginians and join the Romans. Nor was it just the residents who had a sudden change of heart, nearly 1,000 Spaniards in the garrison also decided the taste of Carthaginian salt was now much less to their palate. Though they still had sufficient feeling for those who had been their comrades, they negotiated a safe exit for the rest of the garrison as the price of turning the place over to Romans. These Iberians did well out of their defection, getting double rations for their trouble, though their new employer got the benefit too as 'the Republic availed itself on very many occasions of their courage and fidelity.'

So the disconsolate remnant of the garrison, sold by both their old comrades in arms and the people they had been left to protect, slipped out of the gates unmolested to find a way down the coast to Salapia where their main army was encamped. 'Thus Arpi was restored to the Romans without the loss of a single life, except in the case of one man who had long ago been a traitor and had recently deserted.'[6] The claim of a virtually bloodless coup is almost certainly hyperbole but, whatever the real butcher's bill for the fighting in the streets, the taking of Arpi was a considerable triumph, particularly as the place had been one of the favourite wintering grounds of the Carthaginian army of Italy in the past few years. Now Hannibal would have to find his off season comforts somewhere else, as the consul left a force sufficient to ensure against losing the town again.

If Fabius junior had done something with his father's old legions, this was one of the very few Roman successes of that campaigning season. Yet if this fifth year of the Second Great Punic War was not very eventful perhaps the need for a rest was understandable; certainly what had led up to that time had been extraordinary enough. It seemed like the Roman military machine in the south was taking a breath after years of endless fighting since Hannibal had crossed the snow-capped Alps to arrive in northern Italy, and priming itself for a climactic struggle against an enemy whose career of conquest did not yet seem to be faltering. At a time when the military situation remained extremely uncertain the army the consul had commanded the years before, based at Luceria and taken over by a new praetor, did nothing at all. Nor were these men alone in their lassitude; another praetor, Centumalus, who had been left in charge of some of Marcellus' men at the Claudian camp apparently was equally inactive. Even Gracchus who had done so well, with his army made up partly of ex slaves, at Cumae and Beneventum, had continued on in Lucania, but achieved little more than the taking of a few small communities and fighting a couple of unimportant skirmishes with roving segments of the enemy's military. Elsewhere though, this lack of pace was less evident. In the north another new praetor, Sempronius Tuditanus, took command in Ariminum, modern Rimini and made his mark, storming the town of Atrinum and capturing more than 7,000 prisoners and a good deal of coined money. Two legions also remained holding Sardinia, while Varro continued with one legion at Picenum and in Sicily there was action too with Marcellus continuing his war against Syracuse and Otacilius seconded him with his fleet, while in Greece M. Valerius with his ships and one legion kept up the good fight.

Nor does it seem that Hannibal was particularly vigorous during this fighting season either. Certainly he did not try to hit the Romans with everything he had, to bring them to their knees, knowing by now that they had learnt important lessons and that another Cannae would be much more difficult to achieve. Presumably the spring and summer of 213 was occupied with entrenching his position amongst the many communities who had thrown in their lot with the Carthaginians. There would have been plenty of flesh to press amongst the elites in Campania, Samnium, Bruttium, Lucania, Apulia, and the Greek cities. There was much need of persuasion to bring on board key local players, who could unlock the door to the financial resources and most importantly manpower that he would need to face the military might that Rome had shown itself capable of mobilizing, despite the massive losses he had already inflicted on them. There surely were skirmishes and sieges to occupy the veterans of Trebbia, Trasimene and Cannae but the histories suggest no detail. No hints can be derived from Sosylus and Silenus, Hannibal's campaign historians, whose voices we occasionally hear transmitted through Roman accents.

All we know about most of the first of Hannibal's last ten years in Italy is that, while his men had sat encamped on the coast of Apulia, in what would have been the rising heat and dust of early summer, swatting ubiquitous insects, the great Carthaginian himself would have received news that Arpi had fallen. That the Iberian warriors left to defend the place had let him down was worrying, something that probably frayed his temper more than the behaviour of the citizenry whose fickleness might be more predictable. He was not far away but there is no suggestion of a response to this hostile takeover. In fact the next we hear of him is further south around the very instep of the Italian boot. And it is activity here that would ensure that if the year had begun with disappointment in Apulia it would still end in a winter high-water mark.

From soon after the triumph at Cannae, Carthaginian progress in the far south had been marked. First Mago, then Hanno, had paraded through Lucania and Bruttium, accepting the adherence of towns and people to newcomers who had smashed the power of a Rome they had had to kowtow to for the last fifty-odd years. In the Italian toe most of the local tribes rose in their support too, partly seeing their arrival as an opportunity to take a hit at the rich coastal cities. Yet it had not all been plain sailing. Petelia just a little to the north of Croton, had held out, afraid of being despoiled by local Bruttium enemies who had eagerly joined the invaders' side. After even desperate tearful pleas to the Senate at Rome brought no succour, the eventual outcome was never in doubt. Yet it took an eleven-month siege by an officer called Himilco to accomplish it, with both sides suffering the horrors of famine in a devastated land. Other places showed much less resistance; after a show of force Consentia, the main market town in the high inland heart of Bruttium, fell in a couple of days. Then Croton, Caulonia and Locri, Greek ports on the sole of the Italian boot joined the cause, with only Rhegium left clinging on for the Republic. Nor was it just the locals who had stumped up resources to bolster the scourge of their erstwhile Roman overlord, Hannibal's homefolk came up trumps too. For the first and only time we hear of during the conqueror's years in Italy he got significant reinforcements from Carthage, when a commander called Bomilcar arrived at the port of Locri with 4,000 Numidians, forty elephants, Libyan infantry, money and supplies. A restocking of the Italian War with which Appius Claudius, in charge of an army in Sicily, tried to interfere, sailing up from Messene to surprise Locri, but only to find Bomilcar gone and the city gates closed against him.

But as Capua was the plum prize in Campania, so it was Tarentum that really counted in Magna Graecia. And if after Cannae his lieutenants had mainly carried the load down the far south, it could only be a matter of time before Hannibal himself ventured there. The reason when it came

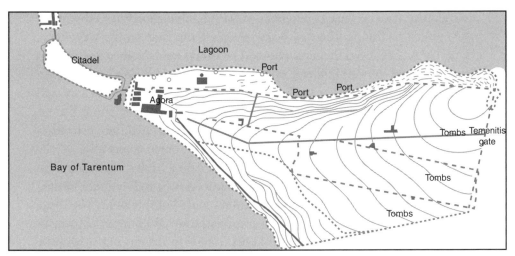

Tarentum.

was an invitation he received from some key people coming from that great city. When in 214 he had been preparing to dash at Puteoli, the army was encamped at the lovely circular lake of Avernus, a volcanic crater near the Campi Flegrei, which had an awesome reputation as the entrance to Hades and was a well known place of pilgrimage and sacrifice. While he was making appropriate obeisance in this mystical landscape some interesting visitors made their presence known at the entrance of his camp. Five young Tarentine nobles arrived, weary from a journey of hundreds of miles and eager to meet the man who had ordered their release when they were captured fighting for Rome at Trasimene and Cannae. The policy of treating well then releasing, without ransom, all of the Roman allies taken prisoner after his great victories had borne fruit plenty of times before, but this was the jackpot. The new arrivals claimed they came with a commission to invite Hannibal to march on the city, with assurances that once he arrived, the popular assembly would swing the place over to the Carthaginian side without a fight.

This was an opportunity far too good to decline; possession of Tarentum would give him the port he needed to ensure easy contact with both Africa and his new friend across the Adriatic, Philip V of Macedon, who was denied direct communication, because of Roman control of Brundisium. He was not however able to take up the opportunity offered by the young Tarentines straight away, but late in the season when he seemed to have accomplished what he could in Campania he made his move. Two hundred hard miles brought the army to the city and once in the neighbourhood strict discipline was applied to troops who had been living off the land on the way down. Hannibal had believed the men who said he would be welcomed and did not want to offend the landholders, who would make the decision in the citizen assembly, by wreaking their field and burning their farms. With his men well in hand, he camped a mile from the city walls in high expectation. But on this occasion the Carthaginian general was to be frustrated, because either by dumb luck or good intelligence Laevinus, the Roman commander of the fleet at Brundisium, had dispatched an officer called Livius with a garrison and orders to organize the place's defences, to raise a militia force to man the walls and just as important to keep a wary lookout for treachery by those inclined to overthrow the pro Roman administration. With internal security tight Hannibal received no news from his friends in the city and with little option but to accept this rebuff, consoled himself with collecting grain from the rich country west of Tarentum and moving north to Salapia in Apulia. From there the crucial work of finding remounts for his cavalry could be got underway, upwards of 4,000 horses being brought in, some from as far away as the Sallentine heel of the Italian boot.

By 213 Hannibal would have been having problems supplying his army in Campania, not wanting to make life more difficult for his friends in Capua whose own population was suffering from the depredations of enemy armies. So for the two last winters he had taken his main forces to Apulia leaving only garrisons to help out in regional defence and generally dispersing his men as far as possible. And now after the loss of Arpi and with a different focus for his thoughts he transferred his centre of operations down south. Much of the later part of the campaigning season was spent around the Ionian coasts of Apulia, Lucania and Sallentini, where his presence in the region not only seems to have had a beneficial side effect in that 'certain unimportant Calabrian communities went over to him' but meant he could offer support to Hanno who had been continuing to batten the Carthaginians' hold on Bruttium. But this had been far from the main purpose in his summertime sojourn.

but here there is a spacious and commodious harbour, closed in by a great bridge. It is 100 stadia in circuit. This port, at the head of its basin which recedes most inland, forms, with the exterior sea, an isthmus which connects the Peninsula with the land. The city is situated upon this Peninsula. The neck of land is so low that ships are easily hauled over it from either side. The site of the city likewise is extremely low; the ground, however, rises slightly towards the citadel. The old wall of the city has an immense circuit, but now the portion towards the isthmus is deserted, but that standing near the mouth of the harbour, where the citadel is situated, still subsists, and contains a considerable city. It possesses a noble gymnasium and a spacious forum, in which there is set up a brazen colossus of Jupiter, the largest that ever was, with the exception of that of Rhodes.[7]

This description by a Greek geographer, philosopher and historian writing at the very end of the first century BC and the beginning of the first century AD described a town shaped like a cone, with an eastern land wall at its base, sea girt on one side with a large inland basin with port facilities stretching the length of the other, and at the tip a rocky promontory with a citadel that controlled ingress and egress to the harbour. The place was famously prosperous, her elite were a proud horse riding people whose style of fighting even gestated a type of warrior, a cavalryman who skirmished with shield and javelins and whose use spread in the wake of Alexander's conquests over the known world. They thought themselves great these spawn of Sparta, a city that founded hardly any other colonies at all. But unlike their pugnacious progenitors over time they had become much less prepared to develop the military muscle to fight for what they wanted, inclined if anything to concentrate on proficiency in her marine, both military and commercial. To compensate they famously tried to buy in the expertise they needed; two Epirote kings, one an uncle of Alexander the Great, the other one of his most brilliant successors, would fight for the city. The first against local Italian people and the second against the hegemony of Rome spreading inexorably south in the 270s. So now with the ruling magistrates bound to the Republic by ties of interest, and a Roman commandant making sure security was tight both internally and externally, it looked unlikely that these people would risk life and property by hitching their star to a Carthaginian presence that would inevitably mean their involvement in bloody warfare. Despite this, it might promise a return to cherished autonomy.

But it turned out Hannibal's enemies were about to do something that would turn the scales massively in his favour. There were always pro Carthaginians at Tarentum, the five who had visited Lake Avernus had emphasized that the 'common people' in the Assembly and particularly the younger men who remembered that only fifty years before it had been an independent city vying with Rome to be the greatest place in south Italy and were eager for revolution. And now the Romans perpetrated an act of brutality that was bound to make many others in the city rethink their loyalties in a situation where it still looked like the Carthaginians had not only come to Italy to stay, but might end up being the winning side. The Roman psyche is not easy to understand, there seemed to be a recurring inclination to do things that were bound to rebound against themselves. It almost seems typical of them the way they treated the hostages taken from Tarentum. Rome habitually detained citizens from her allies in comfortable captivity to assure the loyalty of their compatriots and when a group of these from Tarentum and Thurii made a bid for freedom but were recaptured, their jailers' resentment and fear over so many of their previous allies jumping ship and joining the Punic cause showed in a most fearsome manner. Blood spreading on the floor of the Comitium at Rome, the original place of communal assembly, as hostages were scourged and the cries as they were thrown to their death from the Tarpeian Rock would have resonated in the minds of their fellow citizens at home when word reached Tarentum. Some of the relatives of the men killed decided on action and we know two of their names: Nicon and Philemenus. These young men, on the pretence of going out to hunt at night, made contact with the Carthaginian pickets and were escorted into Hannibal's camp. Interviewed by the general himself, they offered to engineer an entrance for his army and assured him he would be welcomed by the people once the Roman garrison had been thrown out. All was agreed, and the men's bona fides in enemy eyes, were polished by providing them with cattle they could claim they had driven off from the enemy commissary lines. Communication being established and Hannibal convinced of Philemenus' sincerity, it only remained to get other key Tarentines on board, by assuring them no tribute of men or money would be imposed, that they would not just be exchanging one hard-hand master for another.

With this done, the young revolutionaries were patient. Philemenus visited Hannibal on a number of occasions under the guise of going hunting, little enough to raise notice as he was famed as having a passion for the chase. This ruse had another advantage; coming back with game the hunters shared their Carthaginian-provided catch, with both Livius, the Roman in charge of the garrison, and the junior officer commanding the Temenitis gate in the eastern land wall. Night excursions meant the guard became very used to opening the postern gate to these sportsmen, who announced their approach by a whistled signal agreed between them and whose hunting dogs' barking was looked forward to, an event that meant the sentries would feast on prime meat again.

The seasons dominate in all of ancient life but never more so than in military matters, but Hannibal had always showed he could be flexible. After all this was the man who had begun his crossing of the Alps, with which his name would be indelibly linked, with autumn well advanced and snow about to fall. Now despite the fighting season of 213 being ended and winter approaching he prepared to act. D-Day was decided upon when it became known that the garrison commander was going to be present at a celebration, to take place at the 'temple of the muses' near the marketplace. To ensure his enemy was on as low alert as possible, Hannibal had it put abroad that he was seriously ill, which was why his army was still established within three days' march of the city. But in reality he prepared, ordering his generals to select 10,000 of the best light-armed troops who, with four days' rations, were dispatched in the predawn dark on the road to Tarentum, with eighty Numidian horse riding a few miles in front to cover their movement, either by imprisoning any person found on the way or by giving the impression to any who heard of their activity, that it was just the kind of raid that had been a pattern for some time. About fourteen miles from the city the Numidians sent back word for the main body to halt. Here the men were fed in a river cut gorge, the banks of which were well away from prying eyes, as an officer's council ensured all were aware, from lowly soldiers to the leading generals, that everybody must strictly obey orders and do nothing off their own bat. With this understood Philemenus and his party led them forward as dusk was falling, he and his men carrying the carcass of a wild boar to tempt the palates of the tower guards as they had done so often before.

In the Agora the party had begun early and the suspicion is that near sundown, when information was passed to him that some Numidians were raiding nearby, Livius was pretty drunk. Still intent on his revelry he delegated an officer to take half the available cavalry the next morning to see the raiders off. The plotters, led by 'Nicon and Tragiscus' were waiting for the party to break up and for him to return home before they acted, and to ensure this outcome, a group of them joined the rollicking governor, escorting him to his bed carousing all the way. With the enemy commander sleeping off his debauch the conspirators acted. In three bodies, while leaving a guard outside Livius' house, they took control of the streets leading to the marketplace. And now the shindig was over and most of the citizens back home, they moved towards the Temenitis gate to facilitate the entry of the Carthaginians coming in from the eastern approaches. Due to the dictates of an oracle, unlike most Greek cities the Tarentines buried their dead both inside and outside the city walls. So between the house and their defences lay a necropolis peopled with dark ranks of tombs and it was here the insurgents gathered.

As had been agreed when last in their camp the conspirators looked for a light from a fire that the Carthaginians would build amongst the tombs outside the city walls. The place agreed had been a well known landmark 'called by some the tomb of Hyacinthus, by others the tomb of Apollo Hyacinthus'[8] and soon the blackness of the night was briefly illuminated by this marker. When the signal was seen Tragiscus responded with a fire of his own flashed from inside the walls to show those outside the bearing to take. Then sprinting the short distance to the ramparts, and relieved that the sentries had not noticed either the light inside or outside, they surprised the tower guard and let the Carthaginians in. It was a breeze; the sentries, surprised, put up no defence against an attack from within and with the bolts on the door cut, Hannibal and his task force entered the city. With no one even aware that they were in the neighbourhood and leaving his 2,000 cavalry outside the wall to protect the rear, he marched his men, expectations soaring now, in good order through the tombs into the suburbs and along the main thoroughfare towards the marketplace. But once near there he waited until he knew the other prong of the attack had accomplished its objectives.

This other string to the assailants' bow had been activated just as the fire signals were lit on the cemetery side of the city. Philemenus played his part accompanied by a few of his men. As was his usual practice he brought a huge boar, on a litter to the same postern gate he used when he had gone hunting before. The guard was whistled up, fearing nothing at all as he flung open the door, eager to get his share of the prize the huntsmen were bringing. There were four people in the party, one apparently disguised as a shepherd and once within the walls, Philemenus wearing sporting garb over a breastplate, himself ran the sentry through with a hunting spear, or they massacred him with barred knives depending on the version, just as he was inspecting the boar. When this was accomplished thirty Libyans were called up, they had been waiting in a thicket close to the walls just out of sight and they entered the postern, swiftly killing the somnolent guards in the towers by the main entrance. Again the bolts were cut and gates thrown open. A prearranged signal alerted a much larger body of Libyans who entered the town rushing down the road to the marketplace to join their comrades already there.

The attackers were now well in charge of a city not yet even roused. And three groups of about 700 Celts each, led by two young Tarentine insurgents apiece, were ordered to take up positions on the roads running out from the marketplace and cut down all the Romans they came across, while warning the locals to stay put and safe until the garrison had been ousted and the takeover complete. This had largely been achieved before those who had been at the party were aware of any danger, but this could not last. When word got about that the Carthaginians were inside the walls there was pandemonium. Livius, recognizing he was too drunk to do anything, slipped away and stumbled away from his house, helped by some servants and down to the harbour. There he found a boat with which he crossed over to the citadel. He was more fortunate than many of his compatriots who responding to a Roman bugle sounded by one of the insurrectionists from the seats in the theatre, hurried along the streets in disorderly groups to the citadel, their normal place of assembly, looking to find safety but only to be cut down by the waiting Celts or others of Hannibal's men.

Dawn found most of the locals hiding in their houses, not absolutely sure of what had occurred and for most it was the sight of Roman corpses that first alerted them that the Carthaginian army had arrived. Hannibal had been careful, keeping his men concentrated, encamped in the market to avoid confusion in the night. From there he could almost have seen the citadel looming off in the dark, but to attack before dawn was just too risky. With daylight, he called the citizens to come unarmed to the agora and encouraged Nicon, Philemenus and the others to reassure their compatriots that they had come as friends. By now most people showing themselves were well disposed, any Roman loyalists had hotfooted it for the safety of the fortress still held by Livius, so Hannibal was roared on as he met them with honeyed words, 'and reminded them of the way he had treated their compatriots whom he had taken in the battle of Cannae.' And assuring everybody that anyone who put 'A Tarentine' on his door would not be molested, though any who tried to help a Roman by doing so would be executed. Now the disorder of the night was over and with some men in arms to keep guard, the bulk of the soldiers plundered the unmarked houses. A day's looting that provided plenty of value to keep the men happy and eager as after another night of rest under arms their general prepared to round off his control of Tarentum.

The Carthaginians advanced to deal with the garrison of the citadel, which clung to its rocky promontory laved by the sea and was defended from the land side by walls and a deep moat. The passage to the fortress from the city was narrow, no more than a couple of hundred yards, and with the many hands of both his own men and locals a wall was begun, to cut it off from the town, and with a palisade and deep fosse to protect the citizens from possible sorties by the Roman garrison. But Hannibal's intentions were not just defensive, he hoped for more. From the start the garrison had showed aggression, opening the gates and attacking the working parties throwing up the ramparts, so he planned a surprise. Anticipating his enemy would soon make another sortie against the works he held his best troops back and when the enemy emerged, feigning a retreat, he lured them on. Then once most of them were beyond the moat he turned his men about and returned to the attack. 'A stubborn engagement followed, as the fighting took place in a narrow space between two walls, but in the end the Romans were forced back and put to flight. Many of them fell in the action, but the largest number perished by being hurled back and precipitated into the moat.'[9]

It is not difficult to imagine the struggle, looking today over the channel from the city towards the handsome Spanish fort refurbished from an Angevin castle covering the left half of where the Roman defences stood. There where the tourist can now stand on the city side of the bridge would have been the broken wooden barriers and half dug trenches that obstructed the Roman soldiers trying to get to safety, desperate enough to jump headlong into the fosse to try and get away. After this interruption the construction continued apace without a break and indeed another wall was erected parallel, inside the city reaching a street called 'Saviour to the Deep Street'. Defences ended up looking so robust that locals' morale reached sky-high, with the more daring Tarentines considering themselves capable of taking on the Romans on their own. Hannibal not quite sharing this confidence, when he decided to move on, left a force of cavalry and enough of a garrison both to help the citizens complete and defend their works, while he led the main army away to camp by the River Galaesus, about five miles from the town.

Despite decamping the Carthaginians had by no means despaired of digging out Livius and his men from their fortress. They had moved their main numbers out to ease the pressure on the city's granaries, particularly as the citadel sitting as it did on the narrow entrance to the harbour was able to interdict anything coming in by sea, almost subjecting the town to a blockade. But once he heard the walls between town and fortress had been completed Hannibal returned to try again. By now however the defenders had been boosted by the arrival of men shipped in from outside. It may be the Roman garrison was originally about 5,000 strong and though suffering casualties not a few loyal Tarentines had joined them and now so had half the garrison of Metapontum equipped with artillery, small scorpions, throwing bolts hardly heavier than javelins, to large ballista that might cast heavy stone shot into the enemy ranks. So now they were in considerable numbers and well equipped to defend the walls. Succour in the form of men and machines may explain the confidence with which the garrison now faced Hannibal when he brought up his own siege machines to the assault. Appian gives a real flavour of this second battle outside the citadel:

> The Carthaginians brought up towers, catapults, and tortoises with which he shook some of the walls, pulled off the parapets with hooks attached to ropes, and laid bare the defences. The garrison hurled stones down upon the engines and broke many of them, turned aside the hooks with slip-knots, and making frequent and sudden sallies always threw the besiegers into confusion and returned after killing many. One day when they noticed that the wind was violent some of the Romans threw down firebrands, flax, and pitch upon the engines, while others darted out and put fire under them. Hannibal, despairing of his attempt, threw a wall around the city except on the sea side, where it was not possible to do so. Then turning the siege over to Hanno he advanced into Apulia.[10]

But if Hannibal was stymied in this attempt to capture the citadel, the end of his 'attempts to storm the walls' setback did not mean he was not still full of ideas. His project to gain complete control of the whole city might have to be put on hold, but at least he could try and minimize the problems posed by these Romans in their island stronghold. Their control of the narrow passage from the port to the sea was the issue and their occupation of the bridge over this channel effectively obstructed the harbour mouth, cutting Tarentum off from access to the sea. To deal with this grip on the city's windpipe Hannibal decided that they must free the warships that were bottled up in the inland harbour, to use them to turn the tables so the defenders in the citadel might themselves be blockaded. To get the manpower required he called the city leaders together persuading them of his project as the only way they could force the surrender by starvation of the Roman garrison. He proposed they dig out a passage along the highway in the middle of the town and drag the fleet over to the seaside shore, smugly exclaiming, 'Many things which nature makes difficult become easy to the man who uses his brains.'[11]

There was no lack of enthusiasm, after all Livius' people were cutting them off from their natural element, everybody from lowly matelots to moneyed merchants would suffer from being denied access to the outer sea. Soon under eager hands, slow creaking wagons were fastened together to construct boat carriages and tackles hauled the warships out of the water while draught animals were hooked up and helped by thousands of willing workers; they dragged the burdens away. With everyone from all classes flocking to gawp at, if not assist in the enterprise, it took only a few days to drag the heavily laden transports through the city streets and relaunch the ships into the sea properly equipped for fighting and anchor them outside the sea mouth of the harbour.

Now it was a real role reversal with the citadel cordoned off, making the provisioning of the garrison a very difficult prospect. And even if this still did not mean open access for sea traffic into the city, at least it was now the Romans who were threatened with famine because the Tarentines did not totally depend on importing supplies; they could always bring provender in from the countryside. Previously Livius had, by controlling the bridges over the narrow passage into the harbour, gripped the city by the throat, but now with Tarentine warships patrolling the harbour mouth and the walls of the citadel they ensured little could get through to the blockaded men. So understandably with considerable satisfaction Hannibal was able to return to winter quarters, three days' march away, the very place he had been based when Nico and Philemenus found him before this late year action began. Hannibal had won almost full control of another great city in Italy and the details coming from the Carthaginian side that are recorded make it very probable that our extant sources took much from Silenus' field record of Hannibal's campaigns. Though it is telling that not wishing to advertise his namesake and probable antecedents' failings our main source, though concurring with Polybius in most of the details, redacted all references to the governor Livius' drinking.

The fighting season that followed this spectacular coup saw plenty more activity in the deep south. First the Romans managed to slip a convoy of corn purchased in Etruria into the harbour at Tarentum to sustain the garrison in the citadel there. But this setback was not a pattern and most inhabitants in the Italian south were not slow in understanding the direction of events. A new context exercised the minds of people who had never felt great warmth for despotic folk from central Italy and now could begin to imagine the days when Roman hegemony might be over, an attitude next made apparent at Metapontum, a port town in rich corn country just round the instep from Tarentum. With half its garrison gone to help Livius the people there took the opportunity to invite Hannibal to set them free and on top of this Heraclea still further along the coast threw in their lot with the Carthaginians too. Not only did these additions give the Carthaginian commander control of that part of the country, they encouraged disaffection in other dissatisfied Greek places too. So when the leading families at Thurii, already incensed when their relatives held hostage at Rome were butchered, made contact with the Tarentines they were won over. Communication had been instigated to try and ransom some citizens who had been captured when part of a convoy taking food to Livius was ambushed and scooped up. No question of the fact they were both originally founded by Achaean colonists helped and after being offered free restitution of the captives, they agreed to return home and persuade their compatriots to open the gates to the Punic forces.

Two Carthaginian officers were deputed to capture the place and arrangements were made for them to approach in secret and in sufficient numbers to take care of the Roman garrison under Marcus Atinius. Well schooled by friendly Thurians on the terrain and what to expect from the enemy Hanno appeared in the open in front of the town with his infantry while another Mago, not Hannibal's brother, and his cavalry hid behind some adjoining hills in ambush. Hannibal was not the only owner of a box of Punic tricks as these two now showed. Hanno trailed his coat by marching the foot soldiers through the wide rich valley made by the Crathis and the Sybaris rivers, in sight of the enemy scouts and waiting for a reaction. He had been informed that Atinius had only a small force of his own men, and would depend on the locals he had trained up and equipped with arms; knowing these militia would in all probability not be dependable Hanno was happy to deploy against the enemy when they emerged out of the city gates. He had not misjudged the situation, the bait was taken and Atinius came on with the small Roman force ahead of the Thurians in line behind.

As agreed in the command tent before the fight Hanno withdrew his foot soldiers to draw on the enemy into the trap prepared. Waiting in ambush Mago kept his men low with the horses quiet and gleaming corselets and helmets hidden. He knew what his role was and carried it out perfectly as he watched the enemy march past his hiding place in plodding columns. The local militia came on encouraged by the men who had trained them and once they were passed the hill he pounced. Mago knew he had got them where he wanted as his hallooing horsemen came out of hiding and crashed into the rear of their ranks. They first dispersed the Thurians, men with little heart in the fight, and then the Romans, who caught between two fires buckled after a brave and desperate resistance. Then they ran as fast as the locals, but unlike them many were caught outside the walls to be killed or captured when the men who had called the Carthaginians in closed the gates. The Roman general was somewhat more fortunate; he and few of his men had got inside the town and once there found they still had some friends on their side, people who argued hard against a Carthaginian takeover before the revolutionists prevailed. And these people who appreciated Atinius for his 'mild and just rule' were able to rush him and a number of his followers down to the port and smuggle them onto ships waiting in the harbour, ensuring he could depart with his life if not his reputation intact.

The Carthaginian officers met in the marketplace with the local principals, who had let them in discarding their Roman connection and admitting the new power in south Italy, on the promise of a light touch regime. And this happy interaction signalled that now Hannibal was in control from the inside heel to the toe on the Italian boot, with Greeks, Bruttians and Lucanians eager to court his pleasure. These peoples who so often in the past had been at each other's throats found in association that they shared a detestation of a Rome that for at least two generations had been throwing her weight around in their region. And that in Carthage they might have a champion who would ensure the Republic would never be able to return to oppress them. Tarentum, Metapontum, Heraclea and Thurii, this was a ringing statement of intent, the Tiber town's dominant position was under threat from the Volturnus in Campania to Syracuse in Sicily. Indeed south of Latium it was only in a few strongholds, like Luceria and Arpi in Apulia, the coastal towns and Nola in Campania, Beneventum, Venusia and the Pentri in Samnium, and some places in Lucania and Rhegium in Bruttium, where she was still hanging on.

Chapter 3

One Hanno amongst Many

Our ancestors, Conscript Fathers, were never deficient in conduct or courage; nor did pride prevent them from imitating the customs of other nations, if they appeared deserving of regard. Their armour, and weapons of war, they borrowed from the Samnites; their ensigns of authority, for the most part, from the Etrurians; and, in short, whatever appeared eligible to them, whether among allies or among enemies, they adopted at home with the greatest readiness, being more inclined to emulate merit than to be jealous of it.

Sallust, *The Conspiracy of Catiline*, 51.38.

Yet if it seemed in late 213 that a high-water mark had been reached with the great metropolises Capua, Syracuse and Tarentum fighting against Rome, the tide would not stay in for long. The resources that the Republic was able to deploy began almost from the moment of Carthaginian triumph, and made a start on clawing back the grand strategic initiative. And just as Hannibal and his officers glad-handed their new friends in the broad agora of Tarentum they began to get the first indication that the years of triumph might not result in the swift victory they hoped for. Word from even further south would have reached them warning that, though Carthaginian agents and their supporters had been in charge at Syracuse since 214 at least, they were now finding times hard in a Sicilian war where Marcellus, directed to that front from Campania, had orchestrated a Roman revival that would culminate in the successful siege of the city itself. But still it might be useful to imagine what would have happened if at this time, when the Carthaginian wave was cresting, some of Rome's key allies had jumped ship. If Luceria, Beneventum, Venusia, the lynchpins of the defence of Apulia, Samnium and Lucania, the seaside places Neapolis, Puteoli and Paestum had gone over. Could this have been a tipping point? Surely it is only in retrospect that the possibility of a Carthaginian success seems far-fetched and considering what this might have been like is not a wholly fruitless exercise. How many colonies would have had to go on strike, as twelve did in 209 to only pull themselves out of the war, not even join the other side, for the dynamic to have altered? There is of course no way of knowing, but clearly even Rome's closest supporters must have had a breaking point when they had spent blood enough and war weariness made anything thinkable.

The intransigence in adversity of the Republic's leaders may be lauded in a contest that had been so brutal for so long, but still without the resources of wealth and manpower provided by these places she could never have survived as a local central Italian power, never mind the hegemon of Italy. It is difficult to put oneself into the head of the people in places like Praeneste and Fregellae who showed such loyalty *in extremis*, when prospects were terrifying, but the point must surely have come when the number of their sons who had to die would have become too much. Though it cannot be coincidence that when signs of battle fatigue were manifested by the colonies in Rome's central heartland it was after the possibility of a Carthaginian triumph had almost completely receded. When there was little real risk of Hannibal with thousands of Africans, Iberians and other assorted barbarians arriving on their doorstep, and if this had not been the case they might well have kept their noses to the grindstone despite the butchering of their best and brightest.

Hannibal had many officers under him in the Italian Wars, both in independent command and those leading the units in his own army, but we know little about the background and doings of most of them. Amongst these were several Hannos of whom it is not always clear which is which. The paucity of names amongst the Carthaginian leadership makes absolute attestation tricky at times. One of them was a son of Bomilcar, who had been a chief magistrate at Carthage, and of one of Hannibal's sisters, a nephew who was noted doing well at the crossing of the Rhone on the march to Italy and who crucially at Cannae fought his Numidians with great dash and skill against the Italian allied horse, allowing time for the heavy Iberian and African cavalry from the other wing to ride round and complete their triumph. A Hanno who may have been the same man but maybe not headed south with Mago to bring over Lucania and Bruttium to the Punic cause soon after Cannae and it is this man whose career can be followed in some detail. This considerable officer it seemed may have suffered something of a bloody nose in 215, going to join Hannibal in Campania after he had pulled back from his attempt on Cumae, when he bumped into a Roman army near Grumentum in central Lucania. He found himself confronted by Tiberius

Sempronius Longus, and forced back to Bruttium, where in that same year he was able to welcome another Bomilcar, who brought the one significant reinforcement from home we know Hannibal received when in Italy. And taking over these forces Hanno led them to join his commander near Nola. Here he was even deputed by his leader to attempt to contact the town's chief magistrates to persuade them to turn their coats and join the Punic cause. This attempted subversion, delivered through an interpreter, and unbelievably reported as facilitated by Marcellus, failed and when a military solution also proved unachievable he returned to Bruttium, probably with the same men and elephants he had brought with him, as the main army went into winter quarters in Apulia.

This man had remained a stalwart in the south and had already been active in the year 212. Recently he had to deal with both some undependable allies and an outbreak of privatized belligerence in the region. Consentia in the interior and Taurianum on the Tyrrhenian Sea which had joined the Carthaginians over the last few years had now returned to the Roman fold and apparently more would have done so as well except for a prefect of Roman allies and an ex tax farmer with a reputation for dishonesty, whose activities had become a real headache for many in the territory. This man after some marauding, though profitable, had alienated many potential friends, had persuaded prospective recruits that he was a real military leader with a chance of taking on Hanno's tried and trusted army. Rhegium was the only strong place that had remained consistently true to Rome in Bruttium and it may be that its governor was happy for this man to take the war to an enemy; he felt he was not strong enough to deal with himself, no doubt lending some proper soldiers to give an amount of backbone to his band of brigands. All we know is that this Pomponius 'scraped together some sort of an army' but to what extent they were trained or what arms they had we just don't know. But the suggestion is they were mostly ill-prepared, untrained runaway slaves and peasants, something pretty much confirmed when Hanno, far from resting on his laurels, decided to take the threat seriously, swamping them, destroying or dispersing the lot and capturing their leader to boot.

While Hanno had been fighting these fires in the Italian toe Hannibal had been caught in a Capua Tarentum conundrum. A circle even this brilliant man could not quite square. If he had managed to take the citadel in the great southern port it might have been different, but he could never do it. Livius, sober now and staying away from parties, held out and while he continued to do so the Carthaginian general could not happily leave the town and its environs to concentrate on helping his friends in Campania. Despite that news continued to arrive in his camp about the huge enterprises being mooted in Rome, that the consuls Appius Claudius and Quintus Fulvius Flaccus would both be sent to encompass the downfall of a city they hated in a quite exceptional way. The desire to destroy Capua was felt deeply and personally, theirs had been a relationship so close that when it broke down the fallout was tidal. The city had come into the Roman fold after a threat from nearby Samnites; the fear of being engulfed by mountain men had persuaded the leadership there to put themselves under Roman protection back in the fourth century. Only this local threat made subservience to the strong power on the Tiber acceptable, if not palatable, to many. Though others in this rich and powerful place with its smiling cornfields and pale green vineyards, once an Etruscan foundation, had entered the relationship with her new patron with a will. The rich and well born of the two cities frequently intermarried and plenty of noble Capuans had full Roman citizenship, owning houses in the capital and linked financially in exploiting the riches of fruitful Campania. And these close collaborators had shown themselves sound before, even staying loyal when the commons had been caught up with a revolt by the Latins in the 340s. There is even a suggestion that it could have been a faction in Rome with close Campanian links that had pushed hard to get her involved in the First Punic War because of a desire to exploit the riches that would come from controlling trade with, and the resources of, the far south of Italy and Sicily. It had been this closeness that made Capua's disaffection after Cannae so deeply hurtful for a people who considered they had treated the community to the south like a sister. And that the leader of the revolt was actually married doubly into the family of the consul Appius Claudius could have only compounded the distress.

But it was not just motivation, it was opportunity too, as in the previous year a group of nobles from Capua had left town on the excuse of plundering the property of nearby pro Romans, but in fact had ridden hard to reach Gnaeus Fulvius Centumalus' camp above Suessula, saying that they and plenty of their like would be prepared to come over if their property could be guaranteed after a Roman victory. So with division in the enemy ranks the opportunity seemed golden to try for a hit at this lynchpin of the nascent Carthaginian confederation of south Italy. But these crucial allies could not be left to swing in the wind, Capua was as important as Tarentum, not just because the city and its hinterland was wealthy and populous, but because, if it fell, it would make the likelihood of new recruits to the Carthaginian cause amongst the Italian peoples much less probable. In this crisis Hannibal turned to his capable lieutenant in Bruttium and orders were sent to Hanno to go to the aid of the Campanians. When called upon the task he was given was tough enough, to face the six legions and their allies that were moving on Capua, not to mention Gracchus' slave army which was holding its own in Lucania and advantageously positioned to help the consuls as well.

Hanno was a hard marcher and knew the importance of his task. Managing to slip past Gracchus he kept well clear of the consuls. These two after the 'flamens' made the appropriate sacrifices at the Temple of Mars as tradition demanded, and left Rome for Bovianum in the hills of north Samnium, on the far side of Mount Tifernus, enjoying the hospitality of the loyal people of the Pentri, while planning the campaign against Capua. Hanno made it, without encountering trouble, to Beneventum, a place he knew well from events two years before. This frequent visitation is understandable as the town, in a bowl below surrounding hills, with great knuckled mountains looming, frequently snow-flecked, to the north-west, had been, and would continue as a strategic node for centuries. A key staging post on the road, the Appian Way, would soon follow this Samnium town as had been colonized in 268, the citizens receiving Latin rights, and remained faithful to the Republic during all the traumatic events affecting her people and those around her in the Second Punic War. The importance of this provincial centre has been evinced down the ages by just how many great and decisive battles had been fought in the fields around. In 274 Pyrrhus of Epirus had been finally defeated by the Romans just outside the city, warranting its change of name from Maleventum to Beneventum (bad wind to good wind), and 1,500 odd years later the army of the French duke of Anjou had trounced the sitting Hohenstaufen ruler, attacking east over the bridge crossing the River Calor into the town and by these efforts introducing Angevin dominance to southern Italy.

But never was there so much action around the town as in this Hannibalic war for Italy. The first of the Roman Carthaginian battles of Beneventum occurred in 214; two years earlier this same Hanno had marched up the leg of Italy from Bruttium with a good-sized army hoping to join his commander-in-chief in some decisive activity around Nola, but instead bumped into a body of men with a point to prove. Their commander was Gracchus, consul the previous year and master of horse before that, just arrived from Luceria in Apulia. He had pushed his men hard to reach Beneventum and they had responded well considering that a good many of them, two legions' worth, were made up of slave volunteers, with a leavening of debtors and criminals, recruited to help compensate for the huge loss of manpower suffered between 218–216. Hearing from the locals when he passed through the city gates that the Carthaginians were camped three miles away on the Calor River he sent out scouts. These men, while the main body refreshed themselves amongst friendly locals, spread out riding along the river valley that snaked east of the town and soon found what they were looking for. They returned with word that the enemy were indeed not far away and potentially vulnerable with so many of their men out raiding the lands of the Rome-loyal burghers of the district. Gracchus needed no more prompting and putting all his men into marching column led them out, only halting to order them to make camp a mile away from his target.

Peering along the foam-flecked river to where the enemy occupied the wide green fields running gently down to the water, he knew that at this range it would be difficult for the Carthaginians to withdraw without exposing the rear of their marching order to a slashing attack. To try and give himself an edge in the battle to come, Gracchus had got permission from the Senate to free his slave soldiers if he thought it would make them fight better. Now addressing the assembled men before the butchery began, he told them that anyone could earn his manumission in the coming battle by bringing an enemy head back from the fight. So with his men suitably fired, when Hanno deployed his 17,000 Bruttium and Lucanian infantry and 1,200 horse, some few Italian and the rest African, Gracchus' men attacked immediately. This was no cunningly crafted plan, just a brute battering attack and indeed it is suggested that they responded so enthusiastically to the offer their general had made them that some of these warriors, after four hours of trying to secure victims, were so preoccupied with retaining hold on an enemy head that they had no hands free to wield their weapons. But the general having this reported to him by the tribunes, rectified matters by announcing that any fighter would be freed without the need of a head as long as the army routed the Carthaginians. Once relieved of this disadvantage, the servile warriors piled once more into an enemy who had stiffened their fighting line by rallying routed men and bringing in their reserves. As blow was traded for blow between brave Italians, combatants each holding up the side they had committed to, Gracchus tried for a decision with his cavalry. The Roman and allied bluebloods who comprised the mounted arm were in considerable numbers, but charging forward they found themselves held at bay by the nimble Numidians whose accurate volleys of javelins brought down horses and men despite the large round shields carried and the mail shirts worn by the attackers.

The story is that all along the lines and on the wings too, the battle was finely balanced, until Gracchus relayed the word to his sweating and hard breathing men that one last effort that pushed the enemy off the field would win them their freedom. 'These words were the torch which finally set them on fire' and the slave warriors charged again, bowling over the exhausted enemy in the front lines and when these turned and fled it was infectious. They pushed further into the Punic line, taking standards and rupturing the reserve line, until 'After that it was a clean route'. Even those who made it back to their camp found no respite and a second struggle commenced as the fleeing troops jammed the gates and, unable to manoeuvre, were slaughtered like cattle. The worst was that a considerable number of prisoners had been kept in the camp and now these men escaped their bonds, found weapons and attacked in the back any of Hanno's soldiers who were standing and fighting. Almost all of his infantry were eliminated, thirty-eight standards were taken, and the 2,000 men who escaped with their general were almost all his cavalry. The Romans reported 2,000 men lost altogether and those slaves who had done well received full freedom, with even 4,000 who had lagged back in the fight being eventually manumitted, though they had to threaten mutiny to get their due, taking up a stance on a hill outside the army camp, before receiving their freedom. And even then the donation was not untrammelled, but involved having to take their meals standing up for the rest of the war as penance. A circumstance that Gracchus had painted up as decoration for a temple he dedicated to liberty on the Aventine Hill.

All this is a fine anecdote but it has to be less than the whole truth. There must have been much exaggeration here. To begin with it is just impossible to picture the whole front rank of the Roman battle line with the men desperately trying to fight while holding an enemy head. Much more likely there were just a few instances where this headcount took over from the usual cut and thrust, where killing the enemy in front and surviving oneself was the imperative. Still perhaps even this would have been enough to worry the general and make him reconsider what he had enjoined. Secondly we learn that the same Hanno, who had suffered this apparently decisive defeat, quite soon after, caught some of Gracchus' men out ravaging the country and beat them up to such good effect that their losses came near to equalling the casualties inflicted upon him at the Beneventum fight. Now as the claim is that almost 17,000 troops were lost on that occasion, casualties of near

Trasimene proportions, how is it feasible that Hanno scraped together, in double quick time, a whole new army that then could inflict the same damage on the troops of the man who had just defeated him? Clearly in both actions a considerable amount of overstatement can be assumed though Gracchus had certainly done well in terms of grand strategy by preventing Hanno from joining his commander-in-chief at Nola.

But if the exact details of this Hanno/Gracchus confrontation are opaque, the equivalent cannot be said for the next encounter around the same windy city in the beautiful hills of Samnium. Back again in 212 the Carthaginian commander had been given the job of provisioning Capua, something the city's representatives had been begging to be done before the Roman consul's armies arrived to block the roads into town. He again moved in from the east along the Calor where heavy winter rain ensured his army was accompanied by the music of water rushing over stone as the river ran on towards its junction with the Volturnus above Casilinum, before running down to the sea. Camping on high ground three miles short of Beneventum on its western side Hanno sent out his men to gather all the supplies they could find, particularly grain stored from the year before by Puniphiles in the country around and providing troops to protect the men from Roman loyalists. There are plenty of defensible hills that could be the spot Hanno occupied, but a prime candidate is just on the outskirts of the modern city in the Naples direction. This knoll, with a cliff dropping off towards the road and its other sides steep and defensible, was just the size to contain a large encampment capable of holding not only Hanno's men but all the provender, supplies and transports needed to fill Capua's granaries. It was also right by the Appian Way, an excellent road for the great convoy that was being built, to travel the forty-odd miles it was to the Campanian capital. When his commissariat considered they had enough provisions to do the job, the authorities in Capua were notified, telling them to send plenty of wagons to supplement the ones that had been requisitioned from the local people, to transport the supplies from camp to city. But the response was not good, despite the desperate need to prepare for the coming blockade, the people under threat were dilatory and only just over 400 transports were dispatched, far from sufficient for the task. Hanno, while incensed at their lack of urgency and commitment, knew the importance of keeping these people on side, so despite the setback arranged another date for them to organize an adequate wagon train to bring to the Beneventum camp, where the pile of grain was growing rapidly.

The reason given for the failure is that it was just another instance of Campanian lethargy that Romans enjoyed reporting, fitting as it did into their picture of this effete, treacherous people, so different from their own image of themselves as hard driving strivers. Every eventuality was fair game to denigrate the people of Capua for the crime of deserting the Roman cause. There is even a claim that Hannibal's army, after spending their first winter after Cannae in the comforts of the town, were never the same men again. Soldiers who had crossed the Pyrenees, the Rhone and the Alps and had never been defeated in battle were ruined by their winter in the fleshpots of the Campanian capital, even deserting to return to the women they had found there when Hannibal tried to mobilize them for the next year's fighting. While no doubt there were instances of this very human behaviour the whole contention is evidenced as foolish by exactly the number of times this same army would thrash their Roman enemies in the years to come, never in fact enduring a significant verifiable defeat when Hannibal was at their head.

In fact on this occasion it is harsh to blame the Campanians too much. After all it was a longish hike up the Caudine Valley to get to Hanno's camp and all along the way they might be exposed to attacks from the several Roman armies within striking distance. A large escort would have been needed and they would have found it difficult to take that number of cavalry away from the job of defending the city and its farming hinterland. But still this failure at the first attempt was critical, as the job of assembling a new caravan took time and there were plenty of Roman sympathizers in the Beneventum neighbourhood, and with both consuls now concentrated at Bovianum they were well able to alert them to what was happening.

The consul Quintus Fulvius Flaccus acted when messengers arrived at his camp from Beneventum, and hoping to keep his opponent in the dark he marched after sundown, only entering the town when all his men had come up. Swiftly learning the latest news he realized he had stumbled on a real opportunity, as Hanno was out of his camp with part of the army collecting more grain, and the whole enemy post was highly vulnerable, a mass of 2,000 wagons with drivers, drovers and peasants from the countryside bringing in their wares. The troops left on guard he heard were thoroughly disrupted, so without waiting and hoping to catch the Carthaginians at a disadvantage he ordered his men to drop any heavy equipment they had with them, to speed their passage and march straight out with just the arms they carried. After filing out of the town's night-dark streets and with the sun just coming up the legionaries and their attached allies were soon within sight of the enemy camp. But the Romans though gratified by the evidence that they had stolen a march, found their approach was up steep and difficult slopes and that the defenders were well placed, denying the attackers, however eager and prompt, any easy way of getting in. Despite the surprise, when dawn broke and the attackers announced their arrival the units left to guard the milling mass of civilians and transports were somehow able to make a fist of resisting the assault, showering the Romans with javelins as they charged up the hill against them. Drawn up on the slope in front of the camp they almost stopped them cold. But accepting casualties as the price of success, the attackers pushed on up the hill. These were proper legionaries, not the slave soldiers of Gracchus armed with whatever could be found, and their morale was high, confident in a general who, already renowned, would soon make himself one of the great figures in the war.

Each of the Roman legions entering the battle amounted, when recruited to full strength, to between 4,200 and 5,000 men divided into four kinds of soldier and the allies who fought with them came in similar numbers and were similarly organized. The way these warriors were arranged was something different, unlike Greeks who fought in a phalanx alongside neighbours they knew well from civilian life, or Gauls or Iberians who were brigaded together in war bands based around family and clan. When the legions were raised the drafted men were picked in turn, by the officers of the different units, almost akin to schoolchildren picking teams to compete against each other. A system that not only ensured the best recruits were evenly distributed but intentionally broke up any previous social connection and ensured the primary allegiance of any recruit would be to his new unit rather than to friend, family or neighbourhood.

The first type of these soldiers, the Velites, led the way into battle. Up the steep green grass slope, young men of the lowest property qualification, some distinguished by a wolf's pelt worn over their helmet to attract the notice of officers who might reward their bravery, but all carrying several javelins with long thin iron heads, round shield and sword. Interestingly by a year after Cannae the property qualification for serving in the legion was dropped to a third of its former level (from 11,000 to 4,000 asses) and this is almost certainly meant something like a doubling of the number of light armed Velites in the legions. These even less affluent citizens would clearly not be able to afford the panoplies worn by the heavy infantry and were anyway needed to try and counter the good missile men deployed by the Carthaginian army, a factor that would soon have the Republic even occasionally hiring foreign archers and slingers to plug a perceived area of weakness.

Their javelins would have been thrown in volleys at the enemy lines before the Velites fell back hastily to the protection of the first lines of the heavy infantry, as they took up the gage. These were the Hastati, again younger men carrying the long oval body shield or scutum, a convex affair 2.5ft wide, 4ft deep, made of glued wood covered in canvass and leather edged with a boss of iron making it near 10kg in weight. Also protected by a helmet topped with three black or red 18in. tall plumes, they often wore a greave on their forward leg; generally less prosperous than their elders they only stretched to a bronze pectoral or square breastplate, worn over a rust red tunic and just covering the chest. They too flung their 3.5kg pilum at 15yds from the enemy, but far from then withdrawing they took out their short swords and broke into a trot to attack the defenders hand-to-hand. This was a stabbing weapon and would now most likely have been the very effective 20in. Spanish sword that the Romans had been re-equipping with since they encountered it while fighting in the Iberian Peninsula. But with some flinching from the risk of contact and others cut down they were thrown back to be replaced by a second line coming up the steep sward. These Principes were more mature men, usually with the wherewithal to afford a chain mail shirt, weighing 15kg, made of interlinked steel rings, a technology borrowed from the Celts, as was the pot-like head protection, the Montefortino helmet, with metal ear flaps that many wore. Of the four sorts of warriors that lined up behind each other when the legion deployed for battle, the last were the Triarii. These mature veterans numbered only about half as many as were counted in the Hastati and Principes and instead of the pilum retained a thrusting spear as their main weapon and their role was commonly to remain as reserve to cover the retreat of their comrades in the event of defeat, or sometimes even left as camp guards while the rest went into battle. But still if the need arose they could also be flung in as a final throw of the dice by a commander prepared to gamble everything on victory. They also would have worn mail shirts, helmets and shield like the rest and by this time, though all these different legionaries had to fund their equipment, they may well have actually been drawn from state arsenals.

Whatever the minutiae of the outfitting of these men, the Principes too now flung their pila before supporting their juniors with scutum covering them from knee to shoulder and deadly sword ready to push into any exposed enemy in front. The combined pressure as they crashed into the enemy line with their shield bosses was effective, the Romans driving forward up the slope and the Punic battle line pressed back. First they took up another position further up towards the camp until many were forced behind their walls with a number of attackers getting into the ditch under the ramparts. But the defenders still held the gate so their assailants were stymied in their design to overrun them. Getting there and getting in were very different things and it seems Fulvius became disheartened and conferring with his officers seems to have concluded he had bitten off more than he could chew. He would have consulted with those senior legionary commanders, and with those of the six tribunes in each legion who were near enough, and those men with experience who accompanied the consul on his staff. This was an informal group, no doubt some trusted friends and young men related, or sons of friends serving out their apprenticeship years in the army like such exquisites in any age preferring the comfort of a headquarters billet to slumming amongst the rankers. These last would have been useful for taking messages but probably have had little input on tactical discussions and the same would have been true of the lictors, the twelve men who guarded the body and carried out the disciplinary mandates of their consul, though some might have been recruited from time-served centurions and so capable of offering not a little insight for any commander with the humility to ask them.

In this situation Fulvius, who may have anticipated a walkover with so many enemy away, now agreed with the officers around him that it might be better to first withdraw to Beneventum to reorganize, then return and surround the enemy camp, making sure the Campanian wagon train was trapped and Hanno could not get back to succour them. Then to send for the other consul Appius' army to come up, to join them and so ensure they could crush the enemy if he tried to make a match of it. Yet despite the fact the trumpets had already blown to order a withdrawal, some of Fulvius' followers were in a different mood, confidence engendered by the presence of 20,000 men deployed in deep ranks in a half mile crescent round an enemy who were clearly beginning to feel the pressure. And an officer of one of the allied units from Pelignia took charge, throwing his unit's standard over the rampart and calling over the battle racket that his men should charge the defences to retrieve it. These daredevils crouching low for traction ascended the earthen banks and somehow clambered over the wooden walls. Once in, they were joined by legionaries from the 3rd Legion encouraged by their own commander who with his men was ashamed to be shown up as less courageous than their allied comrades.

This encounter is an original for a number of reasons. It seems to be not only the first time in this war that Livy mentions either the ethnicity of allies or tribunes in his narrative and also alludes to legions by number in battle, though on a couple of occasions enumeration had been applied to units when their distribution is described.[1] Logic might suggest that the need to mobilize legions and keep them under arms for many years might be behind this development but it has been convincingly argued that it in fact reflects the sources he is using.[2] Such details are merely the parroting of Roman historians known as the younger annalists, most particularly Valerius Antias. Our chronicler from Padua was not hugely interested in military minutiae or tactical terminology, being far more concerned about presentation and style.

This Valerius Flaccus who had egged on his men from the 3rd Legion was almost certainly the same who would have a great career ahead of him that reached its heights after the end of the Second Punic War. He was consul in 195, fought the Insubres Gauls before then serving in Greece against Antiochus the Great at Thermopylae in 191. In the 180s he became censor alongside his lifetime friend Cato the Elder. Both were hard-line traditionalists eager to pounce on anybody who was overly fond of things Greek and Flaccus ended his career at the top, raised to 'Princeps Senatus', father of the Senate, in 183. Encouraged by this man, the 3rd Legion were led in the attack by the chief centurion of their Principes, called Titus Pedanius, who clutching the standard climbed the rampart and called on his soldiers to aid him if they did not want the insignia to be taken. Men stood on each other's shoulders to get over the defences as their comrades protected themselves with their shields from the rain of missiles coming down from defenders on the fighting platforms and towers. Long though the fight seemed in the balance once some of the attackers got inside, the enemy lost heart and the Romans, despite considerable losses in the fighting in front of the fosse and on the walls, forced the palisade and the camp was taken. With these assailants pressing, their officers shouting orders above the tumult, everywhere was in disorder, with wagons pushed over and civilians desperately looking for a way out. It was so difficult for the Carthaginian troops to escape that in the course of the melee many were butchered where they stood. Six thousand were claimed as killed and 7,000 made prisoner but some of these would have been the Campanians coming to transport the grain rather than regular combatants. And whooping and yelling in celebration the victors, walking over the bloody corpses of their enemies, destroyed the place, while the wagons, livestock and grain and the booty plundered by Hanno in recent days from pro Romans in the region were taken as spoils to Beneventum. There the other consul Appius Claudius, himself fresh from Sicily where he had been seconding Marcellus' campaign, soon arrived with the other army to oversee the distribution of the spoils and decorate the brave men who had spearheaded the assault on the walls of Hanno's camp.

That general had been at a place called Cominium Ocritum, the exact position is unknown but presumably reasonably nearby, when the action took place and soon enough learnt from fugitives of the disaster that had befallen his army. With few men left and without any hope of revictualling Capua he had little option but to return to his base in Bruttium to lick his wounds. This was while the city leadership only increased its desperate pleas for help to Hannibal, warning that the two consuls were now at Beneventum, hardly more than a couple of days' easy march from Capua and threatening to take the fight all the way to their walls. Nor was it just the threat of two consular armies arriving intent on a siege; raiding parties were already keeping the people out of the fields so crops could not be sown. When he heard, Hannibal was still too tied up in the deep south but at least dispatched 2,000 cavalry back with the delegates to help keep off those intent on riving the Campanian hinterland. It was action well warranted, if insufficient, as Appius and Fulvius began to show eager in their efforts to give instruction on what would happen to those who broke with Rome. They had determined on a push directly against Capua and to cover the manoeuvre they summoned Gracchus to come from Lucania, where he had taken up the cudgel, skirmishing with local Puniphiles and storming a few small communities, when the call for help came. He was required to come at once to defend their flank at Beneventum once the consular armies left that place for Campania.

It was when the shoots planted by harassed country folk had begun to show above ground in early summer that the two consuls moved from Beneventum to ravage the countryside down the Appian Way, past Caudium, sitting on its knoll under a huge dome of rock today called Mount Taburna and then past the site of the Caudine Forks where Roman legions had gone under the yoke in 321. And once arrived they began to throw siege lines round the city of Capua itself. This was not taken lying down as the defenders sortied out and attacked these invaders trying to wreck their bountiful farmland, super productive volcanic earth that yielded some of the best grapes and grain in Italy. They came out in force, not just the excellent Campanian horse,

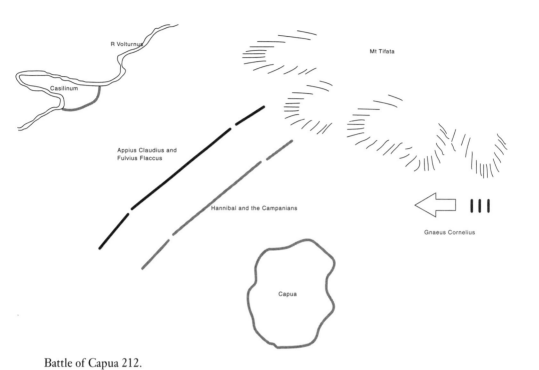

Battle of Capua 212.

but the 2,000 already sent by Hannibal and more cavalry under another Mago, seconded from Hanno in Bruttium and just marched up to join the defenders. The consuls had not expected such an aggressive response and their officers desperately had to drag men, scattered looking for plunder, back into formation, to try and form a line against these caracolling cavaliers. Many of the intruders were caught in open order, hardly able to fight at all and in no time 1,500 of the looters were casualties and even more running the roads or into rough country where they might find a chance of escape. By the time both sides left off fighting the Roman generals were a much more circumspect pair, with a great deal more respect for the men they had come to conquer. The morale of their soldiers was hit too, a fact that could not be hidden even by an anecdote about two old pre-war friends, now on different sides, organizing a joist. And even if the victory of the champion from the besieging army did something to revive Roman spirits, it was not before time because Hannibal with the main Carthaginian army was about to materialize on the scene.

He had come at last to protect his key ally, route marching through Apulia and Samnium, bypassing Beneventum and reaching Capua a few days after the successful sortie. And all this done despite a cordon of armies comprising eight legions who, with allies and auxiliaries, would have numbered somewhere between 80,000 to 100,000 men, lying between him and his Campanian friends. After the step off was ordered he had slipped past the main armies in Lucania and at Suessula, brushing aside any of the enemy detachments he encountered, before near his goal he got through the troops actually encircling Capua before they knew it, to join his allies in the town. An American civil war veteran called Theodore Ayrault Dodge, who made a considerable name as a military historian of the war he himself fought in before registering an epic output on the great captains of history, waxed absolutely lyrical on the achievement of Hannibal in this march to relieve Capua. 'But nothing except the rarest ability, and the power of making the enemy dread his very approach, can explain such a march as this last one of the Punic leader.'[3] Nor is this unreasonable; Hannibal's manoeuvring through a mesh of enemy armies positioned on his flanks and front and outnumbering him many fold is one of the great feats of the war. Yet he hardly rested on his laurels, taking only three days after descending from his old camp at Tifata to organize his own and the Campanian troops, before he moved to build on the success of his confederates to break the stranglehold the Romans were tightening round the city. Deciding any delay could only allow the enemy to grow stronger and that boldness was his best protection Hannibal offered battle and the enemy were willing. A major set piece encounter developed, with the two consular armies around Capua on one side and the Carthaginians and Campanians on the other. Well over 40,000 legionaries and their allies would have deployed between Capua and the Volturnus River where the ground was open and the road back towards Rome held at Casilinum if things went badly for the consuls.

On the battlefield numbers were against him but not hugely, Hannibal had come in decent force despite leaving part of his army, almost certainly his elephants and some of his heavy baggage as well, in the south. He would have wanted to keep the men in hand fairly trim to ensure the best possible chance of avoiding the enemy on route, but now he could call on the Campanians; mobilizing every man capable of wielding a weapon in defence of hearth and home. But the question remains as to what kind of army it was that emerged from the gates of the Campanian capital in what threatened to be the greatest clash since Cannae. The tussling around Nola, Neapolis and Cumae had not involved the kind of numbers that were now dressing their lines in the flat country between Mount Tifata and the Volturnus River. Those at most had been the contest between one consular army and whatever Hannibal had in the field, but now it was one of those unusual occasions when both of Rome's top commanders, as at Cannae, were present with all the troops they could muster, facing the main Carthaginian army of Italy buttressed by allies fighting for their very survival under the walls of their capital.

In the occidental world during ancient historical times we can be fairly sure most of the time how participants squared up to fight each other. When Greek cities came to blows it was in phalanx formation, blocks of soldiers at least eight deep, going up to fifty in extreme instances such as when the Thebans fought the Spartans at the Battle of Leuctra in 371. With this core a variable number of light infantry and cavalry might be involved, troop types that actually comprised the majority of the Persian armies the Greeks contended with in the great wars against the Achaemenids recorded most extensively by Herodotus and Xenophon. Persian cavalry was very good, mostly much superior to their Greek opponents, but their infantry was less so, usually lightly armoured with only wicker shields. With the advent of Macedonian power again we know very well how they organized and fought, the deep infantry phalanx with its long pike or sarissa was not only extremely effective, it also appealed to the arithmetic inclinations of many who came after. Becoming something a of a philosophical ideal for writers on tactics in the Roman imperial age that probably bore little enough resemblance to the reality of the regiments that squared up to Thracians, Illyrians, Greeks and Persians under Phillip II and Alexander III. Again in the age of Alexander's successors there were military elaborations on a theme, but it is pretty clear how their wars were fought. Elephants, Gallic mercenary bands, Tarentines, Hellenistic Thureophoroi, medium spear armed infantry with a shield based on a Gallic pattern, all became an accepted part of the military, but there is little dispute about their equipment, role or deployment.

But the same cannot be proclaimed with quite such confidence in the campaigning we are considering. Indeed question marks hover over the development of the Roman military from the start. It is generally reckoned that early Rome was either ruled directly or very strongly influenced by the Etruscans to the north, from whom she filched not only religious ritual and sculptural techniques, but the idea of gladiatorial combat and possibly even the arch that allowed such developments in architecture in both the Republic and empire, and whose Greek style hoplite military establishment she also copied. But over time, during the fourth and fifth centuries, while Rome warred almost continually with her close neighbours in Latium, with

Volsci and Aequi, with rampaging Gauls from the north and the many tribes of Samnium, the tactical posture of her legionaries evolved. They morphed from hoplite spearmen fighting in a single mass, (possibly with missile men incorporated in the main body as shown in visual representations of Archaic Greek battle lines), into mainly javelin toting swordsmen, who did not cover the comrade on the left with their round hoplon but fought individually, defending themselves with a long body shield. A stance that meant they occupied somewhat more space than a Phalangite, to be able to effectively cut, thrust and parry, rather than just pushing forward with their spear. Space that also needed to be allowed for the usually five to seven ranks behind, where the men were positioned to step in and replace the front ranks, when they were downed or wearied, as opposed to pushing forward and making a shield wall that rolled over the enemy in front. The other key change was that the single line was divided, no longer one mass of men, but at least initially formed in a series of maniples of 120 men each, placed in a chequerboard pattern with the second and third lines covering the gaps in those in front of them.

But it is not so much how the Republic's warriors behaved that is difficult in our period, though issues certainly remain as to whether they actually fought with gaps between the maniples or before contact formed a continuous line to protect their flanks. It is possible the maniples deployed with each of its two centuries six to twelve deep lined up behind each other, as is suggested by the centurions in each maniple being described as of the front and back. Which might mean if this was the case then the century behind could move forward beside the one in front on contact, to show a continuous face. But apart from this we have detailed and impressive reports on their organization, on their camps, and to some extent on how they fought. It is the Carthaginians that we are much less clear about. Historically it is known that from fairly early on the African power depended largely on foreign mercenaries from all round the Mediterranean Sea, who once enrolled in the Punic army, commonly fought in the normal fashion of their people. Amongst the best known types are Balearic slingers, extremely effective skirmishers and Gallic warriors fighting with long sword and body shield in their traditional war bands, awful in the first assault but with little staying power. The cavalry comprised light Numidian horsemen fighting with javelins as well as heavier troopers from Iberia and Carthage itself. Heavy infantry stalwarts were recruited from Libyan and Iberian subject allies, occasionally from Greece and the home population of Carthage itself, though since the previous century that last resource had been used sparingly, largely *in extremis*, as the population of Punic descent were generally employed in the commercial and military marine.

In the first years after Hannibal crossed the Alps, in the epic years of sanguine triumph, the picture is reasonably clear. It is convincingly recorded that the African heavy infantry and perhaps some of the Spanish, fought in a phalanx formation. It was these men who were posted in the main line at the Trebbia and closed in on the exposed flanks of the great block of Roman and allied infantry at Cannae after they had been sucked in by the slowly withdrawing Gauls and Spaniards. What is not clear is whether these regiments were equipped as traditional Greek hoplites or followed the Macedonian style, using a long pike with small round shield. There is no absolute proof, either in the written sources, archaeological finds or in visual evidence that they were the latter, no actual reference to sarissa or pelte that are the hallmark of this formation, but the tendency to follow the fashion of successful military establishments is always very strong. Even the most hidebound of traditionalists in Greece, the Spartans, had reformed their army along Macedonian lines by the 220s and for the preceding century the Carthaginians had been in close contact with the great successor powers of the east, whose armies were always centred on a Macedonian style phalanx. They had even felt the force of just such a formation in their Sicilian war with Pyrrhus in the late 270s and though that prince eventually left the island frustrated, it was due to his failure to retain the support of his allies rather than the result of defeat at the hands of any Punic army.

There would seem to be no practical reason why these troops could not have been pike men, they were not after all citizen soldiers who would find it difficult to spare the time to train in the use of a difficult weapon, to practice on the training ground the evolutions required to manoeuvre in battle. No, these were professionals who would have found it no harder than their equivalents in Macedonia when Phillip introduced the new panoply there. They would have needed instructors but in the fluid and interconnected world they inhabited this would have been easy enough. Drill sergeants could be brought from Greece or Anatolia with ease, just as a Spartan general had been hired in to the lead the defence of Carthage against a Roman invasion in the First Punic War. So the balance of probabilities errs on the side of pike and pelte rather than hoplon and spear but this is far from conclusive and anyway does not affect the real problem under discussion, because both these styles of fighting involved the deployment of the men in a phalanx.

The point is well made that most armies do not change a winning formula, to take on the characteristics of a beaten enemy, yet the evidence is unequivocal that Hannibal started to rearm his army beginning with his African infantry in the Roman fashion after the victory at Lake Trasimene. This could of course just mean that they began to wear the better armour, stripped from the corpses of the many enemy soldiers they had killed, but the feeling is more than this, that after Cannae they re-equipped themselves to fight in the Roman fashion. The question is what motivation would these men, having marched out from Spain to victory at Trebbia, Trasimene and Cannae, have to change their style of fighting? They might have been impressed by the performance of the enemy legionaries, particularly when they burst through the Carthaginian centre at Trebbia, but would this have been enough to persuade the officers and men to dump the panoplies they were used to and start afresh a new fighting style in mid campaign?

But if they had not changed their style by Cannae, what about the forces that fought Marcellus around Nola and Fulvius and Appius around Capua? Whether these men who had come with Hannibal retained the battering ram deployment of the phalanx or changed to the more flexible manipular style is impossible to be sure of. But what is certain is the whole army anyway would have been changing, haemorrhaging not just Africans but Spaniards and Gauls as well and replacing them with local recruits. Carthaginian losses between 218 and 216 had been tiny compared with Roman casualties but still significant in a force that seldom reached 50,000 ensuring that despite one infusion of more traditional Punic warrior types in 215, the Carthaginian army of Italy almost certainly soon became a clean different thing, with Italians, from Samnium, Campania, Lucania, Apulia and Bruttium, not to mention enemy deserters aplenty, becoming very well represented in the ranks. And these Italians had traditionally always fought in a looser formation, indeed it is almost certain the Romans had picked up the manipular style of fighting when battling against many of these same people in the two centuries previously.

The advantages of the manipular method with its flexibility and ability to offer several layers of resistance had been clear to most that arrived in the Peninsula; even Pyrrhus had kept his Italian auxiliaries fighting in this manner when he recruited them to support his own home-grown pike phalanx, allowing him to dish out some bloody noses to a couple of Roman generals before experiencing a rare defeat at Beneventum. And Hannibal was nothing if not adaptable, the evidence suggests that in the years we are discussing and perhaps quite early on in them, most of his soldiers would have looked very like Romans or allies with mail shirts, pot helmets with long body shields, and deployed very much like them too. Some would probably have retained the spear rather than jettisoned it for javelins but then the Triarii, the third line of the Roman battle formation, also carried an 8ft spear to form a last line of defence as well.

But this, like the hoplon or pelte dilemma, is very far from certain and Dodge[4] for one asserts with nineteenth century confidence that Hannibal's army in Italy continued to fight in phalanx formation all through the war and indeed claims the impact of his veterans in this Sunday punch deployment was what caused the Romans to begin to double-bank their legions, placing one in reserve behind the one that was actually in contact with the enemy. He imagines Spaniards, Italians and Africans, certainly togged out in the best defensive equipment they could have stripped from the enemy, but fighting in long, little articulated lines, thrusting with spears or stabbing with swords looking like, but fighting very differently from, their enemies. And there is evidence to support his contention, as the information we get on how Hannibal's veterans deployed at Zama suggests, that these men brought back from Italy to defend Carthage, did indeed form in an essentially solid uninterrupted third line as they waited to play out the final chapter in the drama of that decisive battle.

When this fight for Capua began between Appius Claudius and Fulvius Flaccus on one side and the combined military muscle of Hannibal and the Campanians on the other it was the Numidians who kicked things off. As the sun burned down, the men of the two consular armies waited, deployed deep with the Velites in front, then Hastati, Principes and Triarii behind but still covering going on for two miles because of the very numbers of legions present and the cavalry spreading out wide to cover their flanks. Seeing this daunting spectacle of military might, of massed ranks of infantry glittering and bristling with shining spears, armour and helmets and wheeling masses of horsemen, Hannibal, conferring with Hanno, Mago, his other officers and the senior Campanians present, decided he must depend on his cavalry again. To throw his infantry into the fight without the expectation of support from his horsemen, disrupting the front ranks and coming in on the enemy wings, would be to court the kind of casualties he could just not afford. So while there was a wide stretch of dusty plain to cross before the infantry came to blows he ordered in his veteran troopers.

They were effective as usual, with the Numidians manoeuvring along the enemy front pressing on the Roman infantry and raining missiles down on their line and withdrawing in an agile display of horsemanship before returning to throw again. The Roman and allied horse on the wings tried to respond, pushing into the Numidians and the heavier Spanish and Campanian cavalry, but these were of good quality and made an effective show, driving back against the best the enemy could throw against them. With horsemen on both sides fighting their corner, with beasts crashing down and riders unseated on both sides, finally the infantry lines also made contact. They began hundreds of yards apart but the tramp of hard marching men soon covered the ground as the opposing ranks moved towards each other. Messengers were sent to the officers commanding the Velites to begin things, skirmishing in the fields between the armies, while Balearic slingers and other lights returned fire from the Carthaginian side. As these unarmoured men withdrew back through the front ranks of the heavy infantry, this line pushed forward to encounter their enemy equivalents. Spanish and African veterans, knowing from years of experience what was expected, would have thrown their javelins hoping that a lucky strike might find a vulnerable spot, but knowing that at least the missiles sticking in the Romans' shields would make them unwieldy, so their owners could not easily both protect themselves and strike back with their swords. The pilum of the Romans functioned in the same way, and these projectiles with their long iron head were particularly difficult to break or cut off, once well driven into the shields they had hit. Gauls, Campanians and other Italians would also have been noticed bracing themselves for battle in Hannibal's ranks as well, either in the front rank fighting with the rest or held in reserve in a second line.

The contending armies took turns, to first drive and then to be themselves driven, but we understand the Roman line of battle was eventually hard-pressed, shuddering under repeated assaults, and as they finally suffered more casualties it is probable they were not too far from losing this gruelling fight when word arrived that another army could be seen off in the distance marching towards the combat. The scene would have been of confusion: 'both sides were equally alarmed by the thought that they might be a reinforcement for the enemy' as the messengers brought in the word to headquarters that there were horsemen coming from the east that both sides would soon be able to make out appearing from the indiscriminate dust. The potential threat was coming from the direction of Beneventum and once past Capua itself Hannibal was able to see these newcomers would arrive in the rear of his army. He saw absolute ruin if another enemy force appeared booming into the backs of his men, while the Romans already in trouble might anticipate a repeat of Cannae if their brilliant opponent had reinforcements to deploy against their already fully committed regiments. Neither party could see enough of the banners nor insignia of these newcomers to determine who they were and it was just too much of a risk waiting to see who was under the cloud of dust that clearly advertised the imminent arrival of many men that would inevitably turn the battle.

Fear was the dominant emotion amongst the commanders in both armies, so orders were given to pull apart. The cavalry turned their horses reconstituting their squadrons, helping their wounded comrades while swordsmen sweating in their armour disentangled themselves from the scrummage. Many of these men fighting as individuals, each with a fair amount of space both around and behind them, found this easier than a spear or pike wielding Phalangite, who would have had the rank in his rear pressing him forward and impeding his stepping back. With officers ordering the standards to the rear on both sides, realization quickly came that the fighting was over and no longer threatened; with no defensive stance required, both parties were pulled back to the safety of their bases.

In fact when pickets, who had been patrolling near the Appian Way, materialized with definitive information it turned out the cavalcade just arrived on the scene were the rump of Gracchus' army led by a quaestor called Gnaeus Cornelius. Quaestors were officers who had done at least their ten years' military service and though concentrating on financial tasks could aid and deputize for consuls and praetors at home and in the field. But by the time his outriders had been recognized as enemies by the Carthaginians and reported as friends in the consuls' camps the fight was over and neither side inclined to take up cudgels again. Hannibal watched as the ranks of battalions of fresh and ready soldiers Roman and allies with their cavalry support joined with the army he had just been fighting, feeling that with these enemy reinforcements appearing he needed to think again about a stand-up fight that might cost him many casualties; indeed might be potentially suicidal, particularly as his actions already had effectively raised the siege, his primary objective when he had set out from Tarentum in the first place. While the Romans, even though strengthened, had been shaken by how close they had come to defeat, the recent apprehension of the worst could only underscore an understandable dread of facing the great Carthaginian again in battle.

Fulvius and Appius met in conference after the battle to plan their next step. Thinking over the issues they realized it would be well-nigh impossible to make progress in investing Capua while the main enemy battalions were present in force. They might be safe enough in their own camps, but once they tried to join them up with trenches and palisades, to make lines of contravallation and circumvallation around the town, the defenders would be able to pounce on their working parties at will and in terrific strength. Hard-riding Numidian and Campanian cavaliers would sting like gadflies any legionaries out of unit formation and throwing up the palisades and digging the ditches they would need to if they wanted to reduce the city. Certainly some might burrow while others protected them but this would require so many men that elsewhere around the walls the Romans would be outnumbered and vulnerable.

It was always the case when a besieged city contained large forces, an extreme example of interior lines. The units inside the walls could concentrate where they pleased to come out and attack while the besiegers would need to march miles around the circumference of the long ramparts to support any of their comrades who came under attack. In these circumstances the consuls decided to separate and try and lure Hannibal away. The thinking was that by manoeuvring separately they could not only threaten the enemy's lines of communication to the south, but also that a single consular army would offer a tempting target to that enemy who would follow hoping to catch it at a disadvantage or try and entangle them in a Punic ruse. With the decision made Fulvius took his army on the road west towards the coast at Cumae, while Appius headed down the Nola road putting it about that he was heading for Lucania. Hannibal was never impercipient but this time he took the bait, and after learning the enemy camps were deserted, decided that he should try and chase down Appius, who had not got too far ahead and seemed to offer the most promising target. The Carthaginians moving towards Lucania in pursuit actually lost their man, who had circled back to Campania on another road. But once down the southbound highway scouts brought news that a different opportunity had arisen to deal the enemy a blow, another potential victory of annihilation of the kind that might finally wear the Romans down.

Chapter 4

Three More Blows

PYRGOPOLINICES Take ye care that the lustre of my shield is more bright than the rays of the sun are wont to be at the time when the sky is clear; that when occasion comes, the battle being joined, 'mid the fierce ranks right opposite it may dazzle the eyesight of the enemy. But, I wish to console this sabre of mine, that it may not lament nor be downcast in spirits, because I have thus long been wearing it keeping holiday, which so longs right dreadfully to make havoc of the enemy.

Plautus, *Miles Gloriosus*, or *The Braggart Captain*

Tiberius Sempronius Gracchus first emerged during the Hannibal war and in a short career won signal honours and great glory. His was a family that did not boast generations of high office holders, though we know his father had secured the consulship in 238. This grandfather of the glamorous Brothers Gracchi famed would be land reformers of the later second century whose reputation has remained despite denigration by that awful, old, Tory hypocrite Cicero, was first noticed as *curule aedile* in the year 216. The norm was that this office, responsible for regulating festivals and public building in the capital, was occupied by a candidate who had reached his mid thirties and as he was elected consul the following year, a post usually reserved for those over forty years, all suggests he was a man in his early middle age. And one of considerable standing and military reputation from the fact when Pera was made dictator in the wake of Cannae, Gracchus was chosen as his master of horse. He made a decent contribution to the war by defending Casilinum, the key crossing of the Volturnus on the road leading from Capua to Rome. In the autumn of 216 he was voted in as consul along with Postumius, who would soon die under a Boii sword, as his colleague. When this casual vacancy was filled, not without some controversy, by Fabius Maximus and their provinces allocated, Gracchus campaigned actively in defence of Cumae, knocking about a Campanian army that was trying to catch its neighbours off guard, then slipping away when Hannibal attempted to pounce and tried to catch his men still celebrating their victory.

More than this, he even took on the great Carthaginian himself after he brought his main army down from Mount Tifata to attack Cumae. Hannibal threw everything at the home of the celebrated Sibyl with a succession of assaults mounted against the defences then bringing a famously large siege tower right up to the walls. But Gracchus was up to the challenge, building his own even higher belfry on top of the city's ramparts. Throwing everything they could find down from this structure the defence was so effective that Hannibal ordered his construction moved along the ramparts away from the enemy tower. But this was countered first by a firestorm of burning brands, then by the defenders sallying out from the gates and driving off the besiegers who had grown disheartened by the sight of their own men, fearful of burning to death, leaping from the siege tower. The Carthaginians lost more than a thousand men in this debacle, but subsequently they still offered battle, thinking that the enemy buoyed by their success might risk a fight in the open. Gracchus was having none of this, he for one had absorbed the lesson that it was not wise to take on Hannibal without the advantage of walls.

Having seen off even this illustrious opponent Gracchus moved to Luceria, the solid Roman colony in northern Apulia, though just before this he became involved tangentially with another dimension of this expanding war, when some captured Macedonian envoys were dragged up to his headquarters at Cumae after being sighted sailing by. He sent them on straight to Rome when he realized these captives were required there for interrogation. Once in the capital a reading of their correspondence made it clear what the Macedonian king had signed up to as the latest of Carthage's allies; information that allowed a squadron to be dispatched for Tarentum to commence the collection of forces to counter any threat from across the Adriatic that the new situation might involve. After Gracchus' armies transferred from Cumae to Apulia, with the weather becoming less clement and the troops settled down into their winter camps, news filtered in that a Carthaginian army under Hanno had suffered some kind of reverse at Grumentum in Lucania while three communities in the Hirpini had also been retaken. But if this was satisfactory stuff for the men who heard it their active general still had plenty to think about, finding himself again facing Hannibal who, at the end of the year's campaign, had based himself not far away at Arpi.

Gracchus kept his two legion army in Apulia over the off season and was deputed to continue holding up that front as proconsul in the following year. Then when Hannibal moved from Arpi to Campania, Gracchus was sent for by Fabius to come from Luceria and shadow any Carthaginian move towards Beneventum. There as we know he met and defeated Hanno and in the larger scheme of things held that flank tight, even being positioned and prepared to send help to defend Nola when Marcellus left that place to aid Fabius at the siege Casilinum. The year 213 saw him get his men back on the Appian Way to return to Lucania where in that largely uneventful year he at least fought a few minor engagements and stormed a number of small towns. Exploits that only burnished the reputation of his belligerent ex slaves whose story had become so well known that when the exiled remnants of the Cannae army, rotting on punishment duty in Sicily, pleaded their cause they used them as an example. Declaring that if even slaves should be given a chance to win freedom by brave service why should they not have the opportunity to win forgiveness by their actions in battle.

In 212 he was still in Lucania ready and willing to respond when orders arrived to again guard Beneventum while the consuls advanced on Capua. This very effective officer again acted with alacrity and was soon in the process of bringing his light troops and cavalry through the high country of east Samnium. But in the end this apparently routine bit of military housekeeping turned out to have a tragic denouement, it was at this time that Gracchus lost his life. The exact details are difficult, but probably the events transpired in Lucania when a local magistrate called Flavus, in an effort to improve the terms of his people's alliance with the Carthaginians, arranged with General Mago to lure Gracchus into an ambush. They were careful and in preparation the Carthaginian came up from Bruttium to inspect the ambush ground with the treacherous Flavus. Then the latter contacted Gracchus offering to lead him to this same place to meet with what he claimed were leaders from communities that now regretted siding with the invaders and despite a traditional policy of coolness, might be open to being brought back into the Roman fold.

So it was without suspicion that Gracchus took his lictors, a proconsular eleven and a guard of cavalry and headed out to meet what he expected to be a delegation of repentant Lucanian magistrates. But on arrival at the rendezvous point, deep within a rugged gully, what he found was a large number of enemy cavalry and foot soldiers arising out of cover, appearing from beech forests and crags, not just on his front and flank, but cutting off his road back as well. Deciding there was no hope of escape and unprepared to be captured, Gracchus slipped off his mount to organize his gallant band to sell their lives dearly. But it was not just a glorious death he wanted but revenge too, ordering his men to try and find and kill Flavus if he came within range of any of their swords. But the reality was that, without even any shields, they could do little but stand and die under a hail of missiles. These had been left in camp so little did they expect a fight and the only protection Gracchus had was to wrap his cloak round his left arm. But in fact what really kept the general from going down like most of his men was the determination of his attackers to take him alive. Yet despite being all alone and surrounded he refused to succumb and seeing Flavus standing in the front rank of his enemies, keen to observe the completion of his scheme, Gracchus rushed upon him with such ferocity that in order to save their own lives and despite intending to disarm and restrain him his enemies had to strike at their attacker until one of their weapons found a mortal spot.

When Hannibal further down in the south heard the news of his enemy's death it must have been a considerable consolation that, though the Romans had seemed to have found a couple of generals who could actually defeat Carthaginians in open battle, one of these now had come to a sticky end. But if he was lucky he was classy too because, if we accept Polyaenus, when the Numidians, who had taken possession of the general's corpse, brought it to Hannibal and were preparing to desecrate it, he stopped them, saying the deceased had been a good general who deserved better.[1] And the respect must have been genuine enough as the Carthaginians arranged funerary rites with full honours, with Gracchus' remains burned on a high pyre outside the camp, Hannibal's whole army marching by in full armour and his Spanish troops performing military dances in tribute to a fallen enemy.

There are other versions of the death of this man. That he was not downed in a treacherous ensnarement by Mago's warriors, but was just caught by accident, half a mile from his Lucanian base looking for a propitious site to make sacrifice; or that he had already arrived at Beneventum, when purely by chance he was discovered river bathing by a Numidian patrol, who were lurking in the willows on the banks of the Calor, and dispatched. Whichever was true, all were unedifying ends for this man who had achieved much with very unpromising material. To exit so tamely, particularly as he had been given good warning of trouble (if we believe the stories of snakes repeatedly eating the livers of the sacrificial animals being offered) before the journey out of Lucania. Though he would not be the last Roman commander to suffer fatally for such carelessness, in a few years two full consuls would find themselves similarly endangered, caught ill protected in the open, to similar effect.

Prior to his untimely demise, in the previous couple of years it had been mainly on the open plains of Apulia or the rolling uplands of northern Lucania that Gracchus had plied his trade, the other side of the Apennine spine from Campania that with Tarentum had been, apart from when in winter quarters, the centre of Hannibal's attention. But now this eastern section of the Italian leg where the Carthaginian general had fought his greatest battle was again about to become the scene of two more victories; the kind of battles of annihilation that had almost brought the Republic to its knees four years before. The incubation of the first encounter was not unconnected with the death of Gracchus, because if his demise, however it came about, had not been bad enough in itself, it also resulted in the disintegration of his army of liberated slaves. These men, once manumitted, were soon eying up job vacancies across central Italy. With so many of the young men off their farms and in the army they could easily find lucrative employment, so with their respected leader dead and reluctant to follow another, they slipped away, demobbing themselves in a most effective manner. What their contractual obligations were is not exactly clear, though initially they do not seem to have been castigated as deserters, even if considerable efforts would soon be made to round them up and return them to the colours after it became even more essential to plug gaps caused by the bloody victories won by Hannibal.

In the wake of this the Roman establishment showed how flexible these people could be when circumstance demanded, how they could adapt when they were up against it. According to the rule book only elected magistrates should command armies and then only after they had done ten years of military service as a junior officer, reaching at least late thirties for a praetor and forties for a consul. Yet only eight years after the start of the war the future Scipio Africanus would show just how far the constitution could be bent, when he was sent to Iberia in command of an army at the tender age of 24. But at least, if a very young man, he came from one of the great senatorial families, with consulships and senior military command the norm for those bearing his family name. Yet now something truly extraordinary happened. There was a senior centurion, a hard case veteran, named Marcus Centennius Paenula who was not only famous for his courage but remarkable for his great height. Romans were not generally tall, not much over 5½ft on average, so though this man might not have stood out in our day, at the time he certainly did. He also had contacts amongst the city's office holders and one of these called Sulla sponsored his protégé to take the proposal he was canvassing for examination before the Senate. Not at all overawed in front of this august body, he asked to be given a force of 5,000 troops, claiming, because he knew the country down in Lucania where he intended to campaign and had studied the enemy's behaviour, he could achieve against the Carthaginians the victories others had failed to deliver.

This certainly exceptional proposition showed when absolute necessity drove, anything might be possible now the Lucanian front had become fearfully unstable. So they decided to entrust an army to a man who had never held a magistracy and only had experience as a company commander, a policy derided as stupid by our main source. But there was surely more to it than just foolishness; the decision to give this junior officer his head was a result of the two legion hole that had emerged out east in Apulia and Lucania. With Gracchus' freed slaves no longer to be counted on, the strategists in Rome knew they must try and shore up the situation any way they could. And the soldier who had pushed himself forward must have been impressive, and most importantly, he was ready and willing. The probability of this being a gamble borne of dire necessity is corroborated by the fact that he was given more troops than he asked for, 8,000 men in all, half Roman levies and half raised by the allies. The Senate had already been sending out commissioners to every community within fifty miles of Rome to dig out malingerers and bring in anybody who had escaped conscription and even willing underage recruits too; these men, apart from manning the new city legions and bringing old ones up to strength, may well have supplied many of the units allotted to Paenula. The Roman high command eventually furnished the mint new general with the best part of a legion with its allied contingent, nor was this all they allowed this enthusiast; when they sent him off to harry the enemy, he was granted the authority to raise as many more men as he could both on the march and after he reached his destination.

From the time this self-assured man led his new-found army out of the gates of Rome and arrived in Lucania he managed to recruit another 8,000 volunteers to match the men he had already been given. How he found so many willing recruits after years of war is not recorded, but perhaps it does give some credence to his having a considerable amount of charisma. Once on the spot he searched hard to establish the whereabouts of Hannibal who he had found out had paused to rest in the area. But it turned out he was pretty unsubtle when put to the test. It had been no bluff in front of the Senate; Paenula was determined to smash the enemy up wherever he found them and had the blind conviction that he and his men could do it. We do not know where the fight began, but perhaps not that far from the

Campanian and Lucania border on the Capua road, as it had been near there that Appius Claudius had thrown the chasing Hannibal off his scent and doubled back to rejoin his fellow consul near Capua . Whether he had sent out scouts who were incompetent or whether he just had such confidence in his own ability, the ex centurion did not have the sort of plan that he ought to have had for one soon to be in the presence of the victor of Cannae. With an insouciance verging on stupidity when he approached near enough to be able to reconnoitre his enemy's position, he pushed on, knowing though he must by then, that Hannibal's army almost certainly outnumbered his own 16,000 men, many of whom were raw recruits and a far cry from the veteran warriors his enemy could deploy.

This region was generally friendly to the Carthaginians, so with detailed reports from both local sympathizers and his own guides Hannibal was pretty cognisant of the composition of Paenula's army. He would have known that even if the men who had left Rome were well armoured and knew their drills those recruited on the march, apart from a leavening of old soldiers returning to the colours, could have had little training and would have been equipped with only whatever armour and weapons they could have appropriated in the places they passed. So Hannibal, ever aggressive, now had every reason for confidence as he deployed his army into line on the broad Lucanian slopes where he intended to fight. Unusually he did not feel the need to make any special arrangements to deal with the opposition. He arranged his army with no great tactical refinement, no attempt here to plant some Numidians in ambush behind a hill or in broken tree-swathed country. Instead he deployed his veteran Spaniards, Africans and Gauls, who had fought under his victorious banner for years, filled out with newer recruits from the warrior peoples of southern Italy, and climbing onto the saddle blanket of his magnificent warhorse remained himself behind the serried ranks prepared to feed in support to his front line where it was needed.

At first it was difficult to tell where the fight was heading. The engagement was soon general as for over two hours the sides fought, the air thick with javelins, arrows and slingshot and swordsmen hacking at each other from behind their long body shields as they came on for an all hands attack; the ranks behind clashing their swords against their shields to encourage those in front and to terrify the enemy. The noise of war cries and the clatter of weapons swelled along the line then diminished as men took a break to draw breath or were relieved by comrades behind them. The Carthaginians found the enemy a considerably tougher nut to crack than they had supposed at the outset and when this became apparent to the high command Hannibal would have sent in the troops held back in his second line; these would have backed up the men in front against an enemy who, part cocooned in enclosing helmets and with comrades pressing in on all sides, found the sound of braying trumpets and yelling men only made for confusion. Their ability to hear orders was small and it would have been the pressure from comrades behind as much as the sight of their standards going forward that would have impelled them on. Dread, overborne at least for a time by adrenalin intoxication, would have been the experience of most as they were buffeted across fields that many would have expected to end stained with their blood, following unit emblems that at this time Pliny the Elder tells us would have included eagles, wolves, minotaurs, horses and boars.[2] Terror would have been palpable on both sides but amongst the Romans it was worse.

The contest could not last, as it turned out there was no need of any Punic tricks to win out, these were Hannibal's best men in large numbers against one of the motliest armies he ever took on in his many years of campaigning. Paenula, with the combat exploding in his face and it beginning to sink in where his policy of an all out offensive had led him, was nothing if not super brave. With defeat imminent the tall, hulking, muscular soldier, distinctive in the just acquired burnished and decorated cuirass and helmet of a commanding general found himself in an awful conundrum. He was not one of the inner circle; no senator like Varro who could even survive a Cannae, there was little future for him as a defeated leader. The choice was slaughter or surrender and instead of ignominy and shame, he took himself to where the fighting was hottest, looking for a glorious death. Charging into the depths of the Carthaginian lines to be struck down by the missiles raining down on the ranks of his men; dying like a Roman should.

This man who had thought to crush Hannibal, who had deluded himself he could take whatever the Carthaginians threw at him was dead and when the news of their leader's demise filtered rearwards men looked round in desperation. They might have hoped for inspiration but none was found and the ranks crumbled; 'the result was utter and immediate rout.' This was not the usual process where men at the back of the line began to slip away and gradually the movement spread through the ranks, eventually reaching the men in brutal contact at the front. No, it seems, in this instance, in a moment almost every man on the Roman side, interested only in personal survival, took to their heels, with even those inclined to stay and fight swept away by the mob. Unfortunately very few were going to find the safety they were looking for, the enemy cut them off, blocking the road along which they were trying to flee and hardly even 1,000 lived to tell the tale. The rest were cut down as they tried to scramble through the fields and copses in the unfamiliar terrain in the rear of the battleground, probably spooking not just flighty animals but perhaps even local peasants who had hidden in the woods to escape the soldiers and observe the battle unfolding on their doorstep. And that the casualties were so awful is hardly surprising considering the routes leading from the bruising encounter were awash with cavaliers from Hannibal's army who were not going to be over-gentle with inveterate enemies in a vulnerable condition.

Hannibal had gobbled up another posturing bravo and his satisfaction must have had an extra piquancy after he heard what the man had boasted of doing to him in front of the Senate. But even while his men stripped the enemy corpses and dealt with the dead and wounded on his own side he knew this victory had changed the strategic picture hardly at all, indeed had not done much more than add to the awful arithmetic of the Republic's casualty list. He also remained very aware of the threat to his friends in Capua and would soon hear that the enemy were throwing their tentacles out round the town again and that the people there were in real danger. Over the years he had begun to understand the fortitude of his foe and learnt from long experience that even his success on the battlefield could translate into grand strategy bonuses for the Romans. This would certainly be the case if he lost Campania, but equally the attraction of more battles of attrition round the walls of Capua against two consuls whose armies considerably outnumbered his own, was not great. With perhaps the wish being the father of the computation, despite what calls for help came from his allies and despite him being not that far away he decided that the local military, supported by his men under Hanno would be able to hold out. So weighing the options open to him he did not immediately turn in their direction. Banking from past experience that he could get back to Capua whenever he needed to disrupt the siege was anyway a calculation that allowed him an amount of time he intended to make good use of.

Nor were these opportunities all exactly hypothetical or potential and rather than immediately turning in the direction of Capua Hannibal responded to an extremely tempting prospect he smelled on the wind from the east. There had been plenty of success due to the rashness of one enemy commander and now it looked like he would never have a better chance to achieve the same result against a second. He had known for some time that another Roman army was pressing forward in Apulia, hardly more than forty miles from his current position. The decision to march and come to grips with this particular enemy force was based again on good intelligence. He had eyes and ears everywhere in this region and the condition of this force operating against his allies in the region was reported by Apulian friends who had been bringing news for some time from the threatened places. The troops concerned were led by a praetor called Gnaeus Fulvius Flaccus who had taken over the two legion army based at Luceria. He was the brother of the consul Quintus Fulvius Flaccus and this command had become something of a family affair as Quintus, when praetor, had actually been in charge of these men a couple of years before. Gnaeus would soon show he had little of his brother's ability but he at least started with some inherited kudos and in fact initially did quite well, attacking and looting a number of unnamed towns as his army marched south from their headquarters at Luceria. But since then discipline had become lax. They were approaching Herdonia when Hannibal took notice and indeed some said that the Romans would have been drawn to that place by a pro Carthaginian local who informed Gnaeus that the people would go over if he arrived there in strength.[3]

This community, sitting on a ridge above the plain along the main route through Apulia, was important enough to be the site of two major battles in the Hannibal war. Today the Roman remains of the town are interesting but hardly visited at all by tourists, with only a small grubby sign pointing through a farmer's yard to give a hint of the extensive sight. The pre Roman Daunii community that had seen its best days a century before and had come into the Roman fold after the Pyrrhus War in 270s, was far enough from the river that there was plenty of room to camp on the flat water meadows. And it was there the Romans had settled, eager to strike where they assumed there were plenty of sympathetic folk impatient to welcome them. Joining Hannibal after Cannae, Herdonia had been lost to Rome in 214, and then swiftly regained, so now the Carthaginian was very reluctant to let it go again. So with information that seemed sufficiently trustworthy to act upon, his army stepped out smartly, trailing down from the highlands round Mount Vulture back up to Aquilonia before turning into the Apulian plains. After a couple of days or so they arrived, making camp in the vicinity of the town but off to the west away from the enemy encampment. Hannibal, relaxing in the tent his men had just raised, was pleased to find information reaching his headquarters that confirmed the earlier reports of the condition of the enemy host.

Under a lightweight sibling of a great man there had occurred something that was not that unusual in the Roman military, despite its reputation for ferocious discipline. As has been well pointed out by JE Lendon in *Soldiers and Ghosts* the tension between the demand to show bravery and to keep military order was frequently demonstrable in Roman armed forces. On this occasion when it was learnt with some surprise that the enemy were nearby, unruly soldiers acted almost off their own bat, grabbing their standards, arming themselves and demanding to be led immediately against the Carthaginian army they had learnt was now encamped not far from their own station. The praetor, knowing what a tricky customer he was facing in Hannibal, somehow managed with his officers to restrain the men from heading pell-mell into battle, though they were only able to get agreement to this restraint because the soldiers believed they could have their way, to initiate a fight, anytime they wanted. So anticipating the following day, if the men in the Roman army slept well, their leader, feeling the strain of waiting, certainly did not.

Hannibal knew this region well, the site of his greatest triumph was not so far off, with fine open country suitable for the manoeuvring at which he excelled. And now registering the lack of control amongst Gnaeus' men, that the enemy's soldiers were likely to instigate a battle whatever their generals wanted, he resolved to ensnare these eager but incautious foes. Deciding to accept battle next day, during the night he ordered 3,000 of his lightly armed men to conceal themselves in some nearby farm buildings and in the scrub and woodland that surrounded them, to keep in hiding until the battle was in full swing. More than this, he also ordered Mago, who must have joined up and left with him after the combat at Capua, to take 2,000 cavalry and guard the roads along which the enemy would take if they tried to escape. The largely flat or rolling terrain of this part of Apulia favoured his horsemen, a fact shown most devastatingly at Cannae and he had no reason to believe the troopers in his enemy's ranks had either improved in quality since that battle or were even present in particularly large numbers.

With these preparations made, the Carthaginians deployed for battle as the roseate light of dawn broke the next day and Hannibal waited with his men in good order, taking note of the unfamiliar and disorganized nature of the foe that faced him. There are some hints on the kind of strength he was in during these years of combative peregrination round Italy; if it is right that he led something over 40,000 at Cannae, the suggestion is that in these later encounters he certainly did not keep up this strength. However gung-ho they were, these generals who he defeated so decisively would surely not have gone into battle with under 20,000 soldiers against over double their numbers. That his main army was perhaps not kept up to much more than 20,000 is made even more likely by the fact that he split his army as early as 216, sending a strong force to Bruttium. We are told of a number of occasions that he left detachments to garrison newly won allied towns, indeed as many as 2,000 cavalry were allocated on just one occasion to defend the Campanian lands alone. To fill depleted ranks Hannibal of course constantly recruited amongst Italian allies many of whom were of a very warlike bent, and still it must be that during these years he received some reinforcements, though the issue of how many and what variety of replacements came his way is difficult. Bomilcar arrived in 215 and while this might be the only occasion when numbers were significant enough to get a notice, brute arithmetic suggests other convoys must have got through at other times to beef up his military. It is only necessary to add up the numbers of Numidians mentioned at various times, including the 1,200 reported as deserters fighting for Rome the following year. This is conclusive; Hannibal's army must have received considerable reinforcements of these nimble and effective horsemen as only 6,000 cavalry, many of which were Iberian horse, made it over the Alps and these troopers, even if victorious in hard fights at Trebbia and Cannae, still must have taken considerable casualties who required replacing.

To keep up anything of a cavalry corps there must have been plenty of other reinforcements that reached Italy during these years, a suggestion of contact between Italy and other Punic holdings, underlined by the frequency with which Hannibal's Spanish veterans are mentioned at the forefront in almost all his battles where details are recorded, supports this view. Now the evidence is firm that only 8,000 of these troops arrived in the Po Valley in 218 and this number just could not have remained so significant without new drafts filling in for the soldiers subtracted not just through battle casualties, but through illness, desertion and the numberless other eventualities of life in an army on the move over many years. We also know that plenty of good-quality money got to Italy from Africa to pay Hannibal's men and soldiers who must have gone along to protect the specie for this if for no other reason. Additionally the mention of elephants on a number of occasions during these years, the first as early as the siege of Casilinum in 216, is suggestive too as there were none with the army at Cannae, so if the reports are exact, in the few months between some must have been shipped in.

The other imperative was logistics, however many men Hannibal commanded, as a whole the need to supply them would be bound to encourage him to spread his men about, only calling his lieutenants to return to him when he needed numbers to fight the main consular armies. He had any way to keep on the move to feed the men he had with him, so as not to impose too much of a burden on newly won friends. There was good cause to keep as trim as was consistent with his strategic aims. As for the other side that was shaping up for battle outside Herdonia, it is surprising there was not more of a real sense of dread to fight again on a field so near to where perhaps as many as 70,000 and certainly more than 40,000 of their comrades had perished just four years before. Yet there seemed no such precautionary instincts amongst the soldiers, whose confidence was such they were deciding the direction of the army themselves. Gnaeus Fulvius must have known he was outnumbered and in danger of being outgeneralled, something suggested by his reluctance to fight the day before, but now he accepted battle because the men demanded it. But these eager spirits did not match motivation with competence, their lines were formed haphazardly hardly getting set at all, as standards were raised amid great cheering as they surged impulsively forward, with many soldiers not taking their normal places in the battle line and indeed the less belligerent moving post if they thought they were dangerously exposed. The First Legion with its allies on the left took the front, but even here at the cutting edge it was all indiscipline, with the formations overextended and too shallow to fight well. It seems, against their officers' orders, the legionaries were not keeping to their normal three lines with Velites in advance but were all pushing to the front. Those in charge knew this would make them vulnerable to be broken at the first attack, but they could do little to control the men.

Hannibal waited with his soldiers in good order and maintaining their discipline in the river meadows below the town where there was ample room to fight a battle, taking note of the unfamiliar and disorganized nature of the disposition of those who faced him. Then he ordered the attack, war cries on their lips and trumpets sounding the charge with the Balearic slingers and other light troops softening up the defenders with salvos of slingshot and javelins. With traction gained on the ground by heavy military sandals, the front rank of African spearmen and Spanish swordsmen went forward. Would they have run the last yards or gone at a steady pace? We don't know. But armour was heavy and in the summer heat it must have been almost unbearable with dust and sweat in their eyes and certainly sufficient to ensure any real effort could only be kept up for a short time. Only the heads and shins of the men in this bronze stitched tide would, behind their shields, have been visible to the enemy offering little in the way of targets for the pila of the men from the First Legion and their allied comrades. In every segment of the extended line the fighting was intense with the clash of the men at the front felt like a shiver all along the ranks as men stabbed, grabbed and pushed at enemies they could smell and feel, as well as see through the film of sweat running into their eyes. Hearing would have been muffled by the earpieces of their helmets, with just the rasp of their own heavy breathing, for the rest the other senses were overwhelmed in this awful body close combat.

The Romans might be disordered and reckless but there were sufficient veterans or just brave and hardy novices among them; enough to make the start of the fight an even enough affair. But the lack of cohesion or even much control by the senior officers became very significant once the encounter was taken beyond the first visceral coming together of the forward ranks, with men sinking spear and sword into exposed flesh and the sound of steel striking bone through mail shirts where links had become frayed and worn. In these circumstances there was virtually no manoeuvring to be done until the ambush was triggered. Then the men positioned in the night came into play, with light infantry and horse falling on the flanks and tearing into the rear of the Roman troops. Swelled to a furious climax the battle turned into a disaster almost from the start of this attack and any chance of making a stand was lost, despite the shouts and curses of the centurions desperately trying to get their men to fight on or rally those who had been driven back by enemy pressure. Gnaeus Fulvius had observed with horror the emergence of the figures of ambushing troops, rising from prone positions or coming out from hiding behind bushes and trees and moving in for the kill against the great mass of his men who were clearly incapable of responding to the threat. The attackers were lightly equipped, with javelins, small shields and swords but the element of surprise would make up for any inadequacy of equipment and they were determined too, to tear the heart out of their enemy. Apart from this savage assault there were also Numidians soon seen on the Roman flanks in rough tunics with only a small shield for protection and clutching their javelins, backed by heavier Iberian lancers and local Italian cavaliers. With this precision tripping of a prearranged manoeuvre and with wings and rear threatened it was all disintegration. The Roman commander had been disinclined to fight from the start, forced into it by his men and now he was not going to own the results of other people's decisions. There was no staying to try for a counterpunch, or even a glorious death amongst his men, instead he clambered aboard his horse, called together 200 troopers as a bodyguard and galloped from the battlefield, somehow avoiding the pickets of Numidian and Spanish horse blocking the roads. But he was one of the few who did get out with his skin intact.

Careful planning had paid off handsomely and before long the Romans' formations changed from just steadily leaking killed and wounded to wholesale collapse. Soon the army of 18,000 was practically annihilated with hardly 2,000 getting to safety amongst the woods and scrubland. All this while their arms, goods and booty was lost as the Carthaginians walked calmly into the undefended camp and his men dragged anything of value out of the Romans' tents to add to their ever increasing hoard of booty. As the evening deepened Hannibal again looked out on a battlefield with piles of Roman dead all around him, with his own men ghostly in the gloom stripping the corpses, as the pleas for help and moans of the wounded propped up against rocks or trees echoed on the wind around the plain below Herdonia. Once again he had emerged as the battlefield star and in just a short part of this fighting season three consular size armies had either been dispersed or decimated. As a result the eastern patch of the war, in the plains of Apulia and on that edge of the Apennines covered by Lucania, the Republic's military had worn very thin indeed. The result looked approximately final for that front with only a few strongholds like Luceria and Venusia hanging on and hardly any organized forces in the field at all. But was the resolution in the war any nearer? Hannibal surely must have expected at the least that this must have affected his enemy's stance, that if nothing more, the scare thrown into them by these defeats would bring strong pressure to siphon off manpower from Campania to patch up where things had gone so badly wrong.

Hannibal had been called in to assist the Capuans once Hanno, baulked at Beneventum, had failed to succour the city and he had seen off the consuls. Chasing Appius into the hills had taken him close to the ragtag army that an elevated centurion had brought like lambs to the slaughter. On a roll now he surely expected that the effect of his victories was bound to relieve any pressure put on the Campanians by Appius and Fulvius and the other Roman armies, so he did not put his men in motion for Campania but in the diametrically opposite direction. This confidence alone makes understandable his move south to Tarentum. The strategic judgement was twofold, firstly it was a crucial matter to dig the obstinate enemy out of their stronghold in Tarentum, and secondly considering the Roman setbacks the likelihood had to be that they would concentrate on shoring up where they had been battered rather than showing any further aggressive intent against Carthaginian allies.

News of these latest shocking setbacks on the luckless plains of Apulia and Lucania had indeed spread rapidly through the other armies of the Republic, to the allied towns and the capital itself. But when word reached Rome that once again promised victories had turned into alarming defeats, the military establishment kept its nerve. They might have been excused if spirits had sunk but instead they reacted with great energy and sense. Starting with the basics, orders were sent to the consuls to organize the rounding up of the survivors of the two armies overcome by Hannibal and officers sent to chase down Gracchus' old freed slave volunteers and get them back on the military roster. All the stops were pulled out by local officials to find these veteran soldiers who had fought so well for the dead general and the clues are that the efforts were pretty successful. But this was only a sideshow, alongside what had always been at the forefront of the republican establishment's military thinking. They had decided to mass and commit and they stuck with it. Capua it had been and Capua it would remain.

Now Naples is the big city, dominating the whole of what was Campania. But in the third century that place was hardly bigger than other Greek ports like Cumae and Puteoli, maritime communities of decent sizes clinging to the coast, but the megalopolis was Capua, perhaps most famous for its later connection with Spartacus, he who led the breakout from one of the famed gladiator schools in the city that instigated a servile war that brought fear and panic to much of south Italy for several years in the first century. There were miles of walls round the city that encompassed an area over half the size of that within the Servian walls of Rome and that sat in a flat plain just below the plateau of Tifata where the church of Sant'Angelo in Formis, boasting some lovely medieval fresco, still stands on the remains of a temple to Diane. There Hannibal had for years kept his vertiginous military encampment that strangely the Romans never tried to occupy, even when the Carthaginians had deserted the place to find winter quarters or fight campaigns elsewhere. From there the view shows the lush flat agricultural lands around the town and up just a few miles in the direction of Rome was the River Volturnus. The river crossing at the town of Casilinum was now firmly in Roman hands, ensuring they could both bring resources down the road without let and hindrance and ensure that any attacks up that way would be far from easy. The coastline had remained in the hands of Rome's friends, often secured by legionary garrisons through even the worst of days. A charming shorefront with distinctive towns perched on steep conical hills was already becoming a playground for the Roman elite and their friends and, when security returned in centuries to come, places like Baiae would become a byword for luxury and excess, as well as superb seafood and centres for healing around the hot mineral springs. Inland further south around Nola and other Campanian places the Romans were pretty securely entrenched too. So it was just the big city.

While Hannibal was annihilating yet more of their colleagues' armies the consuls themselves had been far from idle. The Siege of Capua, which had always been at the heart of their strategy, began to be reconstituted. Now it was meticulous stuff, a programme where the seriousness of their intent was shown from the start. News of the most disturbing kind reached the main Carthaginian camp near Tarentum that eight legions were concentrating and unloading at various centres around the city, all they needed to begin a regular siege. The Roman commanders prepared to press the blockade, making very good use of the time generously allowed them. After Hannibal departed Campania and Appius returned from his circuitous march, they took up the vital task of digging their works around the city, but before this could be started they needed to secure their lines of supply. A grain depot was constructed at the camp at Casilinum, while other troops were sent to the mouth of the Volturnus River where a fort was constructed and another refurbished from the original, built by the older Fabius at Puteoli. These bases were made even more secure by posting Decimus Junius at the former with a garrison with the same at the latter on the coast at the north of the Bay of Naples, under Marcus Aurelius Cotta. These officers worked hard to set up the necessary supply chain to transport grain brought by ship from Sardinia and Etruria to the main army camp at Casilinum. The corollary of ensuring that the besieging armies could have supplies from the sea up the Volturnus was that it made it possible to keep Capua's access to the coast restricted, allowing the establishment of something like an embargo even before the siege lines were completed.

Appius Claudius took up the gage in front of Capua itself, being quickly joined by Quintus Fulvius, who came guarding a huge convoy of material hurried up from Casilinum, required to construct their works around the walls. Two consular armies were now on the spot, but not satisfied with these numbers a third was called in, with orders sent to Nero at the Claudian camp above Suessula, on the main road south from Capua to Nola, to leave only a sufficient garrison and to join the forces concentrating to the north. This vast force now divided up the country around the town into three sections and began to dig a deep ditch bringing in the wood to make ramparts. Work went on quickly to build a huge line of earthworks, with blockhouses, strong points and towers sited regularly along the miles of lines, to imprison the population and their defenders in the town. All this notwithstanding the constant interruptions to fight off sorties directed at them from those inside Capua's walls. So despite the numbers deployed, life was difficult enough with frequent skirmishing between the lines as men were not only unable to relax for fear of the defenders coming out to attack them but even more, dreaded the arrival of Hannibal at any moment fresh from his victories, to do again what he had done earlier in the year. In these circumstances even these hard-handed men from Rome were prepared to offer something less than absolute annihilation to their Campanian enemies expecting that the people already feeling the pinch of hunger would be very receptive to their offer. They proposed to allow any inhabitants who wanted to leave, to take what possessions they could with them and that such people should also retain rights to property in the city and environs when it was taken, as long as they left before the lines of circumvallation were finished. This certainly hints at some desperation, as this kind of leniency was not at all typical, particularly for a people the Romans reviled as much as these inhabitants of the capital of Campania. The offer anyway elicited no response, except contumely from a people who not only expected help to arrive anytime but who far from absolutely trusted the clemency their attackers were peddling.

Yet despite this activity that he heard about from his worried friends there was little sense of urgency, Hannibal had not marched from Herdonia to Campania but instead had set his compass south towards Tarentum. Still thinking he had time to deal with developments on the other front, he had decided on an attempt to take the garrison in the citadel of Tarentum by surprise. Hoping they would have gone to sleep when they heard he was in Apulia, he force marched along the well-travelled road south only to find on arrival that the defenders were as vigilant as ever and no more likely to concede defeat than the last time he tried. Frustrated, he took his men to Brundisium knowing if he could get into that place it would mean control of a key port on the Adriatic coast. But this turned out a fruitless effort too and while there, desperate envoys from Capua arrived entreating him with increasing despondency to help them. Hannibal's reply showed that as the fighting season waned he remained confident he could move to their relief at any time he wanted, just as he had before. Or perhaps he was not absolutely convinced of the reports of how close the consuls were to surrounding the whole place with their siege lines. His mindset was still about the offensive; to be pulled from pillar to post to defend new-found friends had no appeal. His calculations remained that he must bleed the Republic even more, to bring such a pall of despair over the city of Rome that would finally force this intransigent people to the bargaining table.

Chapter 5

Under the Servian Walls

Next they laid waste the land of Allifae, dear to Bacchus, and the country where the nymphs of Casinum dwell; and soon the speedy columns passed Aquinum, and Fregellae where a buried Giant sends up smoke. On they rushed over the heights where the warlike men of Frusino cling to their rugged rocks and where Anagnia rises on a swelling ridge, a fertile land for corn. And at last Hannibal set foot on the plains and corn fields of Labicum and left behind the walls of Telegonus, battered by the ram already but not worth delay at such a crisis. Nor did the beauty of Algidus detain him, nor Gabii, the city of Juno. With furious speed he rushed forwards towards the banks where cold Anio gliding noiselessly, winds smoothly with sulphurous waters towards father Tiber.

Silius Italicus, *Punica*, Book 12.

On a bright day in the summer of 211 in the streets of Rome all was chaos, slaves in rough tunics and citizens sweating in heavy white togas all were rushing here and there to find refuge from what seemed an awful danger. Now events were underway of potentially lethal concern to every order in town, not just the political classes or those with family members involved who followed the progress of the war in detail. The city was heaving with crowds of refugees from the country and even the garrison troops posted on the Capitol were in terror, shouting to all who would hear that the invaders were within the gates, and a worthy source has it that the panic was such that people threw stones or other missiles at anybody in the streets who looked a little unusual, thinking them possible invaders. And even more, that the people of Rome if given the chance would have fled into a life of exile except to do so would have meant to have rushed straight into the arms of the enemy encamped outside. The trigger for this particular alarm had been the sight of horsemen on the Aventine, wiry, curly haired Numidians, the sort who had harried Roman armies and Italian civilians the length and breadth of the country for the past seven years. But in fact these were not an enemy advance guard somehow got in the gates, they were party of 1,200 Numidian deserters, fortuitously in the city when a real threat materialized, and who had been ordered to the Esquiline Gate in an effort to forestall it.

The fear in the streets had been borne of error, but a real threat existed to the city of Rome, that if expected before had never so far materialized in their bloody and bruising war with the armies of Carthage. Hannibal was at the gates, he had not come after the battle of Trasimene, not even after Cannae, but now there could be no doubt, Rome's most dangerous foe was almost within sight of the city walls. These Servian defences had been built in the fourth century, possibly to stop any repetition of the capture of Rome in 390 by the Gauls. Made from Tufa quarried near Veii, it was seven miles in length, over 32ft high and 12ft wide at its base, punctuated with sixteen considerable, well-defended gates and though substantial enough anyway, fortuitously the year before a commission had been charged with refurbishing these fortifications. The Numidians who had caused such a stir in the city streets, had in fact been directed to repulse a reconnaissance force of 2,000 horse that Hannibal had led from his camp on the Anio River towards the Temple of Hercules hard by the Colline Gate. From there he hoped to discover what defensive preparations had been made against his arrival. The deserters had been picked for the task because of their special fighting talents, a facility for nimble skirmishing which was expected to be just the ticket in this part of the suburbs 'amongst the hollows and garden walls and sepulchres and enclosed paths all around that part of the City'.

The arrival at this moment of a Carthaginian army, egged on by the savage cries of their officers below the walls of Rome, with Hannibal now facing some of his old soldiers from Africa, had not been grounded on a caprice. The man who had not descended on the Tiber fortress years before had not just decided to attack his enemy's capital on a whim. The decision had been gestated in the rich plains of Campania where the armies of Fulvius Flaccus and Appius Claudius were still pushing hard their attack on Capua. These Romans had showed themselves all about tenacity and spadework as they worked night and day to throw up siege lines to completely enclose the target city. Even family issues had not put the proconsul Fulvius off his stride. The Romans had been in a 'to encourage the others' groove in what was looking to become a decisive year in Campania. So his brother who had lost his army at Herdonia was being roasted by the folk back home and would end fleeing into exile at Tarquinii to avoid prosecution. This man had not got the kind of treatment that Varro received after the disaster at Cannae, both had ridden off from defeat to save their lives but there could be no forgiveness for a man who had allowed his troops to lose their discipline. Varro had had his men in such biddable order that they walked in tens of thousands to their deaths when he ordered it; this was excusable but not what Gnaeus had allowed. The defendant had wanted to get his brother to come back to Rome to speak for him but reasonably enough this was not allowed. These goings-on in the capital could not help one of the commanders at Capua to concentrate on the matter in hand, but at least though the family reputation was undoubtedly tarnished by his brother's behaviour at Herdonia, the elder sibling would soon bronze it back up again to a considerable degree. That he was involved in the Siege of Capua had made it impossible for him to speak for his brother, but equally his conduct there was what would increase even more the reputation of this man who was already second only to Fabius in the Roman military establishment.

This competent sibling and his partner Appius, as they had worked in tandem as consuls, now as proconsuls pulled tight the noose around Capua. In a year that twenty-five legions were under arms altogether, six were given to them, near 60,000 men including allies around the walls and other armies on hand too; they had plenty of resources to throw at the problem of the Campanian metropolis. The war in this rich region had been going strong for five years and in the last three the attempt on this place had been what it was all about. It had begun with tentative approaches, as much to do with defending the road to Rome as preparing the route into Campania. But two seasons had seen real intent, though even as the net tightened the prey was resisting with all their might. The Campanian defenders came out repeatedly to try and interrupt the Roman working parties. Their infantry made little impact, they threw their javelins and threatened to bust into the enemy lines, but when legionary or allied heavies formed line and prepared to attack they melted back behind the city walls. But with the cavalry it was different. Campania was a country of broad rich plains and the local aristocracy had shown as prime horsemen for centuries. These high-toned, beplumed and richly armoured characters can still be seen in all their glory in frescos at Paestum, Capua and elsewhere. They came from moneyed families with wide acres who could afford not only muscled cuirasses and fine helmets for the rider but bronze head and chest protection for the horses, very partial coverings yet sufficient to guard against glancing blows from edged weapons. The equipment was completed with stout spears, round shields and chopping swords, a protective and offensive array that enabled these troopers to not just indulge in nimble skirmishing, hurling their javelins, but to charge up close to their opponents and fight hand-to-hand too.

These cavalry now showed much better than their infantry counterparts when they sallied out to interrupt an enemy trying to enclose them behind a growing line of ditches and palisades. Drawing down on their Roman opponents who came out to face them these enemies found themselves outclassed, pushed back and routed exposing the working parties and slowing down the pace of digging. These rampant horsemen could not actually halt progress, because as they approached, the labouring legionaries would drop their picks and shovels, pick up spear and shield and show an armoured front to the attackers. But this obviously meant the work of digging the fosse, the implanting of wooden walls and the construction of redoubts could only carry on at a snail's pace, with these intimidating troopers hovering in the vicinity. The many miles of siege works the besiegers would have to construct to fully surround the city meant that the whole enterprise might falter and fail if a solution was not found. Necessity gestating invention, the men in charge were prepared to listen when a centurion called Quintus Navius came up with a plan. It might have owed something to what he had seen Carthaginians doing in the past, but that it was derivative did not count when his ingenuity looked like it might do the trick. This officer suggested the cavalry should each hoist up an infantryman behind them when they went into battle. These men were to be young, agile, carry a shield slightly smaller than a cavalryman's and seven, 4ft iron-tipped javelins just like those the Velites used. Once some training allowed proficiency, the combined force rode out to challenge the Capuan cavaliers to battle in the plain between the city walls and the main Roman camp near the Casilinum road.

As the two battle lines approached the Roman horse stopped and dropped off their loads and the foot soldiers forming up, threw volley after volley of javelins into the ranks of the enemy horse. The Campanians were just not expecting this kind of effective missile attack, so after the projectiles were exhausted and the Roman cavalry charged, they found a foe badly disordered, with men and horses struck and wounded by deadly darts. So hardly waiting to break a lance or exchange sword strokes, the Campanians fled, with the Romans putting spurs to their horses in pursuit with the shaken enemy losing many men as they routed back to the city gates, only finding safety when they got back inside the walls. With the victorious Roman knights looking at their enemy's retreating back the besieger's problems melted away, the defenders' cavalry were just never as effective again and strangely not once tried copying the Romans' tactic. This is odd as the ingenuity here was not such a stretch, light infantry had on occasions fought in amongst their cavalry in the Roman military before. Indeed in the fight by the Ticinus River in 218, when the General Scipio may have been saved by his son, his cavalry corps had set up in just this way, but obviously having the foot soldiers actually up on the horse itself provided extra mobility. Yet whatever the exact reasons for a lack of response the defenders were no longer able to effectively disrupt the besiegers and the digging crews could continue to push the snaking lines of contravallation and circumvallation all around the town.

While this battling around the trench lines had been occupying the beginning of 211, Hannibal had been wintering near Tarentum, still struggling with the problem of how to dig the enemy garrison out of the citadel they possessed and had spent much effort succouring in the past two years. Early in the fighting season a Numidian slipping through the Roman lines at night had got through with a letter urging him once again to come and raise the siege, while the Campanians were still strong enough to second him effectively. Now understanding that this crucial ally was facing a new enemy, hunger, and was in deep trouble, he acted. It was needful as not long before word had arrived that one of his other great allies had gone down. Syracuse despite the best efforts of Archimedes' genius had fallen to Marcellus after an epic siege where the last bastion had been brought from a Spanish mercenary officer, who had lost hope when Syracuse's Carthaginian allies had sailed away and his own employer had left the town seeking safety in Agrigentum on the south coast of Sicily.

With this Sicilian partner removed as a factor, losing Capua was unthinkable so he dumped a good part of his baggage and trains, leaving the southern literal with his best infantry, cavalry and thirty-three elephants. They pushed hard covering the couple of hundred tough miles across Lucania and Samnium, hoping to reach the neighbourhood, before word of their own coming. This they achieved, driving into Lucania, through Samnium country and hard up the Appian Way to emerge out of the Caudine Valley where two outcrops still guard its wide mouth, with a fine square mediaeval castle planted where the Castra Claudiana once stood on the south side and where to the north a far more fairy-tale affair guards the other flank, its walls climbing in most dramatic fashion up the steep slopes above the town. The

Carthaginians arrived in a hidden valley behind Mount Tifata, having only paused to overpower a nearby garrison at Calatia, itself sited virtually where Maddaloni now stands, to ensure nobody there would get away to warn the Romans. Now footsore men and animals had a welcome chance to rest while Hannibal opened communications with the gravely threatened city. Word was sent that as he was coming to break the siege and 'attack the Roman camp' so the Campanians must organize their forces to sortie out to face the enemy and aid the cause.

What is sure is that by the time he arrived Capua was fully invested, with the besiegers snug in their lines facing both in towards the city walls and out toward where any relief might come from. The Roman strategy may have been based on blockade rather than all out assault but it was beginning to look like one that must succeed in the end, if the Carthaginians could be kept from breaking through to their confederates' relief. So the new arrivals could see all too clearly what they were up against, but whatever the odds, with his troops recouped sufficiently Hannibal took the fight to the enemy. Combined much could be hoped for and it was not going to be easy for the besiegers despite having built their lines to cope with just this eventuality. They might have more than two consular armies, perhaps upwards of 60,000 men, but Hannibal's name was still enough to instil terror in the heart of officers, who if not present at Trebbia, Trasimene or Cannae, knew all about them. And now they had not only to face the genius of those victories coming from one direction but the Campanians and their Carthaginian garrison under Bostar and Hanno assailing them from the other. To divide their forces was the only way and after the advice of senior officers was taken, Appius agreed to oppose any enemy emerging from the city while Fulvius took on whatever Hannibal could throw at them. These men knew this might be the turning point of the war and nothing was left undone in this time of crisis. Everybody within range had to do their bit. So to guard the roads the propraetor Nero was ordered to take the cavalry of six legions to secure the way south-east towards Suessula while his subordinate commanding the allied horse stood sentinel on the north-westerly route to the River Volturnus.

On the day decided, with attacks coordinated soon after sunrise, the Campanians exited from the Jupiter Gate to take formation in the 350yds of ground between the walls and the Roman palisades, noisily encouraged by the population crowded on top of the walls who clashed bronze vessels together, as if it were a lunar eclipse.

at the same time burst out of all the gates, he inspired great alarm for on one side he himself attacked, on the other all the Capuans, cavalry and infantry, sallied out, and with them the Carthaginian garrison, commanded by Bostar and Hanno.[1]

These men knew the importance of their role; that it was not just up to Hannibal to break into the Roman lines, but they must smash through both the lines of circumvallation and contravallation and push on into the open country beyond. We have no details of what units were involved on this front but they must have thrown everything they had into the fray. The cavalry surely numbered thousands and the infantry tens of thousands and this apart from the 2,000 cavalry who had been attached to the defenders since the year before and probably other Carthaginian troops as well, lent before the place had been completely surrounded, to give backbone for the crucial part they were required to play.

Where now there are traffic crowded streets in Santa Maria Capua Vetere the high-born knights of Campania exited in their last hurrah of independence. These cavalry were good, as were the ones on loan from Hannibal, who now accompanied them but horsemen were not the troops to force an entrenched line; this was a job for infantry and the fighting before had shown they had come up short when these were tested. So once again while the troopers threw their shafts at whatever target appeared and the foot soldiers discharged their javelins too, when it came to close work, to jumping down into the ditch and trying to pull out and push through the palisades, they showed little enthusiasm. It was always going to be difficult with the enemy up high on ramparts and towers, sited forbiddingly on the top of embankments raised over months of hard work and throwing down on them. It seems they never actually got to cross swords, with the army coming out of the city finding themselves totally unable to penetrate the enemy lines on their front. In fact near the Volturnus Gate the Romans themselves pushed forward so far that the Campanians were forced back to their own walls and only missiles hurled by people and engines from the ramparts stopped them from bursting in on the footsteps of the retreating garrison. It was at this time that Appius, leading his men from the front and encouraging them with promises of the mural crown for the first man on the walls, received the wound that would soon be the end of him: 'the general encouraging his men at the front, when the upper part of his chest was struck by a javelin below the left shoulder'.

In this sudden climax the sortie petered out, a costly affray that saw Campanian bodies scattered across the plain between the walls and the Roman lines. So as it turned out Appius kept his entrenched lines secure without any great difficulty. But if this part of Hannibal's grand plan had foundered it would have surprised no one on the Roman side that it was from outside the besieging lines that the greatest threat came, from a larger army of veteran fighters led by the greatest general of his time. There are a confusing number of versions about what really happened on that crucial day on that side of the pincer attack when Hannibal led his army forward in assault. But what is certain is that as he drew up his men offering battle in front of Fulvius' defences, that his Numidians were in action first, harassing the defenders with volleys of javelins in the hope of drawing them out of their camp into battle. The most detailed account claims this worked and that a Roman army that can't have been far short of 40,000 men emerged to face the enemy coming at them from the direction of Mount Tifata.

We hear of no involvement from the cavalry on either side so it is probable the Roman and allied horse drawn up in their thousands to guard the roads north and south from the siege lines that occupied the attention of the enemy troopers, ensuring most could not be deployed to affect the main encounter. The Carthaginians' approach was thunderous as they hit the enemy with everything they could and the 6th Legion in the centre of the Roman line took the brunt. These soldiers did not do well in the hard stand-up fighting. The Spaniards, encouraged by the shouts of their officers, attacked dressed in their usual white tunics with purple trim and mostly now protected with captured mail. Some would have been pike men crowding forward in serried ranks, a glittering forest of spears backed by a press of bodies to carve a path through the enemy. Others were fearsome sword and buckler men of the kind that the Iberian Peninsula would produce well into early modern times. Yet it was not just these alarming warriors surging forward, fighting with desperate ferocity, they were also supported by three elephants. Standing like bastions amongst the pushing lines of men directed by their mahouts, perhaps with a warrior on their back carrying javelins to hurl down from on high.

The debate on whether Hannibal's elephants would have carried towers on their backs with missile and pike men in them rages on. While it is now the orthodoxy that most of his beasts would have been an African bush elephant now largely extinct, with large ears, only 8ft at the shoulder with a concave back, considerably smaller than either better known African or

Indian elephants, how they fought is yet debated. We know from accounts of the Battle of Raphia, fought on the border of Egypt and the Gaza strip between the armies of the Seleucids and Ptolemies in 217, that these kinds of elephants could carry towers with men in them even if they were at a considerable disadvantage against their larger Indian cousins. On that occasion the two species are reported in combat with men in towers on their backs jousting with Macedonian sarissas. Yet no reliable record of elephant fighting in the Hannibal war mentions such things, any damage done is by the animals' trunks and tusks as their heads swung with the bell hung round their necks clanging, and from their feet and the fear they engendered, not by men on their back. Yet there are some solid pieces of evidence such as a terracotta model in the Naples Archaeological Museum showing exactly such an animal with a tower on its back, though it holds no soldiers and could just have been for used for ceremonial purposes rather than battle.

However they were equipped these animals did much execution as the roar of fighting swelled louder down the line then diminished as the front ranks rested. Brutal combat continued with the sun edging towards the meridian until in one section of their line the Romans, Hastati and Principes, shield arms wearying and spirits sinking were pushed back down the fosse and up the further slope, until they were pressed up against their own palisades. Now the elephants crushed on through throwing the legionaries aside like rag dolls, while the Spanish foot protected their comrades with long shields, as they tried to pull down the watchtowers with hooks or ripped up the defensive stakes, to make a passage into the camp itself. But once almost within they became concerned about becoming exposed or being cut off if they entered. So men dithered in the lee of the defences in the outside fosse. Fulvius, behind his line with his bodyguard and officers beside him on the ramparts, now noticed that after the Spaniards had broken through the ranks of the 6th Legion they were vulnerable on their own flanks to the other Roman units. Feeling the pulse of the battle might be turning his way he called on the same centurion Navius standing nearby, who had suggested the ploy of mounting the infantry in the earlier battle, and on the other senior centurions who could hear him, ordering them to lead any men they could rally against the Spaniards below the earthwork.

These officers were inspired by their general's enthusiasm, who declared that with this supreme effort they could defeat the enemy either by letting them in and destroying them in the camp or drive them back from the position they held under the ramparts. Navius' adrenalin pumped, took the standard of the second maniple of Hastati and threatened to throw it into the enemy ranks, if the men did not follow him in and join the fight. This hoary old trope around legionaries giving all to protect their standard is a part of an extraordinary number of battles of which we have details in this period. But if this should give us pause, still they should not be discounted when we know of similar acts of bravery, well evidenced in more modern times concerning regimental flags. Anyway this huge man's bullyragging had its effect, and together the attackers pressed through the enemy missiles and on to the lines of the Spaniards holding the moat. It was a hard fight with soldiers on both sides involved all along the line, but finally with the rasp of heavy breathing in their ears the legionaries, swords stabbing, pushed over the ramparts as the Carthaginians began to give way under the pressure exerted by their desperate opponents. Then another officer called on his men and backing up the Hastati charged at the head of the first maniple of the Principes of the same legion, carrying its standard straight at the Spaniards. And all this while, the tribunes and centurions left in command of the camp, after halting to rearrange the troops still available, led them up the earthwork ramparts to take on the elephants who were trying to crash through the palisades. The animals were killed and their huge frames crashed down into the ditch where a terrific fight continued between the attacking troops and those of the Romans who could reach them.

But this was far from the only scene of carnage as along the whole of the line the Carthaginians pressed forward. But it was to no avail, despite the clash of the two lines ringing across the field of combat: at no other point could they penetrate the burnished line of armoured enemies. Hannibal had thrown in everything he had to achieve a breakthrough, elite infantry and fearsome war elephants all had been committed to try and drive the Romans away from the beleaguered city. Outnumbered and not able to compensate by adept manoeuvring, this was a contest that had been forced on him, not one he had chosen. Eventually exhaustion ensured the bloodletting on this front faltered, just as the Carthaginian general decided he would not win in this battling in the trenches. So giving instructions for his line to fall back he ordered what little cavalry was to hand to cover the withdrawal. The Romans at first seemed in the mood to pursue until Flaccus, weary of losing what he had already gained by some Punic trick, sounded the recall. Not a defeat but certainly a disappointment and one only compounded, when he heard of the rebuff of his Campanian allies in their sortie against Appius' army.

There are other traditions regarding this fight outside Capua, indeed the most respected source, though sketchy, is extant for these incidents and has it that when the skirmishing Numidians tried to provoke Flaccus to action, the Roman commander stood firm behind his prepared positions, refusing the bait until the Carthaginian forays almost turned into an assault on the camp. The cavalry came on in good order, throwing javelins and the infantry who had first stood by as support, deployed in their ranks before jumping down into the fosse and climbing out the other side, digging at the base of the palisades to try and tear them down. But even this did not make the Romans come out, remaining happy to man their defences, while their main force in ordered ranks, under their standards inside the camp, held up their shields to ward off the incoming missiles while their own light infantry replied against the enemy climbing the palisades. But the Romans would not face Hannibal in open battle; they had had too many defeats at his hands over the last few years, though they were firm enough while they could stay safe behind the security of their field works. Fabius had only been prepared to confront Hannibal from unassailable hills above his enemy's route, but now if they could throw up defences it seemed Roman generals might fight him even in the level country of Campania. Polybius saw both strategies as successful ones because in each case they negated the battle-winning potential of the Carthaginian cavalry, who could not hurt them when the legionaries stayed in their palisaded camp or in their defensive lines around the city.

Others have even less of a bloodbath with panicked troops from both sides careering about to little purpose, where the Spaniards and elephants backed by Numidians as well entered without too much difficulty into Fulvius' camp that had been poorly constructed with hardly more than a ditch for defence. Once inside they caused havoc smashing up tents, causing the animals in the horse line and the other beasts of burden to panic and generally generating mayhem in the whole place. And all this confusion was compounded when Hannibal sent men dressed as Roman soldiers and speaking Latin to claim that the proconsul had declared the camp taken and ordering his men to flee to the first defensible position they could find in the nearby hills. But before disaster befell them the interlopers were discovered as being in no great numbers and driven away, the Numidians pushed back at spear point and the elephants forced away by men waving burning brands at them.

The severest version of the butcher's bill is only recorded for the Carthaginians and Campanians, 11,000 and fifteen standards in all and if this was the case then it is almost certain the Romans would have lost concomitantly as well. Indeed the suspicion is that the subtraction from the Roman ranks was considerably greater than their enemies had suffered, as all accounts agree their lines were entered, and even if the camp was not captured, a penetration implied the main lines of the Roman army facing Hannibal were broken in at least one place, probably suffering the kind of casualties that were usual in such cases. But despite the weariness and wide gaps in the ranks of the men, the spirits at the proconsular headquarters after the fight were almost buoyant. The army had held; they had faced the foe, they had to. The most ferocious attack by the main Carthaginian army, led by Hannibal himself, had failed to break through and what they had done once they saw no reason why they might not repeat if the enemy tried again. One of the proconsuls certainly would have slept well that night even if Appius was in too much pain to enjoy an achievement few of his colleagues had managed: fighting Hannibal and coming out at the end with their army intact. The great Carthaginian had subtracted two armies from the Republic's military roster only the year before, yet despite Fulvius having had a few worrying moments, the armies around Capua would not become part of the awful bloody equation constructed by her enemies from Africa over the last seven years.

There are two contradictory renderings as to what exactly happened next, but on this occasion the usually more reputable account is the less credible. Any tendency to take Polybius as default correct must be resisted because however much he may be the best source available still he needs to be tested, particularly as we know on at least one occasion how wrong he could be. This is the man that claims Mago the Samnite was of equal rank to Hannibal himself, a contention that everything we know about the period contradicts.[2] Both the main versions however concur that Hannibal determined on a march on Rome. That he hoped, by threatening the Republic's capital, to entice away the huge armies that were encircling his crucial friends and allies in the great metropolis of Campania. But the timeframe and direction of the march in this most dramatic turn up of the Italian War are most certainly contested. The Greek historian's narrative has it that, unable to break through the siege lines and affect an entry into the town, the Carthaginian general worried that the new consuls for the year, Galba and Centumalus, with forces raised in Rome would establish themselves in his rear. And that anyway he would be unable to easily supply his crucial horsemen in a country already laid waste, so he had to consider a plan B, to feint as if to attack Rome and so draw most of the enemy away from Capua to defend their capital. Once decided he did not delay. The journey started only five days after he had arrived outside the Campanian capital having sent a letter by a Libyan who pretended to desert to the Romans, to inform the people there of what he was about to do, so they should keep up a stout defence, while he slipped the army away, leaving campfires burning so the enemy should not notice their going. This hike was claimed as going deep into Samnium, around the east of Latium through modern Abruzzo allowing the invaders to arrive, out of the blue, on the Anio River about three miles from Rome's walls and, 'by sending his outposts on each day to reconnoitre and occupy the district near the road', even before the Romans at Capua knew what was happening. Indeed 'the thing being so sudden and so entirely unexpected, as Hannibal had never before been so close to the city' such that people in Rome were shocked and bewildered by the appearance of the enemy so proximate to home and could only believe the armies outside Capua must have been destroyed to allow such a thing to happen.

But if this narrative does not make total sense only two hundred odd years later a more convincing version emerged that has survived. All agree the intention was to draw the enemy away from Campania and so raise the Siege of Capua, rather than to capture Rome itself, and to do this the threat to the capital had to be apparent. To disappear into Samnium and reappear outside Rome, while it might terrorize the citizens, would not immediately affect the actions of Fulvius and Appius who could not learn of these events for some interval after Hannibal's arrival. By which time whatever was going to happen in front of the Servian defences would probably already have played itself out. So this later account is much more believable, though its author happily accepts that when he was writing he was himself drawing on a number of divergent versions of what happened.[3] In this narrative too Hannibal took great care in preparing his coup; he slipped the word by 'a Numidian who was ready for any desperate enterprise', of what he intended to the people trapped inside the Roman siege lines, urging both the locals and his own officers Bostar and Hanno to stand firm while he tried to draw the enemy away.

Then sending a vanguard to scize boats on the Volturnus River, he constructed a bridge near the fort of Casilinum that allowed the rest of the army to cross at night before camping on the other side. So by daybreak the soldiers, carrying ten days' supplies, were over and pushing hard on up the road to Rome. The men were unleashed to lay waste all the way, the route passed Cales, now an overgrown but extensive precinct of ruins in flat

Castle on the site of 'Castra Claudiana' (Claudian camp) just above nearby Suessula.

Looking at the citadel of Tarentum from the town side where Hannibal attacked the garrison under Livius.

Looking down on the River Calor near where Hanno was defeated in the first battle at Beneventum.

Samnite warrior, Castle Museum
Montesarchio.

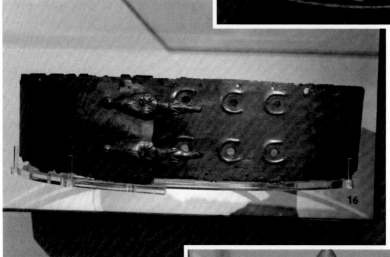

Typical bronze belt
worn by south Italian
warriors, Ashmolean
Museum, Oxford.

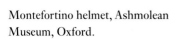

Montefortino helmet, Ashmolean
Museum, Oxford.

Looking at the coast from the citadel of Cumae.

Lake Avernus where Hannibal met representatives from Tarentum who called for him to take over their city.

Looking from the later Roman amphitheatre at Capua, up towards mount Tifata.

The river Volturnus running through Casilinum.

South Italian cavalry helmet at the Archeological Museum, Melfi Castle.

South Italian cavalryman, Paestum Archaeological Museum.

Looking at Monte Cassino above the site of old Casinum.

Later Roman amphitheatre at Casinum.

The Latin way near Aquinum where Hannibal's army would have marched on the way to Rome in 211.

River Liris where the people from Fregellae broke down the bridge to slow Hannibal's progress in the march on Rome in 211.

Muro Lucano above the battlefield of Numistro.

Roman bridge near Canusium in Apulia.

Agora of Tarentum, where a battle took place between Fabius's army and the Carthaginian garrison and defending citizens.

Frieze of a late third century naval battle at Taranto Museum.

Cavalryman's panoply, Archeological Museum, Taranto.

South Italian panoply, Paestum Archaeological Museum.

Column at the promontory of Lacinium, modern Cape Colonne.

The port at Croton.

country under a motorway with a mediaeval castle guarding its entrance. There they did not stay long, or indeed at Teano, a place famous later when on 26 October 1860 the great Italian patriot Garibaldi yielded his republican principles by hailing Victor Emanuel II of Sardinia as King of Italy for the sake of national unity. This town further up in the hills towards volcanic Roccamonfina had, like Cales, long been used as advanced bases along the Via Latium for the Campanian front, though there was presumably little of military value left behind to pick up at these places by the Carthaginians passing by.

But when Hannibal reached the walls of Casinum, where now the extraordinary Monte Cassino monastery looms over the valley road below, the peoples on the town walls saw the intruders prepare for a thorough demolition of their country. The settlement itself on the lower slopes was not taken but still it was grim enough having a destructive enemy so deep in territory long protected and colonized by the Republic. After two days' destroying everything that could not be carried off the invaders moved further along towards the Liris River passing Interamna and Aquino along the Latin Way, that can still be walked to this day, a little overgrown running alongside the modern highway and through an arch of the imperial age. In the shadow of looming great mountains on their right side the Carthaginians had found it easy-going to begin with when they left Casinum, but still this was deeply hostile country and the people at Fregellae were determined to resist, smashing the bridge over the river to try and slow the intruders down, though they suffered for it when Hannibal got over the watercourse and ordered his men to destroy the countryside around, to punish these loyalists, solid for Rome since the town was retaken from the Samnites in the late fourth century.

This route the invaders travelled had been fought over for decades in the Samnite wars and before and the legitimacy Rome's authority had won struck deep. War-weariness might affect in years to come but Hannibal was not going to find any easy adherents in this country and he knew it. This move into the heart of Rome's central Italian power was all about ruin and demolition though always as part of the key strategy of dragging the besieging armies away from Capua. The generals surrounding that place would be receiving constant reports of the invaders' progress, a pressure that Hannibal was sure would lure them away to defend both the capital and the central heartland of the Republic. The raiders deep within enemy territory ensured any engagements with local forces were brief and decisive as they followed hard on the heels of the fugitives they had flushed out. People stumbled desperately into any protected towns to find safety with extravagant claims of the damage done and exaggerated stories of the invaders' strength. Phantoms converging in overwhelming numbers, forcing the surrender of anybody they found in the open, burning or tearing up crops, olive trees and buildings to ensure agricultural production was put out of commission for some time. For the primary assignment of the cavalry and light troops leading the invaders it was a respectable performance, destruction on a wide scale that showed real evidence of their efficiency as wreckers, ensuring a picture was painted of trusted friends being left in the lurch as the interlopers arrived at Frusino first, then Ferentinum and Anagnia, before crossing Mount Algidus to Tusculum. With their gates all closed to them they dropped down to Gabii before reaching within eight miles of Rome itself, all the while with the Numidian horse riding in front, killing or capturing any people they discovered in the path of the army.

Not that this stopped the news of his coming reaching Rome and it was 'a messenger from Fregellae, riding night and day' a horseman sent galloping who brought the dreaded word that the Carthaginian ogre was at the gates and the Senate convened when confirmation came from Quintus Fulvius who had learnt from deserters that Hannibal was marching on Rome. As the dire threat became common knowledge there was desperate preparation for the worst. Fabius was soon on his feet to the Senate. His predominance might not have been what it was; both new consuls Centumalus and Galba were if not his enemies certainly not friends, but the authority was still there. His very presence acted to hold back the flood of desperate men who were calling for the armies from all over to return to save the homeland. Even the like of Publius Cornelius Asina was arguing that the Siege of Capua should be given up and indeed everything else to save the city. This man had clout; part of the Scipio clan he had been consul in 221 and in 217 was *interrex*, a high honour for any senator, to act for a few days as sole head of state to organize elections when no consuls were available. Interestingly the elections he supervised were fraught with class rancour, with Varro elected on an anti–establishment ticket with vociferous plebeian backing. But on this occasion Fabius was having none of this big senatorial beast. Using all his residual political heft and claiming a full understanding of the Carthaginians' intentions, he was determined they should not conform to them, pointing out that if after Trasimene or Cannae the city had not been seriously threatened by the enemy, how could it be so bad now? The effect of the cool old man was enough and a compromise package submitted by P Valerius Flaccus, another heavyweight who had been consul back in 227, was agreed, that the officers in charge of the Siege of Capua should decide what assistance they could dispatch that would not detrimentally affect their progress in Campania. The experienced Fulvius and Appius, the men on the spot, it was agreed, would know what troops Hannibal was taking where and be best placed to respond; to decide what numbers they could afford to detach to defend the homeland while not losing significant ground in what all the long heads in Rome knew was a contest that would be decisive for the advance of their arms in the war.

When these letters outlining the situation arrived in the Roman camps just south of the Volturnus River the proconsuls acted quickly, with Fulvius picking 15,000 foot and 1,000 horse, the best in the army, to rush to the rescue while Appius, still nursing his wound, stayed in place with the remaining what may have been more than 40,000 men to sustain the blockade. The rescue party, learning Hannibal had taken the Latin Way, directed their steps towards the other road to Rome. They stepped out along the Appian Way, a route running west nearer the coast, having sent warnings to the villages along the way to get victuals ready for them as they passed by. And instructing local defence forces to be prepared to protect their own homes should the enemy approach near them. They first had to make rafts to cross the Volturnus as Hannibal had burnt the boats when he passed, which was accomplished with some difficulty as there was little timber nearby. Then it was on or near the Appian Way via Setia and Cora inland of the Pontine marshes to Lavinium, before arriving at the Servian walls under the Caelian hill something more than a mile south of where the Carthaginians were threatening. While this succour had been on its way and even while women were wailing, begging help from the gods and sweeping the temple floors with their loosened hair, the senators remained in session in the forum, from where couriers pounded off to deliver the orders for troops under the city praetor to occupy not only the Capitol and the walls but out to Mount Alban and the Aesula fortress nineteen miles to the north-east, not far from the town of Tibur, too.

The city on the Tiber River that now seemed under threat was one that any visitor from the Greek south might have found initially pretty unimpressive. Populous certainly but hardly grand, there was no grid system of streets that he would most likely have been familiar with from his own home town. This was not the marble city of the imperial age parts of which can still be seen to this day; unplanned, it had just grown, confused thoroughfares followed the lines of hills and valleys; some paved but with many side streets lined with apartments up to eight stories high, dust parched in summer and mud deep after winter rains. This was no thought out orderly pattern centred on a stately Agora, a product of the school of Hippodamus of Miletus, the great if personally eccentric fifth century father of town planning, who famously laid out the port of Piraeus in Attica, but also had his impact on Italy at Thurii and whose ideas were hugely influential in the Hellenistic age of megacities in Asia and Egypt. Still both inside the walls and even beginning outside, on the Campus Martius, numbers of temples and shrines were starting to be influenced by monumental Hellenistic styles, dedicated by generals successful in the Republic's great wars. A process that was beginning to make the townscape more imposing and the impact of which would massively increase after the defeat of Carthage when the Republic's conquest of the Mediterranean world really picked up pace and the riches it brought in funded the ego projects of the city's great men.

But even in the 210s, if the visitor reached the Capitoline or the Palatine hills he would have found much to behold. The former hill where in legendary times an avaricious woman called Tarpeia let in Sabine outsiders who fortified the place to fight the Romans on the Palatine but were soon acculturated and where the sacred geese had saved that one part of the city from the rampaging Gauls in 390. It had long been topped by the ancient temple of the divine triad of Jupiter, Juno and Minerva and by the late third century the great edifice on its high Etruscan style podium had been in place since Tarquin the Proud, 200ft^2 with its well spaced columns, allowed by a flammable wooden roof that ensured that it repeatedly burnt down. But it was the Palatine Hill that was Rome's geographical and ceremonial centre, standing 40m above the forum. People had been living there since 1000 but development had been slow on this original home of the people where there was a cleft in the venerable hill, a cave that was supposed to have belonged to the fire breathing giant Caicus who fatally rustled some of Hercules' bulls and where the wolf who suckled Romulus and Remus had her den. And near where during the Lupercalia youths, many of the most well born, to celebrate the founder twin's mother wolf, ran naked striking young women with leather thongs to encourager fertility and safe delivery.

The attentive ancient tourist would also have seen the rushing water emerging at the cattle market after a twelve mile journey along an underground aqueduct commissioned by Appius Claudius Caecus, at the end of the fourth century. A bit of a dilettante who dabbled in Greek style poetry but who was more famous for the highway that carries his name and an antecedent of the conqueror of Capua. A second conduit also served the thirsty city, some parts raised up on high arches, constructed forty years later to bring water from the River Arno in Etruria to the north and following a tradition of engineering that went back as far as the old Roman kings. The swamps that had filled the valleys below the seven hills had been drained for centuries by the great drain, the Cloaca Maxima, that though allowing habitation did not stop it being unhealthy enough, with a virtually annual visitation of malaria. This was one of the many reasons the well-off built their houses on available higher ground like the Palatine, Esquiline and Caelian hills where on the former there remain traces of their comfortable habitations. Two-storey atrium style houses, many overlooking the forum, are occasionally revealed under the imperial palaces that took over the whole of the eminence in the early centuries AD. So to the Greek visitor the town would have seemed scruffy but perhaps intimidating; we do not know exactly how many people lived within its walls but certainly a great deal more than most of the places he might have known. Though for others it would perhaps have been less daunting, after all any Carthaginian in Hannibal's army waiting outside would have been familiar with a home town that boasted walls almost twice the length of the Servian defences.

This was the place where the consuls Centumalus and Galba had already levied one new legion whose men were expected to report for duty immediately and were enrolling another as well. So these recruits too, frantically mustering even if not thoroughly organized, were on hand for use in this emergency. This activity however only reflected the general endeavour of the city administration with the plebeian aediles sorting out supplies to feed the newly arrived mouths from the country, as senators and magistrates held council in the army camp. They were gathered in hundreds beneath the city's ramparts, surrounded by their *servitors* to wait on them and massed ranks of soldiers for protection while they decided on the tactics that needed to be employed. Yet if the leadership was calm most were not and panicking rustics drove in their cattle for safety, making chaos in the streets, so that anyone who had ever been a senior magistrate was given imperium for the duration of the siege, to put a lid on any alarms that threatened to break out into trouble.

For the man in the street the relief must have been palpable when the army from Capua was seen entering the city precincts through the Porta

Capena. Massed ranks of well-armed confident men, veterans all and the man who led them, though only a proconsul, it is declared, was given full consular powers to lead the defence of the city. Not waiting a moment he pushed his men on through the streets across the southern spur of the Esquiline Hill, named from buildings there looking something like the keels of ships, and out again through the Colline Gate. Here at the northern end of the Servian walls was where the Via Nomentana entered and hard by were the temples of Venus and Fortuna that would witness an awful battle in the 80s in the civil war between Sulla and the Samnite General Telesinus with his army of Samnites and Lucanians fighting in the Marian cause. Here Fulvius joined the rest of the new raised levies and the Numidian deserters who had entrenched themselves on ground just outside the walls between the Colline and Esquiline gates. This covered a considerable part of the north-east section of the town along the slopes of the Esquiline Hill. There were graveyards nearby and the monuments may have been incorporated in the botched up defences and just further south was the 'Agger', formidable fortified double ramparts incorporated within the Servian defences.

With terror abroad it was a balm that Rome's new-found Numidian friends did well, they might fight for a different master but their skirmishing skills were not tarnished. They chivvied Hannibal's reconnaissance force out of the suburbs and herded them back to the protection of their camp. But this small war was only the preamble. Hannibal was camped on the other side of the Anio but crossed to challenge Flaccus and the consuls. The armies drew up ready, the Romans under the walls so they might retire to safety if things went against them. But the soldiers on either side had hardly approached each other when a hailstorm drove both contesting parties to seek shelter as they could hardly hold their weapons. The same thing happened the next day so both sides withdrew again, the Romans behind the city walls and the Carthaginians to their encampment. Hannibal after his failure to thrash the motley army the defenders had sent against him is reported as downcast, particularly when he heard the Romans had actually dispatched regiments to Spain and also sold by auction the land his camp stood on. But these stories are barely believable: while the auction might have been countenanced, it had no downside and encouraged the populace; but that they would send any of their soldiers far away, with the most dangerous enemy they ever faced outside the walls, just beggars belief. Equally improbable is the story that as a quid pro quo the intruders put up for sale lots of land where silver shops stood in the city itself in an effort to show their confidence in their army's ability to take the place. Yet whatever was the truth of these bits of nonsense on both sides, the fact that matters is that after the failed attempts to beat the defenders in the field Hannibal decided to withdraw, initially falling back six miles from the outskirts of the city.

Whether it was really a firm front or even exceptional weather that saved the city is moot. Was it really these two mint new green units boosted by Fulvius' men entering the fields below the city walls that forestalled the Carthaginian attack? 'For the Carthaginians had at first eagerly advanced not without hope of taking Rome itself by assault, but when they saw the enemy drawn up in battle order, and when very soon afterwards they learnt the truth from a prisoner, they abandoned the project of attacking the city and took to overrunning and plundering the country and burning the houses.'[4] The reality was surely that this was bluster, there was never any intention to try and take the town. So having made what impact he could and hoping this would have had its effect on the army outside Capua, Hannibal prepared to terrorize and devastate as widely as was safe before returning to discover if his feint had achieved anything. But he soon found he had stirred up a hornets' nest and that the enemy were not intending to let him fade away untroubled. 'According to his original calculation' he reckoned enough time had passed for the armies at Capua to move, hopefully they might have raised the siege completely, or at least that many of the troops had left to succour the threatened people of Rome and Latium. In the light of this he ordered the army to withdraw, backing off with vast quantities of booty, particularly livestock, collected by men who if they had not had to fight much were certainly prepared to steal, even gutting the nearby wealthy temple grove of Feronia, though when the trove was removed some of the more pious soldiers, worried by curses being brought down by the desecration, left a mass of uncoined brass as offering for protection.

But the consuls had been determined not to let the intruders have an easy passage out; they 'had the extreme boldness to encamp opposite them at a distance of ten stades, Hannibal retired.'[5] Galba had even been out in the countryside harrying these men trashing his homeland and breaking down the bridges over the Anio River that the enemy would need to take to get away. When Hannibal's advanced troops warned him about this interruption he sent out scouts who, quickly finding a ford, guided the rest of the army splashing through the shallows. But Galba turned out more than just an irritant, he took the opportunity to pounce on their rearguard as it was trying to cross and join the main body, many men still waist deep in water. Only large numbers of Carthaginian-loyal Numidians charging up and throwing javelins helped guard the last men over, riding in swiftly to counter the threat and ensured losses were not great. Three hundred men and plenty of loot was left on the field to gladden the hearts of the Romans as they withdrew back to their camp, leaving the enemy to slip away without further molestation.

Still anticipating that the armies at Capua would have hotfooted it for Rome, Hannibal put his men on the road at dawn. The shuffling of weary feet, with horses and other pack animals carrying loot, supplies and any wounded picking their way along the track, was the order of the day. To try and get back to relieve a place they now expected to be being assailed by a much depleted army. But Galba wasn't finished, encouraged by his little victory, he followed on their way back south, keeping to the hills to avoid being easily attacked himself. The invaders marched much faster going out than on the way in, to give themselves as much time as possible to deal a blow against the much reduced enemy in Campania they expected to find and drive off from Capua. There is a suggestion that the invaders took a line of retreat that went deep into the hill country to the east of Rome and through the high mountains of Abruzzo, an itinerary which is very close to that by which Polybius has Hannibal approaching Rome. But while Livy may have had confidence in the route he describes, contending that his source 'Lucius Coelius Antipater' despite living almost a century later could have found locals with folk memories of the passing of 'so famous a leader and so large an army', the historian from Padua reveals that there was no consensus even in his time as to whether this road was taken by the invaders when they advanced on or withdrew from Rome.[6]

But after five days as Hannibal's army descended south towards the Campanian plain it was met by scouts cantering back through scrubland fields, and he learnt that waiting behind their camp defences and siege works were virtually all the enemies who had been there when he left. Forty thousand men at least, even discounting the sixteen thousand that had gone to defend Rome. Learning this truth and with the main plan a busted flush the Carthaginian general decided at least he could give the army following him a bloody nose. No longer so intent on quickly reaching Capua he turned and waited. Then in a night attack crept up on the pursuing force, killed a good number and drove the rest out of their encampment, forcing them to flee, dispersing to high country where they could find safety in this more defensible terrain.

Hannibal was no fantasist, he could face the fact that Capua was about to be lost. Knowing that to throw his men against the Roman fosse, towers and ramparted palisades around the town was to bleed it down in a way he just could not afford in the face of the huge military resources of his enemy. In this year the Roman alliance had mobilized something like a quarter of a million men in their land forces alone. But still if he could accept this setback he might hope to compensate elsewhere. So he listened attentively when news reached the camp about developments down in the very toe of peninsular Italy. And hoping to make the best of a bad job he thought if he could not relieve Capua he might be able, by marching hard far down south, to take Rhegium by surprise. Everything that could be carried from the Tifata camp was packed for moving, Hannibal would never return there, as the caravan set out, swaying elephants and lines of pack animals interspersed between columns of hard and dangerous men. The Carthaginian commander at the head of a column of men and animals snaking backwards out of view as he set out on the longest single march he and his army ever made in the peninsular years. It was mile after mile of country they had passed so often before, through Samnium over the mountainous spine of Italy into Apulia before they crossed Lucania, round the coastal instep and traversing the high country of Bruttium. If he had had to accept the loss of Campania, at least for the moment he wanted recompense elsewhere and intended to entrench his position in the far south by taking the one place of any significance there that still held out for the Republic. Rhegium was a place of great importance, controlling the narrow crossing to Sicily from which direction considerable danger could be anticipated now the Romans had suppressed most opposition on the island. The speed of the approach almost brought complete success; clearly no word of warning had reached the people, many of whom were made prisoner when caught in the country outside the city. Unfortunately for Hannibal the garrison commander was sufficiently on his mettle and though receiving a nasty shock from the appearance of enemy standards below his defences, was still able to close the gates and man the walls just in time. Unable to take the place by a *coup de main* the intruder showed no interest in opening a formal siege.

Back in the famine wracked city of Capua the people were deeply troubled when, realizing their erstwhile defender had left the vicinity, they found out that even the latest desperate message they had sent had failed to reach him. When the Numidian deserter, dispatched by the Carthaginian garrison commanders, now pretty much in charge, who undertook to take it was exposed in the Roman camp by a Campanian woman who had been his mistress, and was killed with seventy others of his comrades who had absconded on earlier occasions. Clearly the amount of desertion from the ranks on both sides was considerable in this war, what with the 1,200 Numidians mentioned earlier in Rome, and that fact that when Hannibal returned to Africa he took many hundreds if not thousands of Roman defectors with him, men who knew they had nothing to expect except death if they had stayed behind. A final offer of partial clemency was offered to the people in the Campanian capital by the enemies who had been besieging their city for so long, that they could come out before a specified date and 'should suffer no harm'. But there were no takers from a population who had little faith in the Romans' preparedness to show mercy, after the hurt they had occasioned over the five years since their secession.

So many of the leading lights who took Capua into the Carthaginian camp, with all hope snuffed out took poison after a drinking party to dull their senses, so they might avoid living to see the desecration of the city and the brutalization of their wives and children. The starving remnant who might have hoped for some clemency now took charge. So the magistrates who had to arrange the final capitulation were inexperienced men who in normal circumstances could not have expected to reach the heady heights of municipal power. These people with some of the old guard who had not been involved in, or hoped they would get away with any participation in the insurgency, made contact with the besiegers to arrange capitulation, offering unconditional surrender to the men outside. The Roman disposition was grimly efficient, Fulvius took a legion and a couple of squadrons of allied cavalry through the Jupiter Gate and occupied all the roads leaving town, and while the garrison with Hanno and Bostar were marched out as prisoners of war over fifty local senators were manacled and taken to Cales and Taenum, towns nearby, for safety. The commons were enslaved or dispersed while the buildings were kept to shelter newcomers who were brought in to till the fertile farmland or service the wants of those who did. The community became Roman property run by an official with no sort of independence or civic rights at all.

The disposal of the imprisoned Campanian senators caused some contention between the two victorious proconsuls. Appius wanted them sent to Rome for interrogation and sentencing so they could establish if other allies or supposed friends of Rome had been involved with them in their treachery. But Fulvius saw absolutely nothing but danger in shining a light into the behaviour of peoples who had remained loyal, for him that they had done so was enough. He was so determined the prisoners would be expeditiously disposed of that he went to the two towns where they had been housed and executed them on the spot. This highlights an interesting matter as to what extent contemplating and preparing for secession was not uncommon amongst many more of the allies and indeed if Fulvius, aware of such activity, was acting to cover it up in a most decisive way. There was little Appius could do in the end to take his old partner to task for his behaviour as he died of his wounds not long after Capua's fall. The great city's demise had other local ramifications as well. For the ancient Oscan town of Atella, halfway between Capua and Neapolis, it meant destruction, with its leaders put to death while the rest suffered slavery or exile with their property utilized to rehouse the citizens of Nuceria, whose own town had been destroyed in the days of Hannibal's dominance when they stayed loyal to Rome. And Calatia seven miles north-east on the Via Appia was another outpost town that surrendered after the Campanian capital fell, a place where a stunning castle still guards the mouth of the Caudine Valley, where too the leaders were executed and the place made secure for the Republic.

The end seems a little feeble with Hannibal, when recognizing that his ploy of marching on Rome had not succeeded, made no further attempts to help his doomed friends, instead leaving Campania completely undefended and turning his attention in the opposite direction. The reasoning here is difficult, he knew what a blow the loss of Capua would be, not just in itself but because of the effect on other communities who had already come over or were contemplating doing so. That he could not defend this crucial ally was bound to be telling. Whether there was any other possible effort he could have made to break the siege is not addressed at all by our histories. Could he not have done more at Rome, perhaps put a blockade in place, so the pressure would be greater for the proconsular armies to come in more numbers to the rescue? Certainly this would have had to be done in the face of enemy action but Flaccus and Appius had achieved it in Campania, though admittedly with a preponderance of men. Or if not that, could he not at least have manoeuvred to harass the remaining Romans surrounding Capua and made their life more difficult for the rest of the siege while awaiting a mistake that might allow him to pounce? What is certain is that he took none of these courses of action though the chronicler who came closest after the action saw no reason to criticize, feeling Hannibal had done all he could but had failed in this because of the stalwartness of his adversaries.

With the great Campanian city fallen, despite the famous flowers still blooming in the gardens of Capua, the people who had tended them were dead or scattered, exiled or enslaved. The question, was this to be a decisive event in this war that had drowned Italy in blood since Hannibal's debouching from the frozen Alps in 218? Whether or not, and great victory though it had been, it would not be the last trouble concocted by those connected with the place. They might no longer be able to fight on the battlefield but enough people remained with fond recollections of a free Campania that there were in the period soon after, incidents of mass arson carried out in Rome by a handful of the sons of the executed senators and more of the same threatened at the army camp of the occupiers outside Capua itself. But this was just police business, military resistance was over and the curtain came down on a front that had been the most fiercely contested in all the war. The rich Campanian country overtopped by the cone of Vesuvius, covered in pine and birch trees, would no longer see either the armies of Hannibal or his allies manoeuvring down its roads or across its fields. The soldiers of Rome had come back for good and Fulvius the man who had led them to triumph would stay for a few years to ensure that any bushfires of resistance were ruthlessly put out. The length and breadth of the region where Hannibal had tried to profit from the windfall of possibilities that had arisen from the adherence of Capua was going to feel the hard hand of rule from a people absolutely determined nothing like it should happen again. Even those with connections to Capua who had stayed absolutely loyal were not to be completely trusted, but were relocated far away, often in communities north of Rome itself.

Further along the Appian Way the story was not so different, no key stronghold had fallen where Hannibal's armies had tramped the roads of Samnium, down through hills covered in handsome mixed deciduous and evergreen woodlands to reach Mount Tifata or to combine with friends and allies from Caudine, Telesia and Saticula. But they would not be seen there again, as the Carthaginians, concentrating on defending in Apulia and Lucania, withdrew and their enemy prepared to replace them. The recovery of central Samnium would be a considerable task for Roman arms to complete but they would achieve it eventually and the suggestion is that even late in 211 both consuls had struck camp and were in Apulia already having pushed well down the road from Campania.[7] This beautiful if physically austere world of jagged outlines and high valleys standing at the knees of the higher peaks of the Apennines or its outliers rising in the sky all round, was a place of stony soil, unproductive compared with neighbouring Campania and the people needed to be inventive and hardy to scrape a living from their homeland. The Samnites had humbled their Roman enemies not that many years before and had not forgotten their days of power when their armies had dominated Capua and penetrated deep up the rivers Liris and Trerus into Latium itself. Some of their most long-lived survivors might even have just been born when the 'Linen Legion' marched out to fight its last gasp battles with the advancing Romans. Recent years would have mingled bittersweet in their cups, to have experienced autonomy again only to find that however much the desire to resist endured, without Hannibal's protection, submission would be inevitable. Not that it was quiescence all the way from now on, Samnite townsfolk, hill farmers and shepherds may have been tamed but there always remained an inclination to flood down into the fair country of Campania. And it is no surprise these same folk would still be prepared to fight an omnipotent Rome in over a hundred years' time in a social war that, though ending in defeat on the battlefield, won for its participants most of those civil rights the refusal of which had begun this, the first of a series of the most bloody civil wars in the history of the Republic and Italy.

Chapter 6

War in Apulia and Lucania

Thinking that before the time thought necessary for destroying Hannibal had elapsed, Italy would insensibly be worn out by him. He thought, too, that Fabius, by making safety his constant aim, was not taking the right course to heal the malady of the country, since the extinction of the war for which he waited would be coincident with the exhaustion of Rome, just as physicians who are timid and afraid to apply remedies, consider the consumption of the patient's powers to be the abatement of the disease.

Plutarch, *Marcellus*

L ooking down from the heights above ancient Numistro where the castle and town of Muro Lucano stand drowsing in summer sunshine above a tumbled, irregular and plunging drop it would be easy to imagine the soldiers of Rome and Carthage in the valley below deploying to fight. The man in 210 who led his legions into this confrontation with Hannibal was Marcellus once again preparing to trade punches with his old opponent from Nola. He was back from Sicily after taking Syracuse, though the pleasure of his triumph was not unalloyed, as important local islanders had followed in numbers on his heels, to lay complaints about the treatment they had received from him in the war. Allegations that Marcellus considered were orchestrated by a hated rival, Cethegus Marcus Cornelius, who had recently been dispatched as praetor to Sicily and would be consul in 204. These islanders claimed they had stood by Rome, but had still been ruined by the general who brought back so much booty from Syracuse that it is purported that this was the beginning of Rome's elite becoming enamoured of Greek art. These supplicants, though unable to get Marcellus prosecuted, did cause sufficient a furore that arrangements had to be adjusted after he was initially allotted Sicily as his consular province. The other new consul was prepared to go along with a responsibility swap. This was Laevinus who had also previously been posted to a front outside mainland Italy and done well enough in the war over the Adriatic. Tying up Philip of Macedon so he could do little to help the man he had allied himself with, after the great victories of the early years of the war. So now he was given Sicily as his province instead of Marcellus who was directed to south Italy, though whether this indicates the complaints from Syracuse and elsewhere were not without foundation, or just that key people saw advantage in this man who had faced Hannibal before without being crushed and should be allowed another crack at him, is not clear.

Not that Marcellus had been alone in facing these kinds of accusations, like almost any successful Roman leader Quintus Fulvius had also accrued plenty of domestic rivals prepared to use any stick to beat him with. He was taken to task by a number of Campanian bigwigs who could show decades of commitment to Rome and claimed they had never wavered in their loyalty, yet had suffered like everyone else at the hands of the commander who conquered Capua. This kind of contention was almost bound to arise as the elites in these towns with long connections with Rome were almost always deeply split and some certainly had risked family and possessions to stay loyal against the run of popular sentiment. In Syracuse in particular Marcellus had had to find his way around something like a civil war, with different sections of the city held by separate factions at different times, some fighting for and some against the Roman army encamped outside the walls. Capua had at least been a more straightforward instance of rebellion, which partly explains the brutal dispositions made once the place was taken. But still there had been staunchly loyal Campanians and these were now not slow to complain that they and theirs had lost as much at the victors' hands as those of their compatriots who had taken them into the Carthaginian camp. And with long-time contacts they were never short of friends and family connections in Rome who might take up their cause in the Senate or the courts. Though Appius Claudius at least was saved the necessity of having to defend his behaviour during the conquest because he died of his wounds straight after and indeed in his defence he could have pointed to his attempts to mollify the brutal behaviour of his colleague as far as he had the power to do so.

At the beginning of the last decade of the third century, as Marcellus and Laevinus prepared to take up their postings, the war was in balance. Triumph matched by defeat on both sides. The Carthaginians had prevailed over the Scipios in Spain, but against that Syracuse in Sicily had been won for Rome, while in Italy if Tarentum had long fallen to Hannibal, Capua had been lost to the Punic cause and in Greece Phillip of Macedon found that once the Aetolians had joined his Italian enemies, his resources were completely tied up holding his own in Greece, quite unable to effect the war over the Adriatic at all. Though this sort of equilibrium had only been achieved by eight years of huge expenditure and massive loss of life, the Roman leadership still showed no signs of contemplating any sort of resolution outside of total victory. They had even been prepared to chance dangerous resentment amongst the ordinary citizenry, increasing financial burdens across a citizen body already despoiled by repeated devaluations, to enable the funding of oarsmen and sailors complete with the rations required for the navy. The risk was apparently so real that only a leader was required for the spectre of real revolution to raise its head amongst the poorer sections and in the end to bring in the funds required those at the very top of the financial pile, the senators and knights, had to show the way by themselves stumping up their precious assets to get the ball rolling. Though these men in control made sure they were recompensed with interest in a few years' time, a facility not made available to the man in the street.

For the Carthaginians, on the debit side the loss of Capua had been the greatest body blow and Hannibal felt it, knowing as he did how it would be bound to affect sentiment in many other Italian communities. Places where he just did not have the men to provide the garrisons needed, both to ensure loyalty and protect the goods of people bound to be worried they might be next on a Roman hit list. It was no personality trait of the great Carthaginian no 'avarice and cruelty' as historians claim or any inclination 'to despoil where he could not protect'. It was a rational act that he wrecked many of those places he could not defend, to get goods for himself and deny them to the Roman armies. Just increasingly this was the nature of his predicament that only wanted more activity from his enemies to expose further. This was not long in coming.

If the destiny of Capua had ensured Campania had been the epicentre for some years, after its fall, the war migrated eastwards to northern Apulia; the scene of not only the Carthaginians' greatest triumph but where at Herdonia two years before they had eliminated another Roman army. Here was a flat country of open expansive plains, with a low lagoon–indented coastline, a favourite country of Hannibal who often wintered in its pleasant clime. Where good horse country allowed him to recruit and recoup an arm that he had shown he could use so effectively. On his first arrival in the country the inclination to cosset valuable horseflesh was well illustrated by the troopers using local wine they discovered in abundance to rub into their animals' skins to protect against mange. One of the most well utilized bases was at Salapia, near where Romans had first set up camp in the run-up to Cannae and a place where it is claimed that on one occasion Hannibal in winter quarters had enjoyed some rest and recreation with a local courtesan, one of the very few attempts to tar the great Carthaginian with the brush of ardent lechery, something the Romans were usually happy to attribute to Africans as a whole.[1]

Early in the campaigning season of 210 an extraordinary comic drama of chicanery and treason was played out at that city, where some trimmers had begun to think the future was no longer looking like a Carthaginian one. These people had taken longer than their like at Arpi to reach this conclusion and indeed far from all of the resident ruling elite were inclined to ditch the Punic connection. Events developed as was so often the case in a tangle of personal strife and bitter rivalry between local big shots. In this application of that general rule one of the antagonists was named Dasius who was thoroughly committed to Hannibal while his home-grown rival, Blattius, had begun to see the future very differently. The latter in pushing his cause managed to muster plenty of local support, even persuading some previously pro Carthaginian compatriots that the only way their community could avoid exemplary punishment was to take their city over to Rome of their own accord. But Dasius was having none of it and reported the matter to Hannibal who arrived, setting up his tribunal in town to adjudicate on the accusation.

Seeing the claims as motivated by private spite the Carthaginian general was inclined to dismiss them, but not before Dasius, with howls of indignation, exclaimed that Blattius had tried once again to suborn him there in front of Hannibal himself. But once more the accused successfully defended himself by claiming he would have had to have been mad to try such a thing in the very presence of the general, who put the whole matter down to bad blood between the two. This may have been the strategy, that Blattius, like water dripping on stone, would finally wear his rival down and that he would consent they should together make representations to the Romans to hand over their town. But the most detailed account has the whole business as a premeditated effort to discredit Dasius that led to a dangerous game of bluff and double bluff.[2] It is asserted that when Hannibal went on his way the man did indeed pretend to agree with Blattius' plan, but in fact only to trap him into betraying himself. Then with the two key community leaders apparently working together the coup was matured. Blattius agreed to contact a Roman army whose commander he knew well, while the other stayed at home to keep an eye on events. But when he had left town Dasius prepared to go and warn Hannibal, though taking his time because the Roman force specified was some way away and could not be expected to arrive for quite some time. But in fact Blattius had approached Marcellus who was encamped much nearer and after leaving his son as hostage, had started back with sufficient troops to deal with the Carthaginian garrison and take over the town. Quick to strike, the upshot was that when Dasius returned with Carthaginian military muscle thought adequate to scupper his rivals' plans the Romans were already in charge, having disposed of the 500 Numidian horse who had made up the garrison. These men had been out of their element in the city streets, without the room they needed to practise their normal skirmishing tactics, and all fell fighting except for fifty who were captured. The crowning glory for Blattius came when his rival returned and believing the Carthaginians to be still in control, entered through a gate left open for him, only to find that once inside he and his troops were brought to grief, ambushed and killed in the narrow streets just inside the walls.

After this Apulian success Marcellus cranked up his campaign. He might have reason to be peeved after his treatment back home, denied a triumph and traduced by men from a city it had taken him so much time and energy to suppress, but if he was he did not let it show. This year we learn was a twenty-one legion year, so not a few men including over 7,000 allies had been demobbed in the year after Capua fell. But this financial retrenchment in the military gave Marcellus no pause. Deciding no longer just to wait for places to fall to him like ripe fruit, he had his men step out on the road to Samnium where he captured Marmoreae and Meles, oppidum built up as supply dumps that would have been crucial for any enemy campaigning in the area. It is also asserted that abundant provisions were secured and booty distributed to the soldiers while 3,000 of Hannibal's garrison troops were killed as well. But when so happily occupied in forcing rebel territory back into the fold Marcellus received intelligence that threatened to overturn all his recent good work. The news spread that his colleague left in command in Apulia had come to grief in a particularly spectacular fashion. Hannibal had not taken the loss of Salapia well, intending retribution and if he could not rain it down on Marcellus there was another officer who looked ripe for the taking. He had learnt from friendly locals that an army under the proconsul Gnaeus Fulvius Centumalus was threatening Herdonia and might be vulnerable to a decisive strike.

This man had been clambering up the '*cursus honorum*' in the war years, recently an aedile, in 213 he was elected praetor and was in command when a number of Campanian cavaliers had visited him at the Suessula camp, wanting to protect their lives and property by making terms with the Romans before they began the attack on their home town. In the previous year he had reached the summit, the consulship, so it was this experienced commander probably well into his forties who had been reported near Herdonia, not more than a couple of easy days' march from Salapia. Where he clearly hoped to repeat what Marcellus had just achieved and bag another Apulian town. Expectations had been specifically raised when agents reported that the locals had become much more Roman inclined now that Hannibal was testified marching south on the Bruttium road. But not all the folk had lost faith and at the sight of the approaching Romans some of these sent to warn the Carthaginians, not only that the enemy were threatening, but also that the way they had disposed themselves in camp in the river meadows below the town meant they might be attacked with a good chance of success.

Hannibal on hearing this news, left his trains behind, and marched swiftly in light order. Once near Herdonia he confirmed his enemy had been tactically unwise, placing their camp near the river but neither well positioned nor well protected and perhaps not even warned of his arrival, hidden as the Carthaginians were behind the ridge the town sat on. So, confident in fighting a second battle where he had done great things only two years before, he led his men forward without even preparing a defended position for them. The Carthaginians were able to immediately deploy for battle yet despite this Fulvius, not even given pause for thought by what had happened to his namesake on the same battlefield, prepared to confront the surprise arrival. Like so many an overconfident opponent in the past, he took up the gage with little care and attention in approaching the trickiest tactical customer going. He had few excuses for underestimating his opponent's military genius but he certainly seems to have done so. The desire to face and overcome the foe in a stand-up fight was so much a part of the Roman DNA that however often they came to grief, overt belligerence was the only option they could imagine. And it may not be a complete coincidence that the older Fabius' faction had had a lesser stranglehold on the top jobs in the last few years, so his strategy of avoiding battle and wearing the enemy down may have gone a little out of fashion.

His plan was simple and with no great thought the Roman commander prepared to plunge into daunting battle. Without anything like a complete idea of the enemy's numbers or quality he just assumed his own 20,000 plus men would be sufficient. The 5th Legion and an allied ala donned their armour and deployed in the flat country around the River Carapelle, that flows gently passed Herdonia towards the salt marshes on the coast and out into the modern Gulf of Manfredonia. Behind them were positioned the 6th Legion, with their allied support and with what cavalry was available divided between the wings. The Carthaginians must have had a very considerable edge in numbers of horsemen, perhaps as many as 6,000 troopers against the enemy's 3,000, and Hannibal intended to use this. Fighting opened with both sides' light infantry skirmishing as the heavy foot arrayed themselves into their formations; these dressed their lines in perfect composure, advancing slowly to begin with. Then the first ranks by prearrangement pushed forward, with slingshot from withdrawing Balearic slingers rattling down on their shields they advanced at pace, the men roaring to reach the enemy line, both sides coming hand-to-hand after those with javelins had discharged them in a deadly hail. The ground was level with no advantage to either side to rule out a fair trial of strength and unlike in the previous contest on this same field the Roman army was an experienced one, which had been campaigning in Apulia for some time. This was neither an army of recently recruited tyros with little equipment and even less training nor one where discipline had collapsed with the ordinary soldiers themselves giving the orders.

When the Roman line became fully engaged, jabbing and feinting to try and gain advantage over the well protected veterans in front of them the contest for a time seemed balanced. Both sides to begin with kept their second lines back so they would not feel the same stress as the men in the ranks actually in contact and so were both physically and psychologically fresh, less likely to run and more able to contribute when called upon. With the front ranks failing the reserves were fed in, continuing to maintain both sides in the contest until something occurred that was another tribute to the battlefield acumen of the great Carthaginian general. He once more showed his skill in affecting a combat already underway. If much of the details are unknowable, one crucial movement is agreed; Hannibal gave orders to his cavalry, riding out, surrounded by his military family, to meet the officers in command of these Numidians, Moors, Iberians, Gauls and Italian locals waiting fresh and eager on both wings as they prepared to deploy into line and advance beyond the enemy wings.

Direction and extortion were bound to take some time to transmit but despite this the troopers were soon in motion, cantering forward against the cavalry Fulvius had put in place to guard his flanks. In dust and disorder these horsemen, led by officers dressed in gorgeous panoplies, assaulted the foes facing them. On both flanks the Roman horse and allies' squadrons would have trotted forward to receive the inevitable clash. Now it was pandemonium, caparisoned mounts flinching and jostling, those who stood thrusting with spears at half seen heads behind protective shields and horses bowling over the men and animals in front of them. Some of the less enthusiastic turning back into their comrades in desperation to get away while unhandy Roman cavaliers were unhorsed and found themselves slashed at from above by heavy *kopis*, single bladed curved swords wielded by Iberian knights, or stabbed with javelins in the hands of nimble Numidians who moved too swiftly to be hit back at. The Carthaginian cavalry was better, more numerous and massed on either wing, still the key was morale and leadership where they excelled. So it did not take an overly long or a heroic effort to overturn the enemy horse, as with the ground shaking under their hooves they cleared a path for victory.

Then the victorious horsemen divided, directing their attacks without hindrance. The encirclement had taken the Romans by surprise and now the main legionary line was pinned, the cavalry dead or dispersed. Some of the victorious squadrons pushed on through the meadows to find the enemy camp before pouring into this hardly defended bivouac, to fire the tents and disperse the occupants while the rest went slashing into the rear of their enemy's infantry lines. This was not luck, they had been kept well under control by their officers, who had been coached earnestly in the need not to waste time in pursuing the defeated cavalry, but to return to make the difference in the main contest in the centre, to ensure the end for an enemy Hannibal now felt he had in his grip. They hauled on their bits, or in the Numidians' case using a stick to guide and their rope harness to swing their horses around, before crashing first into the rear ranks of the 6th Legion, who were terror-struck by the enemy riding through their lines hurling deadly darts into the unprotected rear and flanks of the maniples. More than this, the terrifying uproar from the camp as the Carthaginians' horse cantering towards it entered the gates, did not help as the Romans realized that if defeated they now had no bolthole to return to. As their ranks were cut down, first it was the 6th Legion and the allied contingent with them who suffered, with their commanders hard-pressed to find men to counter the effect of the high horse attackers swirling round them. Finally the Romans, stricken and shattered, broke as even the Triarii with their long spears failed to stand against the chaos of churning troopers stabbing, hacking or throwing at their exposed limbs.

Then it was the turn of the soldiers of the 5th Legion and their auxiliaries in the vanguard. They would have been fighting for hours, the launching and completion of the assaults on the wings must have taken time. So they were weary, many wounded and already committed, with no possibility of men turning to face the menace from their rear. It was hopeless, in front the medley of foreign warriors was terrifying and the fact that so many of them were accoutred with Roman weaponry only emphasized how successful they had been in the past. This already almost intolerable pressure was now compounded when the rear ranks were overwhelmed by enemy cavaliers yelling petrifying paeans of victory in strange Gallic, African and Iberian dialects. The Romans were unable to stand against this, despite they were brave enough, with the clang of swords striking armoured enemies and shouts and screams heralding a slaughter that included eleven military tribunes dying where they stood, holding their ground while others tried for survival, fleeing if they could away from the flailing hooves and awful weapons of the pursuing horsemen. Fulvius too was unprepared to capitulate, he had fought all day, trying to rally what horse were still on the field, to face the enemy squadrons drumming down on them or the allied and Roman foot traumatized by the swarming enemy and streaming back in search of elusive safety. But in the end he also fell, caught by a javelin or hacked down by a Spanish blade, gilded armour dented and his commander's cloak soaked in blood while his high-toned mount mingled in flight, searching desperately for escape from the mayhem.

Both the attacks against the enemy rear and their camp were the result of a conscious decision by Hannibal. The tactic of fixing his enemy's infantry and circling behind to attack with his cavalry had been decisive, the Romans had no answer, despite the 6th Legion having been kept in reserve and might have been expected to be able to turn and make a front against the onrushing horsemen. That they didn't, suggests either incompetence in the Roman command or more likely that the pressure on the front line by the Carthaginian foot had already forced some commitment of these support elements. The whole might seem trite, stuff Hannibal had done so often before most notably at Cannae but to repeatedly orchestrate these kind of successful manoeuvres was just what made him a marvel, to find any other ancient commanders who attempted never mind achieved this kind of silky smooth choreography on such a regular basis is well-nigh impossible.

The Romans had taken on the challenge as they always did, holding beside their comrades as long as flesh and blood would stand an onslaught against front, rear and flank. But in the end the shock from all around deranged even these fighters, they scattered, routed and losses were large, estimates varying between 7,000 and 13,000 against very few for Hannibal's men. And certainly the sequence of actions and outcome casts doubt on any suggestion that the loss of 500 Numidians during the Roman capture of Salapia had badly weakened the Carthaginians' cavalry arm.[3] It was the handling of exactly these troops that had accomplished this latest triumph. That had brought about the second occasion when a Roman army was vanquished in blood near Herdonia, virtually annihilated in this region where Hannibal counted so many successes against his enemies.

The Roman commander had at least on this occasion died where he stood unlike the one before who had fled first from the battle and then into exile when his peers planned to take him to task. But still his conduct was open to criticism, it certainly seems he had allowed himself to be outflanked rather easily and it is a wonder he did not spread out his infantry to occupy more of the ground between the town and river, rather putting half his men, a legion and its allied auxiliaries directly behind the others. In fact the manner of Roman army deployment described by Livy in the later years of the war remains more generally problematic. In most of the combats described by our main source the norm is that, depending on numbers involved, at least one legion and presumably its accompanying allies was kept in reserve, sometimes specifically described as being behind the legion that occupied the front line. This is somewhat odd as the very deep formation in which the Romans deployed with ranks of Velites, then Hastati, Principes and finally Triarii was specifically designed so that each legion could reinforce itself and indeed incorporated in each formation its own reserve. So to line such a legion behind another one, each both deployed in the same fashion, seems not only superfluous but also inevitably meant the Roman battle line was bound to have little width. It would ensure that their depth could easily reach sixty ranks or more, meaning even accepting that a legionary occupied up to double the space of a phalangite and there might be spaces between the maniples, that two legions with an equivalent number of allies would cover far less of a frontage than an equivalent enemy lining up with skirmishers out front and perhaps two lines each eight ranks deep. Sacrificing width in this way seems counter-intuitive in an age when the flanks were always the vulnerable point.

Whichever the manner they had formed up in the Romans had almost been sitting ducks, torn to pieces with refugees from the broken army scattered to all four points of the compass. Some eventually found their way to Marcellus in Samnium, desperate remnants from Fulvius' cavalry would have been the first to reach this security, wild-eyed men who had dumped weapons and armour to lighten their load in an attempt to flee the scene of disaster. Later some few of the infantry, who perhaps had found hiding places in the dusty chaos produced by the shocking collision of over 40,000 men, straggled in. All came with accounts of the battle no doubt amplified by personal trauma, but in their wake a few more organized units, men more used to the professional mayhem handed out by Hannibal's old-timers, with some of the heavier military equipment, following little frequented trails through Samnium found their way back. And with them further information reached Marcellus that was considerably more encouraging. Hannibal despite victory in the field had made little attempt to exploit his success. There had been no all out pursuit of the few survivors as he again faced the problem of not having the resources to defend places like Herdonia, which if he left them alone he feared would soon fall to Rome again. He knew elements amongst the citizenry would push to desert the Carthaginian cause as soon as his army left the locality, so determined on a programme that was logical in the circumstances but fraught with dangers for the future. He ordered the people of this strategically located place that he did not have the resources to garrison, to gather their movable goods and leave their homes, escorting the deported community south to swell the populations at Thurii and Metapontum and then burnt the place itself to the ground to ensure his enemy would find very little of advantage when they returned to the stillness of Herdonia's charred and smoking remains. This was one of the first hints of where the future might lie for many who had taken the Carthaginians' side in the years after Cannae.

The consul Marcellus had not long been in camp, religious duties had kept him at the capital, before first scooping up Salapia then being faced by the need to respond to this latest disaster in the field. As he met with his senior officers in the command tent he seemed animated by the news. The retaking of a significant, but still regional backwater, like Salapia was small beer compared with the epic of Syracuse but still it would have reinvigorated a buoyant personality that years of gruelling warfare had not

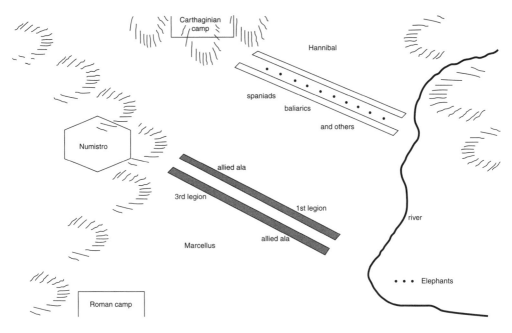

Battle of Numistro 210.

drained of its enthusiasm. And now with Hannibal himself on the radar he took even greater heart. His intention was to pick up where he left off at Nola and confront him on the battlefield. First he did the 'admin', reporting to the Senate of the elimination of another army, but also reassuring them, making much of his old reputation as a Hannibal fighter, that he would not be just another moth to the flame when he marched to find and challenge the victorious enemy. So directing their feet south into Hipirni his soldiers hiked a long road in high summer, the legionaries and allies climbing in and out of verdant basins, old calderas, with high knolls planted with communities of people never very friendly to Rome and openly hostile since the arrival of the Carthaginians. The distance covered through this unfriendly country was over sixty miles with the serrated outline of towering heights sometimes visible off in the distance. Soon though scouts began to find evidence that Hannibal's army was not far away. However unresponsive the locals along the way had been in terms of leaking information, there were always a few who for coin or advancement would tell a tale. And once sufficiently good intelligence was garnered that the enemy was to be found in very hilly country near Numistro in Lucania, Marcellus laid his plans. This place had either remained loyal to Rome or had come back into the fold some time before and now Hannibal was camped nearby putting the squeeze on one of the few pro Roman places in the region. A circumstance that ensured the threatened townsfolk heartily welcomed the newcomers as Marcellus' tired soldiers found some level ground and raised their tents, dug ditches and implanted palisades.

The army surveyors laid out the plan of the camp, a routine followed virtually every day, with flags and upright spears driven into the earth to ensure the tents of the commander were situated in the centre and those of the legionary commanders and tribunes nearby. With these correctly placed around them the accommodation for the infantry maniples and cavalry squadrons could be set out to a pattern the Roman army would follow for centuries. All to be fabricated by the men who erected their own sheepskin tents after first having built the fosse and wooden wall that would make them safe from any attempt at surprise by the enemy. A two legion camp with room for allies as well could be at over 800m² and this one may have been even larger with long stretches of wooden walls for the Velites, customarily allocated this duty, to guard. But if they had arrived now, it had been nervous searching on the road, with plenty of obvious places for an ambush along the route, but Marcellus had finally found his man. And so it is hardly surprising that, well aware of how tricky his enemy could be, he wanted to get a good view of the coming battlefield to get an idea of what they might intend and formulate his own battle plans. Having done so he refuted any disinclination to fight, determined to go ahead regardless of any qualms evidenced by his officers and men, some of whom had experienced defeat before at Hannibal's hands and must have been anxious about facing him again.

The Carthaginians were encamped on a steep conical hill to the north of the town commanding the valley below with a river cramping in the country to the east. Hannibal himself was far from hiding on top his eminence, when he realized his enemy was close, indeed he may, knowing well the character of Marcellus, have intended to draw him into battle in this advantageous situation. Calculating that even if the Roman was not looking to bring on a fight, he would probably be drawn by the need to defend one of the very few places they still controlled thereabouts. The Carthaginian had chosen his terrain well; the country below his camp was one of the rare localities in extremely rugged, hilly country where a stand-up battle could be fought. And with his own camp well placed for defence he could be confident that if things went wrong they would have a very secure bolthole nearby. While the enemy if they could be beaten would find themselves in inimical country, only able to find refuge in Numistro, where Hannibal might hope to pen them in and starve them out. But despite these dangers that old Marcellus must have recognized as well, he had not just come to contain. The Roman general immediately led his men out of their camp gates, to line up against this enemy he had previously tussled with so frequently and furiously in Campania.

With no idea but to get to grips the Romans offered battle, drawing up well within sight of the enemy camp, their left resting on the precipitate knoll where Numistro stood, while on the other side of the field their right was protected by a river, running down the valley. This bold and well ordered front must have given Hannibal some pause, but he had just come off the back of a brilliant victory and was anyway always confident in his own battlefield expertise. He might have had to give up some ground in Apulia and reality forced the acceptance that his resources did not allow him to retake and retain Campania or Samnium, but he was determined not to be squeezed further down the Italian Peninsula. He would draw a line north of Lucania. Numbers are as usual not easy, Marcellus had at least a two legion consular army of well over 20,000 and perhaps plenty more, if he had had time to reconstitute the remains of Fulvius' men. Getting on for 30,000 would not be an unreasonable guesstimate, a fair match if not more for the number the Carthaginians could field. Hannibal moved in the early light after dawn, as soon as he saw the legionary standards moving out of their camp gates, with an army that had been significantly reinforced since the last bloodletting near Herdonia. Not only had he probably recruited up his ranks to compensate for the numbers killed or wounded that day but our main source also reports that he had also been rejoined by his elephants.

The itinerary of the elephant corps in the Italian War is something of a mystery. We know that thirty-seven of the animals crossed the Rhone River but almost all of these were lost in traversing the Alps, in battle at the Trebbia and to winter weather, so that by the time Hannibal passed the Apennines the army was down to just one beast. Even this one, called 'the Syrian' who carried an ailing Hannibal through the Arno marshes, gets no mention at either Trasimene or Cannae so presumably had died sometime on the long march south. The presence of others of these animals is attested at Casilinum in 216 but if the report is true where they came from is not known, presumably shipped into a deep south port sometime in the summer of that year. Then Bomilcar had brought more in 215, bringing them from Africa to Bruttium but their involvement in the great Carthaginians' battles after that are patchy. In 215 in battle at Nola the claim is that Hannibal lost four elephants killed and two captured from the thirty-three that Bomilcar brought over with him. They were also present around Capua in some of the fighting there but are not mentioned on the march to Rome and equally seem to have taken no part in either of the battles at Herdonia. This is perhaps not so much of a surprise because elephants are not easy animals to keep in trim, they hate cold weather and need to get something like 100lb of hay a day to compensate for a very inefficient digestive system and a daily intake of upwards of 100gal. of drinking water is a requisite. It is probable for some of his campaigns it was considered preferable for them to be held out of the firing line, kept back and pampered for use when it really counted. Because despite poor eyesight and a steady pace of not much over five miles an hour that makes them considerably less versatile than horses, their devotees still felt they could be decisive in battle. That the terror they engendered in the enemy ranks, particularly in those of the cavalry where the horses could not tolerate their noise or smell, was sufficient to make up for the drawbacks. And these could be considerable as having no attachment except to their rider, or mahout, if spooked they could run amok trampling anybody who came in their way. Methods of combatting them had been explored by the Romans since they first came across these terrifying creatures fighting for Pyrrhus sixty and more years before. From ox-drawn wagons equipped with long spikes, to fire pots, flaming arrows and driving lighted pigs at them, all had been tried, but these threats could often be defended against by the light infantry guard each animal usually had to protect it. And anyway, in the end as often as not, it was the normal javelins and pila hurled by the regular troops that did the job of seeing these behemoths off.

Yet despite elephants being indelibly linked with Hannibal's name the extent of successful use of the beasts in battle by the tactical master is not impressive. Apart from the Trebbia they played no role in his great early triumphs and in the years this book is covering we know of no instance where they were decisive and a number where they showed that unfortunate tendency to do damage to their own side, routing back into their own ranks to the considerable detriment of the Carthaginian forces on at least one occasion. How exactly he deployed them in these years is mostly guesswork as the details we have are very patchy. We hear of them charging into ranks of enemy infantry and assaulting camp defences but never being used against cavalry for which the animals were particularly reputed. This may be because the Romans during this time never had a significant superiority in the mounted arm, indeed it was as often as not the other way round. Yet even at the Battle of Zama, a contest that so much has been written about, there are few satisfactory explanations of Hannibal's use of these animals. In that final battle in 202 when Scipio defeated Carthage's last army on the plains of North Africa, the Romans were seconded by a significant force of Numidian allies, so could count on both numbers and quality to give them edge in a cavalry fight. But Hannibal though aware of his disadvantage did not try to rectify it by arraying his smelly and noisy beasts against the enemy's wings. A cordon here might have kept the troopers of Masinissa and Laelius from coming back to finish the battle by smashing into the rear of Hannibal's infantry, just as Demetrius the son of Antigonus Monophthalmus, the One-Eyed, was stopped from returning to rescue his father at the Battle of Ipsus in 301. But he did not, instead sending them pell-mell against Scipio's infantry that had been trained to deal with them, by raining down javelins and corralling them along alleys created between the maniples that had lined up behind each other for just this eventuality.

This time when Hannibal deployed his men near Numistro to fight his doughty enemy he thought the risk of using these temperamental animals worth taking and brought his pachyderms along, drawing them up between the two deep ranks of infantry in his main battle line. He also took care to protect his flanks, resting his right wing extended up the hill occupied by his camp, facing the Romans' left which was anchored on Numistro hill. The legion on the right of Marcellus' double line was the first and with their allies they were the foremost to attack. The Roman lights sparred with the enemy Balearics, who let loose a hail of slingshot, before the legionaries encountered the veteran Spaniards comprising the vanguard of the Carthaginian army. The fighting was hard from about nine in the morning and to swing the encounter his way Hannibal deployed his elephants. Though we are given no details of their impact except that the animals must have deepened the tone of the argument and that the infantry fighting remained evenly contested. These Spaniards were the equal of the best swordsmen the Romans could field. The combat seems to have lasted all day 'early morning to nightfall' and to keep up his end Marcellus fed in the men from both the 3rd Legion and the other ala of the allies as the others became exhausted. This was matched by Hannibal, also introducing units from his second line with the battling men breaking their clinch to allow these replacements to manoeuvre into place.

A convincing case was made a few years ago that emphasizes the role of missile exchange on the Roman battlefield.[4] Very reasonably pointing out that an orthodoxy that has the Hastati and Principes discharging their pila before getting down to the real business of swordplay hardly fits the facts. On a number of occasions in various encounters leaders, troops or even elephants are specifically designated as having been killed or wounded by missiles well after the fight had begun and it might be expected the battle would have become all about sword or spearplay. Paenula, the fatally upgraded centurion, Paulus at Cannae, Gnaeus Scipio the uncle of 'Africanus' near Munda in Spain and in a few years in a battle in the Po Valley Mago, all were killed or wounded by missile weapons. And likewise on a number of occasions Roman troops are described driving elephants with missiles, all well after the fighting these troops were involved in had begun. And more than this is the practicality that men just could not fight for hours on end with swords or spears without giving way to exhaustion. Now some of this might be explained by the feeding in of support lines to give a break or the ranks falling apart to allow a hiatus for rest. But equally likely is that in fact many of these encounters were about exchanges of missiles without actually getting to sword or spear thrusts. That this did not apply just to the Velites and other light infantry, but that the heavy foot too spent much of the time throwing their pilum, then gathering up those thrown at them to return them back again. This was more easily believable in this period because the Marian reforms which rendered the pila useless after it had been thrown were 100 years in the future. All of which makes it probable that at this battle near Numistro was this kind of routine, largely exchanges of missiles only occasionally coming hand-to-hand, that could be conceived of as lasting a full summer's day.

The two armies must nevertheless, after a fight still sufficiently brutal and interminable with tempers fraying on all sides, have been worn out by the time darkness brought an end to the combat. The stench of urine and faeces alone must have been bad enough from thousands of men and animals relieving themselves over those long hours as they waited in serried ranks to join the fight. But neither had given way. The battle had been fought to a stalemate with both sides falling back to their camps so the men could recuperate. The wounded who were carried back were cared for, repairs made to dented armour and shields, swords sharpened and missiles collected, while camp servants cooked up the hot unleavened bread, that was eaten like pitta or pizza, with the other dietary staples, cheese and wine. This sustaining fare, which would have differed little whichever side a soldier was on, had its effect as Marcellus was able to get his soldiers up and into line of battle behind their standards for sunup the next day and keep them there until almost noon. The gage he threw down was not however picked up a second time, allowing the Romans to strip the enemy dead left on the battlefield and give the proper rites to their own fallen. Hannibal it turned out was not interested in another battle of attrition. He had clearly not been able to use his cavalry advantage on this occasion and in fact we hear nothing of the doings of horsemen on either side. The country certainly did not suit his hard-riding troopers, here was no wide Apulian plain but just a valley constrained in by high green hills and a river, if not a torrent, still significant enough to constrain movement.

With neither army routing and running casualties would not have been high. No figures are given, this despite our main source's propensity to offer huge piles of Carthaginian dead where it might be at all credible. Hannibal had always been a ruse and manoeuvre man and decided to escape without risking any further battle casualties from within his own ranks, to get once more underway, hoping that in a campaign of movement he could catch Marcellus at a disadvantage. So after the Romans returned again to their camp and with night fallen he got his men in marching order. It must have been time-consuming packing his baggage and preparing the elephants for the march but his officers were proficient veterans for the most part and leaving his cavalry to man the palisades, to make the camp look lived in, he soon got the main body hard down the road east to Apulia. These nimble horsemen could then join him later, having deceived the enemy for a sufficient time to allow plenty of distance to be put between himself and any pursuit.

But Marcellus was nothing if not persistent and after providing a small garrison and doing what he could for the wounded in Numistro, he pushed his army hard on Hannibal's heels. The Carthaginians headed north-east up the glens, a mile-long column of animals and men with elephants repeatedly stopping to stand and drink in shallow water, while the soldiers' cavalry mounts and pack animals, with mule drivers cursing filed by, splashing through runnels cut in the dramatically high and steep wooded sides of the valley where the heady perfume of plants was matched by the colours of flowers in bloom. Soon after reasonably easy marching they ascended to emerge where the terrain opened out and the road swept rolling round, on to folded wold country dotted with pockets of cultivated soil and with the silhouetted cone of Mount Vulture becoming increasingly clear on the skyline. On approaching the main north-south road it became apparent they had not thrown off the pursuing enemy. So again, not twenty-five miles from Numistro, the armies clashed again, skirmishing for days in the shadow of the nearby volcano, not far from the colony of Venusia. But these encounters as the Carthaginians cut across the magical hills of south Samnium never reached the intensity of a full-scale battle before they slipped away once more towards Apulia. While the Romans followed the road with difficulty, they always showed great care, looking out for traps or other trickery in an enemy they very far from underestimated. This jockeying, with Hannibal traversing Apulia at night looking for a place to waylay the enemy and Marcellus following in daylight, his scouts on the lookout for ambuscades, continued right to the end of the year. While the Roman commander remained sufficiently concerned about what Hannibal might do, he decided against leaving the front despite the pressing consular responsibilities calling him back to Rome.

This is not the only version though, there is another tradition concerning the outcome of the Battle of Numistro[5] where Frontinus, an imperial official of the first century AD, clearly reports the encounter as a victory for Hannibal effectively dishevelling his old opponent due to his intelligent choice of a good defensive battleground. But whatever the exact details what was becoming apparent to the communities of central Italy in all this was that Hannibal had been far too occupied by Marcellus in the second half of the campaigning season to interfere with Fulvius Flaccus as he made strides in entrenching the Roman position in Campania. This commander kept his troops on the alert, while organizing the leasing of the confiscated land and helping out partisans who had lost their all when Nuceria and Acerrae were destroyed by Hannibal. It was required as there were still locals around who wanted to hit back at the invaders and a plot to burn down the soldiers' camp, with the men in it, was discovered. And when informers broke the news to the authorities near 200 of those involved suffered the ultimate penalty. That much could be achieved if Hannibal himself could be kept tied up while not risking an all out battle was now the orthodox strategy for the authorities at Rome. This distracting of the main man while making progress against his allies and lieutenants is a little reminiscent of the strategy of the Sixth Coalition's armies against Napoleon in Germany in 1813; the Trachenberg Plan that finally ended in the absolute dissolution of the French emperor's cause in Germany at the Battle of Leipzig.

Despite the fighting season coming to a close Marcellus was unable to leave his army, confronted as he was by the main enemy army. It was becoming a learning curve for these proto imperialists from the Tiber town now wars were far from seasonal affairs any more when the inclement months had been spent back home in the comfort of Palatine Hill mansions, wheeling and dealing for political advantage and social cache. They had begun to get an inkling of this change with their wars against Illyrians and Ligurians in the 220s and 230s. There is even a suggestion that it was in the 320s in a war around the Greek city of Neapolis that the Romans first extended a consul's tenure of military command making him a proconsul for another campaign. But now what had been an aberration was becoming an institution. It was the same for the soldiers too, no longer going home to get the harvest in, they were all-year round warriors now, though some were not so happy about it, as stuck in camp the winter they saw no opportunity for plunder. These months were for refitting and training, perfecting manoeuvres that in a manipular army were considerably more complex than in one based on a solid phalanx. It was no longer a case of eight to ten or more men lining up behind each other and only having to learn how to move from column into line. Now three lines of troops, each one separated into maniples of 120 men, were required to form with those behind covering the gaps in the line in front. Within battle the first maniples filtered back through the gaps in the second when they were exhausted and those behind were required to come to grips with the enemy and the second doing the same while the serried ranks of the Triarii stood as the last reserve. This convoluted cavorting needed plenty of practice, as did the weapon skills these combination javelineers and swordsmen needed to acquire.

Also as service became more permanent so did their encampments with Venusia becoming a real home from home for the armies facing Hannibal at this stage of the war. This fine hilltop town, the birthplace of the poet Horace, perched on its escarpment where modern Venosa still inhabits a community that includes the remains of Roman walls, with an amphitheatre and where exhibits at the museum show that half a million years ago extinct varieties of elephant and rhinoceroses frolicked with specimens of homo erectus in the region. The inhabitants of this place, a colony since the 290s, would have got used to its role as home to camping legionaries at least since the Pyrrhus Wars, becoming blasé at the sight of semi-permanent encampments capable of housing at least two consular armies spreading out in the fields below their walls. So with Marcellus occupied up country recouping his strength the other consul Laevinus had to be withdrawn from his largely routine, garrison duties in Sicily to supervise the autumn elections. Not that he came alone; with him were plenty of soldiers from cushy and safe billets on the island, who would soon see serious action in Italy. Unfortunately he was swiftly forced to return to his old post because of the threat of a Carthaginian invasion and to fill the void Fulvius, the conqueror of Capua, was nominated as dictator. But the protests when he put himself forward as a candidate for the consulship are telling, showing the strains brought about by both trying to maintain normal political life and to find effective commanders to fight the war. Fulvius and the senior Fabius were the candidates proposed, the former for his fourth consulship and the latter for his fifth. Now there could be no denying the massive experience and military skills of these two, but still two tribunes of the plebs argued that it was unconstitutional that a man organizing an election should also stand. These tribunes were ten in number, usually young senators whose role was to protect the interest of the people, with the power to veto legislation and with their persons sacrosanct. Though technically not a magistrate, the role was one in which an ambitious man could make a name and garner a following. On this occasion however their protest failed, there had been precedents before, but what is clear is that with the consular seat being monopolized by admittedly the best generals meant for many the normal road to the highest honours was choked. Senior senators who might expect to be consul were being denied the chance and they resented it, whatever the reasons of state.

For the moment the dominance of the likes of Fabius, Fulvius and Marcellus remained, but this would soon be threatened particularly with the coming of young Scipio, the future 'Africanus'. Much of the support that young patrician would get came without doubt from men frustrated in their ambitions to sit in the Curial chairs cornered by rivals with ready-made military reputations. Like any political system the Roman one was fraught with tensions and subject to seismic change, even if these lovers of tradition and stability always tried to deny it and even if no one realized it at the time, still tremors were being felt, foreshadowing changes that would bring the Republic low in a century and a half's time. Already armies were changing from being comprised of men with half an eye on the harvest back home to something very different, many veterans would find no farms to return to when the war ended. And the men who led them were no longer just magistrates who had drawn the sword for a season, but were becoming much closer to sorts of professional politicians, soldiers and varieties of these would become very dangerous in centuries to come.

Chapter 7

A Fierce Season

The citadel is situated between the forum and the entrance of the harbour, it still preserves some slight relics of its ancient magnificence and gifts, but the chief of them were destroyed either by the Carthaginians when they took the city, or by the Romans when they took it by force and sacked it. Amongst other booty taken on this occasion was the brazen colossus of Hercules, the work of Lysippus, now in the Capitol, which was dedicated as an offering by Fabius Maximus, who took the city.

Strabo, describing *Tarentum*, Geography, Book 6.3.

U nsurprisingly Marcellus' command was extended for the following year. Apart from the practice of repeatedly voting in the same experienced commanders as consul, it was also almost becoming the norm that generals and armies were kept together when serious campaigning was intended. Knowing they could expect the enemy to attempt to regain the initiative in Apulia after the loss of Salapia the year before, in 209 Marcellus was deputed to find the Carthaginian army of Italy and keep it busy, while the consul Fabius 'the delayer' went south to Tarentum and his colleague Fulvius to Lucania. In spring, when forage was available in decent amounts, the general broke up his winter camp at Venusia intent on a circumspect approach towards an enemy who his intelligence agents had learnt was in the region of Canusium in Apulia. There Hannibal had been trying to bring the people over to his side.

This place upriver from the flatland by the sea and right by the Aufidus occupied well-wooded, rolling country where there were occasional real hills like the one upon which the town itself stood. It was one of the strongholds of the Dauni, another of not a few peoples living in Italy who claimed connection to the wolf. They were a hybrid of Illyrians from over the Adriatic and other intruders from Greece arriving in the late Bronze Age and mixing with already instituted locals, established in the area of Luceria, round modern Foggia, south to Canusium and even over towards

Asculum and Venusia. In Canusium a rich elite had been strongly influenced but not conquered by the Greeks who had arrived on the coast to the south and today it is possible to visit their impressive rock-cut tombs strongly reminiscent of those found in Hellenistic Macedon. This leadership who had themselves interred so sumptuously, a generation or so after the last ones were dug came to accommodation with Rome, an arrangement not based on conquest that allowed these Dauni to see their new circumstances as much more partnership than subjection. A relationship that had sufficient sinew that after Cannae the people there gave refuge to many of the survivors of the battle. Now Hannibal was hoping to take possession of this community of considerable strategic importance, particularly as he had firm tidings that Hasdrubal had left Spain and the road through Apulia was likely to be crucial if he was to have chance of linking up with his brother when he arrived in Italy.

On being alerted by his scouts of the arrival of his old protagonist Hannibal decided immediate battle was not the most congenial strategy. He might be at a place only a few miles upstream from where he achieved his greatest triumph, but he knew Marcellus well enough to appreciate that he could not expect him to walk into a trap like Paulus and Varro had seven years before. One consolation of the standing he had with his men, won by years of victory, was that he could ask almost anything of them with complete confidence, that they would cast their vote to follow with hardly a dent in their morale. So when he put the army on the road manoeuvring west of Canusium they knew he was not afraid to fight, only looking for the best possible ground. He searched for it in the dense forested country nearby the town, with Marcellus continuing on from the year before, following, but carefully, with scouts ahead looking for any sign of an ambush. Every day he took up the pursuit and every day, after constructing a marching camp, he ordered out his legions, standards showing, to offer battle. But each time Hannibal refused the overture, he would not come out from his own defended positions, only prepared to skirmish with small numbers of light infantry and horse. It is likely to get away from his stalking nemesis that he even crossed the river below the town that is spanned to this day by a fine Roman bridge, though half hidden from the modern road by bushes and trees, to try and find a position of advantage.

It was beginning to look like another follow-my-leader campaign like the year before as the Carthaginians moved in the direction of Asculum, where in 279 Pyrrhus had led a south Italian alliance to victory against a Roman army.

An encounter that apparently had the king making the famous comment 'One more such victory, and we are undone.'[1] This game of cat and mouse continued with the Roman commander's impatience growing palpable until they managed to catch the Carthaginians on the move. It was near the end of the day, Hannibal had marched all night and more to throw off pursuit, but Marcellus had followed suit and as the light was fading, the Roman Velites pushing forward at pace came on the enemy in travelling column occupying open, level country. Some of Hannibal's men were already preparing to build their marching camp when they found the enemy so proximate it became difficult to carry on the work of construction. Brought to bay and forced to defend themselves, they were obliged to get into battle order, regiments shaking themselves into line, with horns sounding and officers bellowing commands in the twilight. Showers of javelins came in from both sides and the Balearics unwound their slings and shot at what enemies they could see in the shadows. The heavy infantry on both sides, despite the lateness of the hour and tired from a day's marching, took up the challenge, legionary Hastati and their allied equivalents pressing forward into the ranks of Spanish, African and Italian combatants on the Carthaginian side. They fought with ferocity until it became almost impossible to distinguish the shape of the enemy soldiers in front of them. In fact the light soon became so bad that no more real stand-up fighting was possible. Both sides pulled back, giving ground to put a good space between each other. But being still so proximate neither side could risk a full-scale retreat without the possibility of their enemy falling on their rear as they were moving off. So there was little real option but for both to throw up what kind of defensive works they could, while keeping most of their men under arms and facing each other.

The ditches were shallow and the palisaded defences meagre on both sides but at least they gave a semblance of protection as men tried to get some rest in the few hours before they knew they would have to risk a mortal gamble in battle the next morning. As the new day dawned over the two armies, camped almost cheek by jowl, Marcellus left his commanders in no doubt that he expected all his men to be armed and ready to challenge the enemy, to continue the battle from the night before. Whether he expected to see Hannibal again try to slip away we do not know, but this time his wish to fight the man was not to be disappointed. Even for the tricky Carthaginian, to extract his host right from under his enemy's nose without insupportable loss was not going to be possible. So despite his not being able to choose advantageous ground Hannibal accepted the inevitable, and with little time elapsed he emerged from his camp and deployed his veterans with standards showing. Elephants lined up trumpeting, to support the first line of infantry and with his horsemen caracoling on the wings of the array.

Numbers are unknown but probably they almost equalled the Roman two legion consular army of about 25,000, though his cavalry may have been somewhat reduced from the beginning of the year before having lost 500 Numidians when Salapia fell and also others in the many months of hard marching and fighting since then. Denied the chance to manoeuvre if he had to slog it out with Marcellus' legionaries Hannibal hoped that his elephants might give him the edge, that with the terrifying beasts trampling them down, the vaunted battle courage of his enemy might falter. Apart from preparing to use this hopeful trump card he also addressed the men near enough to hear him, an exhortation that reminded them of the great victories they had won over these Romans, from the Trebbia, to Trasimene and Cannae not to mention more recent triumphs in Lucania and Apulia. What is interesting here is that his mentioning of the early battles confirms that at least some of his warriors must still have been those veterans who he had brought across the Alps, still in the ranks despite the years of fighting in Italy or it would have made no sense to mention those battles. On top he geed them up to deal with the specific problem posed by the army facing them, who had been harassing them at every turn, hardly even allowing them to build their marching camps in peace. They were susceptible to this and making it personal apparently had its effect: 'they advanced eagerly to the attack.'

Whatever the specifics, the make-up of his army had certainly changed in the decade Hannibal had been in Italy. We know in the year before he still had enough veteran Spaniards to lead his line and certainly he still had many of his dependable Numidians. But we do not actually hear much of other Africans and not since taking Tarentum in 213 are units of Gauls specifically mentioned. It seems improbable that many of these terrifying swordsmen, with their fearsome war cries and eerie carnyx horns sounding high above the head of the user, were still present. Of the 15,000 plus at Cannae, apart from the 4,000 casualties suffered many would surely have taken the opportunity to go home loaded with booty, after the battle there being little in the way of Roman field armies to stop them. Of those who had remained there would have been an inevitable erosion of their numbers with little chance to recruit fresh drafts, who would have had to make their way across the length of Italy and that after crossing over a northern frontier now well-defended by both garrisons and mobile armies. As has been suggested before, it is certain Iberian and Africans, foots soldiers and horsemen must have been shipped in but in limited numbers. Casualties, disease, desertion and accident all would have taken their toll creating large gaps in the ranks that would have been filled with Italian recruits. Campanians, Samnites, Lucanians and Apulians all were enrolled during the years after Cannae, the inheritors of military traditions going back centuries and distinguished by the broad bronze belts they wore. We hear already in 214 of Samnite and Hipirni elders who are claiming to be defenceless because all their young men had gone to join the Carthaginian army. By 209 Hannibal's army was surely already a majority Italian force, one that had fought hard showing their fighting skills had improved on every chance they had to show them, but also who would already have suffered plenty of erosion of its own. And soon with Carthaginian control squeezed down the Peninsula more and more of the new soldiers required to fill out their regiments would have been found amongst the warrior peoples of Bruttium.

The information is that the Romans facing this enemy had drawn up with one of the legions on the left and the allied ala on the right flank, men who like the Romans fought in three line maniple formation, the second and third lines being available when the first men into the fight had to be replaced. With them were the 'Extraordinarii' who included something over 2,000 of the best of the allied horse and foot brigaded together, men often used for tasks like reconnaissance, picketing and rearguard duty but now expected to fight in the front line. They took up the challenge of the advancing enemy as expected and two hours of hard fighting commenced, with missiles thrown in volleys and lines of swordsmen pushing forward to stab and jab, before taking breaks to get their breath back. But after this time, when the front lines had become tired in this bloody affray the signs were that the Carthaginians were gaining the upper hand. The Roman and allied front was showing symptoms of coming adrift, with shield and sword arms weary, the ranks were fracturing and men dropping out, not just to regain their breath but looking for a way out, with their centurions' exhortations and the whacks from the flat of their swords or swagger sticks having no effect. Fighting was fierce, the butchery considerable and soon Hannibal's veterans in the front ranks were looking to exploit the opportunity of enemy frailty and the gaps this left. His hand was forced and in this moment Marcellus decided to put in his reserve. Ordering the 18th Legion up and into the front line as the allies fell back through the gaps between the legionary maniples coming on at a trot. But this turned out no parade ground manoeuvre at all, the allies broke in route streaming back across the field as the second line tried to move up to replace them. And this was not the end, the panicked men in the front transmitted their fear to the new arrivals and in the resulting chaos Hannibal determined to hit them before they could reform. So in no time the whole of the Roman formation was broken with the enemy driving them before them. Fleeing from the field most reached the safety of their camp but not before 2,700 men had died, including four centurions and two tribunes with four standards captured from the allies and two more from the 18th Legion.

There is no mention by the historians of either the elephants or the horsemen on either side in this day's combat. It seems to have been a victory of hard fighting by tough men, some of whom had walked from Spain nine years before and tramped the whole of Italy since, sufficiently inspired by hatred of the enemy and devotion to their commander. Three-day battles were not the norm in the ancient world, they were in fact extremely unusual. The intensity of personal mauling involved in a pre gunpowder age combat meant that more than a single day's fighting under a burning sun would generally be enough for anybody, however bloodthirsty. But still in two days if the Carthaginians had not destroyed Marcellus' army they had certainly wounded it. Prisoners would have been questioned and the participatory details they gave of how the Romans' morale had given way would have been sweet balm to the Carthaginians' ears. Now there was no question of slipping away. Hannibal and his officers gathering in the evening light occupied themselves with preparing for the next day's attack, before they dispersed to find what few hours' rest they could.

When the dawn broke in rosy light on the following day it was clear Marcellus also had no idea of quitting while behind, he intended to fight again. In the aftermath of the defeat the day before he had been withering in his criticism of his men's behaviour. It was far from flattering, they were chicken-hearted changelings, totally unlike the soldiers who he had led to victory before, despite their faces and equipment showing they were the same men. To punch the point home, those who had left their standards in enemy hands were only given barley to eat and their centurions forced to leave the assembly without their belts and carrying their swords. After this, contrite, they begged to be allowed to redeem themselves and he agreed that they would have the opportunity when he led them into battle again the next day. Though Marcellus' biographer was not quite so sure where the blame lay for the disorderly collapse, seeing the general's own order for the reserve to move forward as the root of their failure on the second day: 'After this they joined battle and fought. And it would seem that Marcellus made an unseasonable movement during the action, and so met with disaster. For when his right wing was hard pressed, he ordered one of his legions to move up to the front. This change of position threw his army into confusion and gave the victory to the enemy, who slew twenty-seven hundred of the Romans.'[2]

In the morning the encampment of these chastened men was a hive of activity, with a scarlet tunic displayed to announce impending battle. The men who had routed the day before were ordered under arms, marched out accompanied by the brassy sounds of the cornu and the tuba, the former a roaring and the latter a howling accompaniment to these men who were posted first, offered a chance to make up for their earlier disgrace. This eager return of his enemy clashing spears against their shields to announce their coming to the half fought confusion of another encounter must have been something of a surprise to Hannibal, though previous experience of Marcellus' tenacity should have suggested this outcome. Nevertheless he remained confident after the previous day's victory and calling on Hercules-Melquart, to remind his Italian friends of his divinely inspired mission to degrade the Roman tyrant, he ordered the men of his army, after a swiftly taken breakfast, to put on their war gear and arrange themselves behind their standards. It promised to be deadly, the encounter about to be staged as the left of the Roman line made up of those who had fled the previous day moved into position, while the 18th Legion was on the right side with the others and their allied support in a second reserve line. Unusually we know the names of the generals who commanded these wings: one called Lentulus on the left and Nero, who would become a hero in two years' time, on the right, either side of their chief, surrounded by his lictors, horse guards and his informal staff of young bluebloods ticking off the necessary years of military service, who remained in the centre of the battle line. The Carthaginians put their best foot forward with what are claimed as the elite troops, there was balance and experience here with the Spaniards prominent at the front. It was these men who first took the fight to the Hastati, the first Romans to reach them after the Velites had flung their javelins and withdrawn through the gaps between the maniples. The combat under broiling sunlight pouring down swung one way then the other, as groups were pushed back before their officers rallied them to try and hold again. When the Hastati were exhausted the Principes came forward in their glistening mail shirts just visible behind their 4ft shields, bolstering the front and holding back the onrushing enemy African spearmen, Spanish swordsmen and south Italian heavies all reciprocating the enemy fury and the latter extra eager to do well on home turf. But wanting a definitive decision, he knew he could not ask much more of his men after three days' hard fighting, Hannibal determined to use his elephants to make the difference.

Preparations had been painstaking in getting the temperamental animals deployed for action and the intention as usual with these beasts was to cause 'panic and confusion'. There might not have been many of them but their very presence, the sight, smell and sound of them did have an effect, with Roman units thrown into turmoil and not a few men, who could not get out of the way, trampled to death. The opposition had no surprise weapons to combat the elephants, no flaming pigs or firepots and many of Marcellus' men could not take the shock of contact and fled. In one section of the line they penetrated deep and a gap opened up. Even an army based on the flexible maniple would not have been able to cope with these living packets of mayhem churning amongst them for long. Some of the officers looking on must have feared the worst, an even greater reverse than the day before, but as it turned out the situation was by no means hopeless. The hour brought forth the man and disaster was averted by the actions of a military tribune. This Gaius Decimius Flavius was at the head of the first maniple of the Hastati and rallying these soldiers, led them forward towards the elephants giving orders to let fly with their pilums.

> Flavius by name, snatched up a standard, confronted the elephants, smote the leader with the iron spike of the standard, and made him wheel about.[3]

A scenario that suggests the beasts must have been bunched very close together, offering an unmissable target, despite that they usually moved separately each with a guard of light infantry to defend exactly against this kind of attack.

Now there is the classic description of elephants being spooked; there were screams of men and animals, then trumpeting in distress, they turned on their own men. The animals careening back, heads swinging and tusks cutting the air, all had an awful effect with the Spaniards in the front and then the others behind them unbalanced and disorganized, only interested in escaping the great feet of the out of control brutes. When the Romans and allies saw what had occurred in this sphere of action their officers led them forward into the breaks in the enemy lines, at a rush to get amongst them before they could recover their composure. They apparently encountered little resistance from an enemy who were falling back with hardly a fight. Marcellus saw his opportunity and ordered the cavalry to take up the pursuit of a mob of men and animals no longer in formation and only intent on finding safety. The refuge they were looking for was not easily achieved, as by the time the fugitives reached the gate of their camp they found the bodies of two elephants blocking the way; animals who had expired from wounds after escaping from the missiles of the Roman Hastati. With this route blocked most of the panicked soldiers had to jump down into the ditch and climb over the palisades before they were safe. And it was during this crush that most of the casualties were sustained; 8,000 men and five elephants were apparently lost on the Carthaginian side while there were 1,700 legionaries and 1,300 allied casualties, and that not counting an even greater proportion of wounded. Despite how worn by fighting the participants must have been, this third day is claimed as a far more ferocious affair than the one before. Indeed Marcellus reported that he was unable to follow on Hannibal's tracks, when he marched away, because so many of his soldiers were unfit for combat. So wisely he did not attempt to pursuit, all that could be done was to send cavalry scouts to trail the enemy, who was soon discovered in marching column on the road south moving in the direction of Bruttium.

In fact there are large question marks over this whole series of events. Apart from the fact that rumour probably inflated the numbers of dead, the narrative fits too neatly in a pattern of reporting that frequently has any defeat suffered by a Roman army almost immediately compensated for by a subsequent victory. And beyond this the evidence suggests that the battle, whether a one-day, two-day or three-day affair, and the details of the third day do suggest veracity, ended as a Carthaginian victory. Not a victory of annihilation but still one that meant Marcellus' army garnered such a grisly harvest of casualties that it was '*hors de combat*' for the rest of the fighting season, while Hannibal was able to continue in effective action, for the rest of the year. It is telling in terms of what really happened at Canusium that while Marcellus was rendered camp-bound Hannibal remained at large and even seemed quite capable of not only marching his army into Bruttium, but also of raising the siege of Caulonia and capturing not a few of an 8,000-man army sent out from Rhegium that had attacked the place. As a much later

Greek biographer of both his own compatriots and of Roman heroes put it succinctly:

> But as Hannibal, having disentangled himself from Marcellus, ranged with his army round about the country, and wasted Italy free from all fear.[4]

All of which is confirmed as authentic not much later by the essential Roman source, who specifies it as Marcellus who had been defeated twice and was not only harried by detractors but dragged before the people's assembly by a tribune of the plebs for his failure in Apulia. The intention was to deprive him of his command, but the prosecution cast their net wide, claiming the whole of the nobility were prolonging the war through incompetence and mendacity. The complaints were dramatically refuted in front of a huge crowd at the Circus Flaminius where Marcellus made such a successful defence that he got elected consul for the following year. Yet even he never maintained that the army he had left wintering at Venusia had not suffered defeat at the hands of Hannibal.

But if tactically Marcellus had fallen down, in terms of the larger strategy a claim could be made for complete success. Fabius had written to Marcellus at the outset of the campaign outlining that he should utilize his army to engage the main enemy so others could make encroachments elsewhere:

> He then made an agreement with Fabius Maximus that, while Fabius should make an attempt upon Tarentum, he himself, by diverting Hannibal and engaging with him, should prevent him from coming to the relief of that place.[5]

What he had achieved at Canusium had given his colleagues time to work in and what they realized was considerable. Quintus Fulvius, the other consul for the fourth time, for his part had made great strides amongst the Hirpini. These people had been firmly hostile when Marcellus had crossed their country getting to Numistro the year before, but now with the Carthaginians unable to protect them and with grim-visaged Roman legionaries coming their way, inevitably there were changes of heart. It was the same in parts of Lucania, particularly in Volceii, a region just south of Numistro not far from Campania and Samnium, whose people also surrendered after imprisoning the garrisons' troops left by Hannibal, giving them up in the hope of ameliorating any punishment coming their way. They ended getting away with only harsh words, which looked like it might be good policy for the Romans, as Fulvius soon found some Bruttium grandees at his camp door hoping to swap back to his side on the same conditions as the Volceii.

But if this was heartening the greatest achievement of the year was realized by old Fabius in this, his fifth and final consulship, and the last great campaign of his long life. The question for the 'delayer' was how to utilize the strategic space he expected the proconsul to win for him. From the beginning it was clear that the target was Tarentum, the greatest city in Magna Graecia and second only to Capua in size, wealth and potential of those mainland Italian places that had sided with the Carthaginians. Tarentum also had had one great advantage over Capua from the start; it was a port that allowed communications with Macedonia, Sicily and Africa. And since 211 it had another that it was still, apart from the citadel, under Carthaginian control, while the other was a desert, eliminated as a community and squatted on by tradesmen and farmers from elsewhere who had won this right by their steady adherence to the Roman cause.

It had been far from quiet there since the city fell to Hannibal by coup in 213. Action centred around the citadel which had remained in Roman hands despite the Carthaginians and their Tarentine friends being firmly in control of the rest of the town. Though cut off in their island fortress, where today a district of most wonderfully decrepit eighteenth century palaces stand between the port and a slight corniche on the seaward side, the commandant Livius and his men had been reinforced sufficiently to hold the walls. But the concern remained; how could they be supplied? This was no minor matter, Tarentum was a key position and the Romans were prepared to pull out all the stops to retain their foothold there. In 210 commitment, if not competence, was shown when one of the few significant sea battles of the war took place as an attempt was made to bring succour to the garrison. A fleet of twenty ships provided partly by Marcellus and partly by the allied towns of Velia, Paestum and Rhegium was collected at the latter place. One Decimus Quinctius, another of those rare soldiers of 'obscure birth' who had been allowed to advance due to the demands of a long war, took command. He had at least two triremes and three quinqueremes apart from fifteen other smaller warships. These he filled with corn and other supplies brought from Sicily and set sail. They reached Sapriportis, an unknown place fifteen miles west along the coast from Tarentum without mishap, but then things went wrong. There they ran into a squadron of twenty Tarentine ships under a commander called Democrates; whether he knew the Romans were coming is not clear, he might just have been guarding the predictable route. But the presence of so many of the city's celebrated leaders in the fight certainly might suggest they knew the enemy was coming and that battle was in the wind.

The crews had been kept in readiness on the Tarentine ships and the officers were eager to attack at once, while Quinctius had hoped he would not have to fight his way through, despite filling out his crews on route near Croton and Thurii with men prepared to risk the ire of the pro Carthaginian authorities to garner good Roman wages. His vessels were moving under sail when they saw the enemy to their front, but a delay was caused by contrary winds, allowing time for the Romans to stow their sailing gear and get ready for combat. When the ships finally made contact the fighting was ferocious, both sides knowing how crucial was the need of the men holding on at Tarentum. The cutting edge of Quinctius' force were three quinqueremes and two triremes, the rest presumably being biremes or perhaps just transports. There was little manoeuvring despite the Tarentines having a proud naval tradition and it might have been expected that her more adept sailors would want to take advantage of more lubberly opponents. But there was no attempt to break through the line or come in on the flanks, it was just 'beak to beak' when the warships collided, as each one grappled its opponent and the soldiers on board fought hand-to-hand. Even when the pilots and oarsmen tried to disengage by 'swinging the sterns this way and that' it turned out impossible, indeed they were packed so closely together that marines were able to cross from one vessel to another with little difficulty, almost as if they were fighting on land.

The most noted contest was a vicious affair between the two lead warships. The Roman was commanded by Quinctius while Nico, one of the men who had let Hannibal into the city in 213, captained the Tarentine. As the men swayed and sweated in confused melee after armoured Romans had clambered on to their enemy's decks the two leaders came to blows. Like antique heroes they fought hand-to-hand on the planking of Nico's vessel until he speared his opponent at a moment when Quinctius had dropped his guard. Then the victor leading his men pushed back the dismayed enemy and boarded their ship, taking control all the way to the afterdeck. There the defenders made a stand, but not for long as a Tarentine trireme, who had broken from the pack, drove for the stern and grappled it 'hemming her completely in'. It was the finish, with the flagship lost, the rest of the fleet gave up the fight looking only to make their escape, many were sunk or ran aground, these unfortunates finding themselves at the mercy of wreakers from Thurii and Metapontum. Though there was some small consolation that the transport ships with the supplies on board seem to have made use of a rising breeze to make their escape out to sea.

Nor was this getaway the only consolation for the Romans in this part of the world. When 4,000 Tarentine raiders left the city to forage in the country around, Livius, wide awake, sent 2,500 of his best men out from the citadel who pounced on the disorganized enemy, chivvied them through the farms and fields, killing many before the remainder got back to safety through the city gates. This same year also saw activity that must have been a real balm after the defeat at sea, when 1,000 soldiers, half Roman and half allied, got through to join the garrison, bringing with them a large quantity of corn that had been purchased at markets in Etruria. Equally they were not forgotten at the beginning of 209 either, when gold reserves were released and distributed to the consular armies, to source cloths and reimburse the armies in Spain, some was set aside to pay up the garrison defending the citadel of Tarentum.

But with Fabius senior consul again in 209, the effort would not just be to sustain the men in the citadel; ambitions were now raised considerably higher for the troops swinging along the long open roads of Sallentini, in Italy's heel, with an old man at their head. Even if he was in his seventies their commander was still spritely and any concerns amongst the troops about his durability were trumped by the feeling that behind this man they were at least likely to survive the campaign and perhaps with wreaths of triumph on their brows. The army had been in the area a while and we know they had just had success at Manduria. That important place just over twenty miles down the road south from Tarentum had been taken by storm and inside 4,000 or so prisoners and plenty of equipment had been scooped up. This feat must have come at some cost considering the extensive and impressive defensive walls that can still be seen by visitors today, and on this occasion desperation would have given the defenders strength. Manduria would be a handy base for the main task in hand; it had after all been a major place in its time, a local challenger to Tarentum in centuries gone by. This limestone flatland dividing the Adriatic from the Ionian Sea had in recent times always been something of a borderland, certainly after Cannae and then with Tarentum falling many towns took advantage to throw off Roman tutelage. Yet at the same time, because of the Macedonian War, Brundisium had remained home to considerable Roman fleets and armies whose presence would have kept other places on the straight and narrow. By 214 Brundisium had become base to Laevinus with at least fifty-five warships and a legion, but now that man had returned to Rome, to take up his consulships and responsibility for the island of Sicily, to be replaced in 210 by the proconsul Galba who had defended Rome against Hannibal the previous year.

Fabius and his men were intent on conquest as they stepped out of the flat, summer-brown fields of Sallentini. The aim now though was to take Tarentum itself and the old consul led his men north all around the lagoon and city walls, where the Carthaginian garrison and local defenders could see the extent of the new-found threat, to camp his men close by the entrance to the harbour, from where he could send agents across in rowboats to communicate with Livius and the garrison still holding out in the citadel. Fabius also liaised, with the commander of the ships left behind, to keep supply lines open to the fortress island, but more than this the vessels were re-equipped, not being needed to fight at sea, because the Carthaginian fleet had departed for Corfu to join the Macedonian War. Missile throwers and assault gear was loaded aboard, with ladders and other artillery packed onto some merchants' vessels, to allow an attack to be made all along the extent of the sea walls. The consul was not interested in a bruising siege, a time-consuming enterprise that might allow Hannibal, way down in the Italian toe at Caulonia, to get over to raise it. He intended to take the place by storm. But as it turned out he did not in the end need to gamble on an all out assault.

He got lucky. A garrison had been left by Hannibal to defend the city and part of it was made up of Bruttians, who as recruiting grounds in Campania and Samnium became less available provided a large proportion of his army's soldiers. Now it was reported to the consul that a captain in their ranks had fallen for the sister of a local Tarentine fighting in his investing army. The brother, with the full cooperation of the Roman high command, arranged to get into the city posing as a deserter. Once welcomed back as a lost sheep returning to the patriotic fold, he laid his plans. Through his sister, this convincing man made contact with the officer, playing the convivial putative brother-in-law for all he was worth. Once he had gained the man's confidence it did not seem to take a great deal to persuade him that his future, that of his lover and his men could only be defeat and death if he stayed to defend a doomed city. The arguments were cogent and it was not even the Bruttians' own people he was risking his life for. Bruttians historically had hardly more love for the colonial cities of Magna Graecia than they did for Rome and the deal was done. As a turncoat he could both save his skin and make his fortune, as the man who had delivered the city back to Rome. The whole story has not a little of the romance about it, yet whether it was love or lucre at the back of it, this key officer was brought over to the Roman side.

Having agreed on arrangements to sell the pass, either this daring agent or one of the Bruttians' men as messenger slipped back at night, past the city guard posts and into the investors' lines again. With preparations made the coup was kicked off. During the dark of night Fabius ordered his main force back on the road they had recently travelled to the eastern landward side of the town, while the men in the citadel and by the harbour were put on high alert and instructed to make a great commotion, with all the noise that trumpets, shouting and clashing of weapons could make, suggesting a seaborne assault coordinated with an attack from the citadel was getting underway. The effect was immediate; Democrates, the naval victor of the previous year and the officer commanding the eastern land wall by the Manduria Gate, was completely deceived. Unaware that most of Fabius' army was now posted opposite his sector and thinking there was no threat on that front, he sent most of his troops to where the racket was coming from on the citadel side, convinced that it was there that the principal assault was underway. When Fabius, waiting in absolute silence, saw in the increasing light of early dawn, that the eastern walls had been largely deserted, the order was given for the ladder men to advance towards that part of the defences where the Bruttium officer was known to be in command. The traitor had persuaded his men to transfer allegiance too and the attackers were helped over the wall by the captain and his squad with no resistance offered and continued, breaking down the nearest gate. This had all been achieved so far without raising any alarm and allowed Fabius' main force to file into the town in decisive numbers.

Yet despite there being no resistance, these circumspect movements had taken time and now dawn was nearly on them. Fabius, discarding any further attempts at secrecy, called on his men to raise their war cry and ordered a rush into the heart of the city. They approached the marketplace with little trouble but once near it the fighting became serious. The attackers, Cato the Elder was amongst them looking to add lustre to a family military reputation that began with a grandfather who had five horses killed under him in battle, now found themselves facing both the Tarentines and the Carthaginian garrison concentrated to oppose what they had originally thought was an attack from the other direction. Getting in had been carnage free but Tarentum was a large, populous city and it must have been with some fear the invaders pushed down the still dark and deserted streets, into the marketplace on the town side of the fosse, not that far from the citadel. There they approached, where still today there is an open plaza with an excellent museum to one side with the main municipal building dominating in the town direction, a spot where it is easy to picture the defenders, Tarentines and the garrison Hannibal had left to stiffen their resolve, all rallied, to try and throw back the attack.

Posted in the streets around and in the open space itself were the defenders, desperate and fearful with little illusion about their fate if the enemy won the day. But most lacked the training and did not have access to the kind of equipment worn by the men they were facing, many possessing only javelins to fight with and even those with swords and shields were not expert in their use. There must have been good fighters amongst then, clearly some professionals had been left to help the defence, the treacherous Bruttium was one such and a man named Cathalo commanded the Carthaginian garrison. But there were not sufficient of them. The locals, unprepared for brutal street fighting, after throwing their missiles at any attacker they could see, fled pell-mell using knowledge of their own streets and alleyways to avoid Fabius' men hunting them down. When the invaders went forward breaking into the marketplace it was all the sound of brass, as the Romans seemed not to use pipes or drums for marshal encouragement. These harsh tones were the signal for a bloodbath with the scene amongst the citizenry one of demoralization bordering on hysteria, 'indiscriminate slaughter'; Roman troops butchering armed and unarmed Carthaginians or Tarentines alike as they fled hoping to find refuge in the streets and houses of the town. Nico, the insurgent of 213, could expect no mercy and suffered in the mayhem dying along with Democrates sword in hand while Philemenus 'the hunter', who had let the Carthaginians in at a postern gate in 213, disappeared after fleeing on his horse, a rumour claiming that he ended up dead at the bottom of a well. It was a bloody denouement, with little hope for citizens found in arms or the garrison troops even after Carthalo ordered them to lay down their arms. And despite Fabius having been a friend of his father in an earlier peaceful time, was himself cut down where he stood by a private soldier before being able to claim the protection of the commanding general. Even the Bruttians, many of whom had helped the Romans into the city, were butchered apparently because of the particular hatred the Romans felt for them. It is even possible there was intent here, to hint that the town had fallen to glorious assault rather than ignominiously betrayed by a number of the defenders.

So the last of the great Greek cities that had joined Hannibal in the years after Cannae was retaken and the walls that had been put up between the citadel and town thrown down. It turned out that Fabius had been very fortunate in being able to wrap up his conquest in double quick time. Though the Roman intention may have been sophisticated, with the idea being for Marcellus to occupy Hannibal and allow Fabius the time he needed, this had not been quite what happened. The main Carthaginian army was actually engaged somewhere else when Fabius made his move. Marcellus was nursing his men after their bruising in Apulia when events panned out and it was only the speed with which the coup had been accomplished that meant Hannibal did not have any real chance to come riding to the rescue. The Carthaginian marching south after battling near Asculum had been putting the squeeze on the enemy attacking Caulonia when Fabius struck. In fact many of these Romans had just surrendered when messengers arrived with news of the threat posed to their Tarentine ally. They reacted as quickly as possible but Caulonia was far off, between Croton and Rhegium, some days' hike away through difficult country. The camp was struck, the wounded or ill left with friends to look after them, and marching 'day and night' the fit and able of the army of Italy pushed hard to make the difference, the column having to push on with all speed round the bay of Scylacium before they even reached Croton, prior to continuing to follow the winding coast road. There was no alternative until they reached where Sybaris used to stand, it was twice the distance but to push inland would have meant crossing the high rugged Sila mountains of central Bruttium. At least further on towards Heraclea and Metapontum the shore road was the most direct way but still they did not make it in time. And Hannibal heard from refugees while still on the way that Fabius was now in complete control of the town and port as well as the citadel the Romans had always retained. He kept going reaching to within five miles of the walls, staying a few days, hoping to find an opportunity to rectify what had occurred and perhaps realizing he had made an error in putting such a distance between his main army and the last great Greek ally he had in the Peninsula.

Based nearby, word reached him that not only had Tarentum fallen but that Fabius' men were already in the process of plundering everything of value with much of the populace corralled and shackled in preparation to being sold on the slave block. Five miles from the city Hannibal, in his stockaded encampment and careful as ever, now he was near the enemy, sent out to gather information on how things stood. It did not take long to discover his opponent was well dug in behind defensive walls and not in the least open to attack with any hope of profit. Hannibal was no Richard the Lionheart looking at a far off Jerusalem he could never hope to capture and keep; he still had hopes for his cause and by staying close by he intended to encourage any potential friends in the town who had survived the hard hand of the Roman occupation. But these few days were enough to convince him he did not have the resources at hand to attempt to retake the place now; it was after all defended by a whole consular army. But if he could draw them out and dispose of a good few, there might yet be an opportunity to return and drive out any that Fabius would have left as garrison.

The great Carthaginian general had been duelling with the old Fabius since 217 and had long esteemed his intelligence and determination, but now the story goes that when he heard the details of what had occurred when Tarentum fell he felt new respect, uttering the assertion that the Romans had found their own Hannibal. Yet this did not stop him from attempting to play a trick of his own on the man. Hannibal withdrew fading back to Metapontum, a place not far down the coast and well known since the people there had joined the Punic cause in 212. Once there he did not let the grass grow and planned his next move. From Metapontum he sent two locals with letters purporting to be from the civic authorities, offering to sell the town with its Carthaginian garrison, if Fabius would forgive them for their previous dallying with the Carthaginian cause and agree a pardon for the people and their leaders. The Roman general, eager for more success, and though a long time later Cicero reiterated his reputation for cunning on this occasion he seemed fallible and jumped at the offer, writing back to the city fathers and giving the day he intended to bring his army to the outskirts of their community.[6]

Hannibal was waiting, having been given the message from Fabius written to what he hoped were the party who would open their gates to him. Preparing a trap, he laid up his whole army, hidden in the woods along the road where it crossed the coastal plain approaching the town. But the old marshal got lucky, his diviners found their sacred birds were repeatedly refusing to give the go-ahead for action and so advised strongly against making the attempt. Fabius took notice; he was an old fashioned, superstitious Roman at heart, despite being famous for innovative strategy as the 'delayer' and when, two days after the appointed time, Hannibal's agents returned to find out the cause of the delay, something in their manner gave them away. Perhaps they seemed a little too eager and finding themselves clapped in irons, just the threat of torture was enough to make them spill the whole story. Though there is a different version less redolent of the usual clichés of improbable doings round the camp altar, where it is suggested Fabius was forewarned by the similarity of the letter sent to him to one Hannibal had previously sent to the Tarentines.[7] Whether true or not, after this the officers planning the Romans' next move were much more circumspect, knowing how close they had come to disaster, with Hannibal lurking outside in a country that for many years past had been his home territory.

Proper Roman triumphs had been pretty thin on the ground in this generation of conflict with Carthage. After all, these honours were generally meant, though the rule was respected as much in the breach as anything, to be granted at the conclusion of a war, not just for some success in battle. Even Marcellus after his blockbuster conclusion of the siege of Syracuse did not get to ride a chariot through the streets of the capital behind his soldiers in triumph. Enough people who mattered were convinced by the argument that he may have taken the town but the war in Sicily was not yet over. Or there may have been sufficient naysayers motivated by jealousy of the extraordinary success of this man over the last few years, his light shone so bright that they faded and shrank in his shadow. There was a practical problem too, as many of his soldiers were still on the island and their testimony was technically required to back the general's claim. So he had to make do with an antique ceremony known as an ovation which was a far lesser event without the winner's soldiers accompanying him in procession, though spoils of war, captured siege engines and eight elephants were part of the show. Also, so nobody missed the point, Marcellus also conducted a full triumph outside of Rome on the Alban mount at Alba Longa, the mythical original home of the Roman people.

There he let loose, processing to the sound of music all day with the sacrificial white oxen, captured enemies in chains, then after great wagonloads of captured armour, gold and silver treasure and vast amounts of statuary followed by great movable pictures of the highlights of the campaign. After this, the year's magistrates and senators usually followed, but how many attended at the Alban mount is not known, though no doubt there were plenty enough of his friends and those who wanted to keep in with the great man to make a show. Lictors escorted the general's chariot, their rods wreathed in laurel and beside the four horse carriage, where the triumphar might have his youngest children or a slave to remind him of his mortality, were friends and family on horseback. Then at last what troops he could get together, who in Rome would always have to be unarmed, but perhaps outside made more of a show in glistening mail and gilded beplumed helmets. Yet despite this the people of Rome would have wanted to celebrate success in their own streets, to register progress as well as toning up morale in years during which the demands on their blood and money was exponential, they had had to come to terms with at least two devaluations in the last few years. Now they could do so and express their joy as Fabius, in full triumphant show, brought the spoils of Tarentum through the Esquiline Gates, the traditional entry point for these parades, with people lining the streets and celebrations, both civic and private, the order of the day.

Chapter 8

Death of a Hero

Thus fell Marcus Marcellus from an act of incautiousness unworthy of a general. I am continually compelled in the course of my history to draw the attention of my readers to occurrences of this sort; for I perceive that it is this, more than anything else connected with the science of tactics, that ruins commanders. And yet the blunder is a very obvious one. For what is the use of a commander or general, who has not learnt that the leader ought to keep as far as possible aloof from those minor operations, in which the whole fortune of the campaign is not involved? Or of one who does not know that, even if circumstances should at times force them to engage in such subordinate movements, the commanders-in-chief should not expose themselves to danger until a large number of their company have fallen? For, as the proverb has it, the experiment should be made 'on the worthless Carian' not on the general.

Polybius, Histories, Book 10, 32.

The conqueror of Tarentum was only one of a surviving triumvirate of Hannibal fighters, commanders who had been directly contesting with the great Carthaginian for years and who had in common that they all were pretty struck in years. But apart from this they were very different men. Fabius in his seventies by now had been the greatest man in Rome for well over half a decade with his son, other relations or political friends almost monopolizing the consulships in this period, and in 209 he had just been elected '*principes senatus*', the father of the Senate, a huge honour. His nickname of 'delayer' had been well-won, he had never been prepared to face Hannibal in open battle, yet still his conduct, as dictator, consul and many other offices had been essential to the survival of Rome. And now he had topped off his career by the taking of Tarentum, scooping up 30,000 slaves, 3,080lb of gold, huge amounts of silver and coins to replenish a sorely tried exchequer, as well as a cache of artworks that almost outdid the booty Marcellus had brought back from Syracuse.

Quintus Fulvius Flaccus, like Fabius, had always managed to avoid destruction, not rushing to face Hannibal in open battle, but instead of digging in his heels and remaining in difficult terrain, he had usually kept to prepared positions to ensure his men did not suffer a Trebbia, Trasimene or a Cannae, most importantly contesting from behind his camp palisades, ditches and towers so he could carry on with his colleague the crucial siege of the Campanian Capital. Both had won reputations before the war; Fulvius had been consul way back in 237, so was probably now in his late sixties at least. Censor a bit later, consul again in 224 campaigning against the Boii, the great war had seen him as praetor, master of horse and consul in 209. So in terms of consulships he was just behind Fabius an incumbent five times. Remembered most for his defeat of Hanno at Beneventum and for his part in the conquest of Capua he had faced Hannibal in battle more than once and even if beaten in the field, his armies had always survived the experience and he had seen through to the end possibly the most significant success of the whole Italian War, gaining with the conclusion of an epic siege in 211 the kind of kudos that would keep him at the head of Roman affairs until his death a couple of years before the end of the war. A reputation that could even stand the taint of his brother who disgraced himself at the first Battle of Herdonia by running away and another of his kin who also lost an army in the same place, though that man at least did have the good grace to perish respectably on the field of blood. So despite stains on the family escutcheon he himself had lost none of the confidence of his peers and now in 208 was directed back to the scene of his greatest success, Campania.

It was only the last of the three who could boast repeated encounters with Hannibal in open battle. He had never beaten him and the victories claimed at Nola were surely really drawn affairs while the fights at Numistro and Canusium were far more probably clear defeats, yet still this dogged old soldier had repeatedly had the conviction to go toe to toe with Hannibal, and at least had never had the army under him annihilated, as had so often been the fate of Rome's other generals. No one the Romans had thrown at Hannibal had managed to defeat him significantly in an open fight but Marcellus had come the closest. This man had fought him to a standstill on several occasions even if it had cost his men enough in blood. This commander in 208 now showed every sign of being prepared to do so again; 'for no man was ever inflamed with so great desire of anything as was he to fight a battle with Hannibal.'[1] Just as he had done the year before, intending to occupy the main enemy army and so enabling his colleagues to push the Republic's cause on other fronts. If this meant his army suffered casualties it was worth it, Rome and her allies were able to absorb losses much more than their enemy. Thus Hannibal facing a truculent Marcellus would not be able to effectively defend elsewhere. Indeed since that man's return from Sicily the Roman hold on Apulia, Samnium and Lucania had been considerably extended and now Fabius had even filched Tarentum, in a manner so scheming it almost replicated how the Carthaginians had gained it in the first place.

Marcellus was now voted consul for the fifth time, if the occasion he was elected but stood down in 216 is counted, and after fighting fires in Etruria, where just his presence suppressed locals excited by the putative approach of Hannibal's brother Hasdrubal, he took the familiar road to Venusia, intending to join his patrician colleague Titus Quinctius Crispinus there. This was an experienced officer who had served under Marcellus when he replaced Appius Claudius in Sicily on his leaving to stand for consul. The ageing commander was now going to war in tandem with his colleague, a double command that had been far from the norm, for both the most senior magistrates to campaign together. But as when Appius Claudius and Quintus Fulvius began the great offensive against Capua it showed that the leadership of Rome had determined on the strongest of efforts at one point. The two generals were given the choice of three armies, the one which Marcellus had left at Venusia and two others of consular size, allowing the third to be allocated to the defence of Tarentum and possibly to look to make further conquests along the southern literal. These however were not the only fields of action. Quintus Fulvius was left with one legion in Campania, a region now felt to be virtually pacified but other parts of the mainland, Etruria and Gaul, were still fractious and vulnerable requiring four legions to be kept *in situ*, even if some rearrangements were made in the personnel in command.

Marcellus arrived accompanied by reinforcements for the battered army he had left licking its wounds over the winter at Venusia but he did not find his colleague present. Crispinus had left Rome for the front in Lucania first and taking up the cudgel seemed intent on making a splash. He attempted a coup by marching far south against Locri. It was a well thought out attempt with siege engines brought over on warships from Sicily, the plan being to assail the sea walls of the town. But things had hardly advanced at all when news arrived that Hannibal had arrived with his main army near Lacinium, north-east of the besieged city. Crispinus cannot have expected such a vigorous response, as he clearly was not prepared to take on the main enemy general with just his own army despite the support he was getting from the Sicilian command. Feeling exposed far down south and expecting his colleague to have arrived at Venusia, he packed up his equipment and marched his men north to find him.

On the border of Lucania and Samnium the two consuls met and though keeping to separate camps remained within three miles of each other, to offer mutual support in the face of an enemy who, having first secured Locri, had now marched north too. After the arrival of the Carthaginians, over a number of days, the Romans drew up both their armies in battle order to offer combat. These challenges were firmly rejected, Hannibal had found himself considerably outnumbered, facing as he was two consular armies that must have numbered 40,000 men and probably many more. The sort of numbers the Carthaginian army of Italy comprised during these years is not specified, but we know that plenty of Roman commanders took him on with the type of two legion army that with allies would not have got far above 25,000 men. So it is reasonable to conclude this was the size of army Hannibal usually fielded in these years. He tried anyway to keep in motion as much as he could to allow him to supply his men and keeping numbers down made sense for the same reason. Dispersal to forage and concentrate to fight was a strategy forced on a man who did not want to overtax the ability or indeed willingness of his Italian friends to provision his men. Though on this occasion, coming from Bruttium, he probably brought some of the troops normally stationed there, to make things more even if it came to battle with the two consuls in full strength.

The two sides settled down to something of a routine with just some skirmishing between small groups of soldiers to test each other's strength in this Samnite border country between Venusia and Bantia, modern Banzi. The Romans feeling they were occupying their main enemy army sufficiently decided they should make use of troops elsewhere and try their luck again in the south. It was Locri again where they hoped to strike. In the middle of the summer the consuls wrote instructing the commander of a squadron of warships based on Sicily, to sail against the town while they also ordered the commander at Tarentum to go to his assistance with part of his garrison. It seemed the Romans were looking to repeat the success of the previous year, a replication of the triumph at Tarentum, this time at Locri, using armies based as far apart as Sicily and Samnium in coordination to achieve success. But Hannibal was impressively well informed and when he received news from his people at Thurii, who would have noticed the activity on the

Tarentum road, of what was afoot, he laid his plans. Arrangements were quickly made for 3,000 cavalry and 2,000 infantry to respond, presumably men stationed nearby as to send soldiers from his own army would surely have taken too much time. But whoever they were these men secreted themselves in the hills at Petelia, just north of Croton, and falling on the Roman force marching heedlessly on the road from Tarentum dispersed them, killing 2,000 and taking 1,500 prisoner in this scrimmage, scuppering this crucial support for the intended attack on Locri.

The Carthaginian had shown once again why he remained a fearsome opponent even after the attrition of so many years in Italy. Almost miraculously well informed and always capable of utilizing the information he received. He might have begun bogged down on the Samnium border but his military organization still had the ability to hand out hard knocks to an enemy over a hundred miles to the south. And this facility to engineer his enemy's downfall was now about to be shown in the most dramatic way. Because when Hannibal had arrived back near Venusia where he campaigned so often before, he had been contemplating the decapitation of Roman leadership that was remarkable even for this man who already boasted consular and proconsular scalps that included Flaminius, Paulus and Gnaeus Fulvius.

So on a high summer morning, well into the campaigning season, a considerable number of Numidian horse, men always capable of arduous and desperate service, were settling themselves under cover on heights that lay between the opposing camps of Hannibal and the two consuls. The actual place was probably where the small town of Palazzo San Gervasio now stands, as this is the only eminence sufficiently extensive in this largely rolling, wold country to contain the action. They had ridden up during the night and dressed in no armour, just their normal rough tunics, were patient, well used to waiting for hours hidden amongst the trees in ambush and now they were about to accomplish one of the greatest coups of these dramatic times. These men who had always provided crucial fighters in Hannibal's and indeed most Carthaginian armies, stayed quiet occupying both the commanding heights and the slopes below, ensuring their small, hardy and bridleless horses did not make any noise that might give their presence away and well placed to off cut anybody who might ride up the road to the top. Their officers had also placed a sentry down the track on picket duty to warn of any approaching enemy and now this man reported exactly what his superiors had been hoping for.

A group of over 220 horsemen were seen approaching, most were Etruscan blueblood cavalry accompanied by forty troopers from Fregellae and according to our most usually reliable source, a force of thirty Velites too. The group were led by six officers, two military tribunes, two prefects of the allies and at their head two purple clad riders, showing very fancy accoutrements. The two consuls were themselves leading the party, their lictors with their rods and axes beside them and accompanied by Marcellus' son. This prestigious group cantered up the slope, clearly intent on reconnoitring the top of the hill to see whether it might be an advantageous place to make camp. As they neared the top a war cry broke the silence, as wiry ferocious men on lean and spritely mounts materialized out of nowhere, a fearsome sight accompanied by a volley of javelins hurled at the unprepared Italians, knocking over horse and man in awful confusion. The first shock was followed by the enemy charging in amongst the party, stabbing with lance and javelins at men hardly able to put up their shields in time to protect themselves. Marcellus was probably wounded at this time, 'run through with a lance'. The trap had been sprung with such elegant efficiency that the officers and their guard had no time or room to deploy in battle order, unable to go forward to the top of the hill nor could they fall back with the Numidians swarming over the track behind them. And soon it was not just Marcellus who was downed, but his son, serving with him, was wounded too, while Crispinus was caught by two well-aimed javelins as the tribunes and prefects around him were killed or taken captive. Lictors, officers, Etruscans and Fregellian troopers were all cut down or dragged from their mounts. Indeed it seems to have been hardly a fight at all with most losses suffered while attempting to escape. Some made it, Crispinus and Marcellus junior amongst them, with a few of the escorting cavalry somehow getting back down the road to the protection of the camp, where troops already alerted to move to the hill if it proved suitable for a new camp, could come to their rescue.

There were other traditions concerning the combat; that Marcellus was cut down in an instant or perhaps made a gallant last stand, with his Fregellae guard in a defensive circle around him, but the outcome was the same. A consul was dead, the other fatally wounded and Hannibal soon aware of how his luck was in, immediately transferred his camp to the hill where the trap had been sprung. The combination of his gaining this dominant ground and the news of their losses in the skirmish devastated Roman morale. Being in such proximity to the enemy now seemed like the height of vulnerable exposure to officers suddenly projected from subservient responsibility to high command and both consular armies were ordered to withdraw to higher ground in mountainous country around Mount Vulture, where the enemy would find it difficult to get at them.

What is almost sure here is that Hannibal had been specifically targeting an enemy commander and this was the first time that he had determined that the general opposing him needed to go. Usually he had been happy to play on the characteristics of the men the Republic put out to face him, using their weakness to his own advantage, but not this time. This Roman was different and the evidence strongly suggests that he was after eliminating a man who, for a third season, threatened to get in his face in a way that allowed his colleagues the freedom to cut great chunks out of the south Italian conglomerate Hannibal had so painstakingly built after 216. And at this moment the continued presence of this tricky opponent was even more of a potential menace when the Carthaginian general would need to have his hands free to manoeuvre effectively to join his brother Hasdrubal when he descended from the Alps, in what he hoped would not be too long a time.

The question might legitimately be asked, had he just got lucky? But his knowledge of his opponent had been at the root of his strategy and tactics in the past and now it is not unreasonable to suspect he did indeed hope just for what occurred on the basis of what he knew of his opponent's character. Marcellus after all had form, he was an up and at them man and a hands-on one too, he had shown this in the past two campaigns they had fought against each other and it is likely that Hannibal depended on this to deal with the particular threat he posed. The impetuous character of the Roman general had frequently been in evidence over his long years campaigning. Hazarding life and limb was the mark of any Roman general aspiring to glory and Marcellus had never been shy in this direction. He was famous for when as a young commander he won the ultimate battlefield trophy, personally fighting and killing the king and commander-in-chief of the Gallic army he was fighting, stripping his body to dedicate the arms to Jupiter. Apart from winning this 'Spolia Opima', an achievement of extreme rarity, he had also accomplished the first and perhaps so far greatest victory of the Second Punic War: the capture of Syracuse. This was a man who even at past sixty years of age would not be unprepared to roll the dice now he had the opportunity of again fighting Rome's greatest enemy. This, despite the usual story of several unpropitious livers, soothsayers and Cassandra warnings now he felt he had brought the enemy to bay and only needed to view the battlefield from the nearby eminence to formulate his battle plans.

Some might suggest the ambush was put in place just to pick up any strays they could, but the numbers employed suggests the object of their attention was altogether more noteworthy. Marcellus' biographer even has it that the steep eminence with wooded hollows and 'springs of water seen trickling down' was intentionally left unoccupied, though the Carthaginians could have camped there, as a lure to suck the enemy in. The Numidians and others had been sent for more significant prey and matters had fallen as well as they could, with not just one consul disposed of, but both.

> Marcellus, it must be confessed, brought this misfortune on himself by behaving not so much like a general as like a simpleton.[2]

The conclusion is harsh but perhaps justified. Both commanders had no need to personally reconnoitre the ground, a competent junior could have gone and with the memory of Gracchus caught in a Numidian ambush not long before the precaution of a much larger bodyguard was surely reasonable. But with peace returned to the hill where Marcellus had met his fate, Hannibal settled in his new-built camp behaved remarkably. Despite the frustration he must have felt when the dead man had dogged his footsteps and knowing what strategic damage had been done by this redoubtable opponent, still he gave all honours to his fallen foe. Even those who would vilify the African menace in every way conceivable, did not deny that on many occasions Hannibal showed the bodies of deceased enemies great consideration, something not reciprocated when very soon the Romans would find themselves in possession of the corpse of a different Carthaginian general. But this show of respect did not stop a determination to wring every drop of profit from good fortune. So using the signet ring he found on Marcellus' finger Hannibal sent a message to the town authorities of Salapia in Apulia, purporting to come from the consul, giving out that Marcellus would be arriving the night after the next day and they should welcome him and his men inside their walls, the intention being that the Roman deserters who had joined Hannibal's army would be dispatched there and on being let in take it over for the Carthaginian cause. But Crispinus, despite being desperately wounded and not far from his own death, still had the prescience to dispatch messengers to warn all nearby cities that his fellow consul had been killed and not to credit any communications purporting to come from him.

So forewarned the Salapians, despite being deeply worried about what Hannibal might do to them after the revolt that had led to his losing 500 of his precious Numidian garrison, prepared a coup of their own. When, near dawn, an army column headed by soldiers in Roman dress approached they were not fooled. The deserters yelled up to the men on the walls in Latin that Marcellus was not far behind and that they should open the gate. But the men peering down, 'pretending to have been awakened by their outcry,' were putting on a show. They responded with apparent welcome pulling on the mechanism to open the gates to the advancing men who pressed to get in, believing the ruse had succeeded and they would presently take over a somnolent town. But as soon as 600 had cleared the entrance the sentries on the wall let down the portcullis 'with a great crash' cutting off those inside from any hope of support from the men outside. Then they fell upon the unsuspecting intruders, who had no time to defend themselves, as all of the garrison and able-bodied locals who could, from the house roofs and city walls deluged them with 'stones, stakes, poles and javelins', anything they could find. Most were killed and those that were captured would anyway have expected little clemency but being deserters the worst was reserved for them, crucified in plain sight of the Carthaginians on the city walls.

The news soon spread of this setback, which would not have helped the Carthaginian cause in nearby cities whose attitude could be important in the fighting season to come, when it would be crucial to keep a road open to the north when Hasdrubal arrived. But Hannibal had little enough time to worry over this as he heard from Mago that Locri continued to be threatened by Lucius Cincius. This resolute man had deployed the artillery and siege paraphernalia he had brought from Sicily to excellent effect around the walls and the garrison were feeling the pinch. They needed help from a leader they had last heard of as far away in northern Apulia and they needed it soon, so desperate pleas for help were relayed along the road that they would be unable to hold on without relief. In the end it turned out not a huge effort was required, Hannibal had only to send a message that some Numidians would be coming to their aid and that he would follow with the infantry after, for events to fall his way. On the day the Numidians arrived they signalled Mago who led his men out in a sortie, taking the Romans by surprise, occupying their much greater numbers until the cavalry deployed themselves in battle order and routed the besiegers, who could only flee to the beach, board their ships and escape with what they could, leaving their siege engines and artillery littering the ground outside the town.

Crispinus, now getting solid word that the enemy had pulled back towards Bruttium, sent the dead consul's army on to its base at Venusia, while he had his own broken body transported by litter escorted by his own troops to Capua. From where he wrote to Rome stating he could not return, not only because of his wounds but also for fear that the enemy might have another go at Tarentum. He was a man in a hurry, he knew he might not have long to live and requested the Senate send a delegation to receive his instructions. The response was appropriately immediate. The younger Fabius was dispatched to take charge of the main camp at Venusia while three other delegates were sent to press Crispinus to appoint a dictator so the elections could be carried out. Yet the folks back home obviously were not clear on quite how serious the consul's wounds were, there was concern he might have actually moved with his army to Tarentum and because of this they had readied a force under the praetor to plug the gap his leaving would have caused. Not that anybody was long left in doubt as to the condition of the second consular victim of the Carthaginian ambuscade near Bantia, as Crispinus finally expired of his wounds near the end of the year.

Chapter 9

A Last Chance

But suddenly Hasdrubal came up, and a squadron white with dust followed him. Brandishing his weapons, he cried to his men: 'Cease your flight! Who is the enemy before whom we are retreating? For shame! A feeble old man is putting our army to flight. Has my arm, I ask, waxed feeble for the first time in this battle, and are you discontented with me? Belus is the author of my line, and I am kin to Dido, the Tyrian queen; Hamilcar, most famous among warriors was my sire; my brother is he whom neither mountains nor lakes, neither plains nor rivers, can withstand; mighty Carthage reckons me as second to Hannibal.'

Silius Italicus, *The Punica* Book 15.

So as the fighting season petered out in the tenth year of the war, the Romans' indefatigable adversary had counted another body blow, not just decapitating their administration by encompassing the death of both the highest magistrates, but also dispatching the only general they had so far found who seemed capable of matching him on the battlefield. Yet the next year was to turn out even more dangerous, as the Carthaginians seemed at last to be about to land a long threatened knockout punch on the tottering Republic. For nearly nine years, from almost straight after Cannae the intention of the Carthaginian high command had been for Hasdrubal to follow his brother to Italy, a policy based on the conviction that with two great Carthaginian generals with their armies loose in the Peninsula the Romans were bound to come to terms. Indeed a general called Hamilcar had been sent with an army to Iberia to release the second Barca brother for his new task as early as 215. But the conception here turned out far easier than the execution. The brothers Scipio arriving in Iberia knocked the Carthaginians' armies there about sufficiently, that not only could no one get away to beef up the Italian front, but in 215 the third Barca brother Mago had to divert an army recruited in Africa to Spain rather than pursuing his original purpose of reinforcing Hannibal. A poorly coordinated Carthaginian command in Spain sparred with the Roman forces until 211. Sometimes winning, sometimes losing, but never able to combine sufficiently to suppress the very able brothers left to carry the war on there with no great surfeit of resources. Even after these two were killed, and their armies almost destroyed, Hasdrubal was unable to put into action that second invasion of Italy that had been planned so long. The Carthaginians permitted a resourceful officer to rally the Roman survivors, allowing time for first, another expeditionary force to be sent under Nero, and then in 210 for the whole front to be reconstituted under the son of the dead Publius Cornelius Scipio who would, over the next few years, not just sustain the Iberian War, but bring it to a successful conclusion.

The particulars of this Scipio's campaigns are no part of this book and have been plentifully detailed elsewhere, but the story of an opponent who slipped away from the Iberian Peninsula on his watch is. The word was soon out that Hasdrubal was at last on his way. The great Hannibal's brother was a man of real talent, even if he and his colleagues had seemed to waste many of the advantages they had possessed at the beginning of the Spanish war, and his imminent arrival in Italy with hordes of Spaniards, Africans and Gauls was the stuff of nightmares. He had been pretty slow in coming, leaving Spain late in 208 after being hammered by the young Scipio at the Battle of Baecula. Marching out over the passes of the western Pyrenees into what is modern France he took as many Spaniards as he could recruit, they were afraid that any left behind would go over to the Romans. Certainly his circuitous route round the north end of the mountain range had saved on casualties but it had been expensive in terms of time. Indeed this man who left his colleagues to the tender mercies of Scipio hardly made haste at all to reach Italy and a brother who was in very great need of succour. There was little sign of hurry in anything he did, during 208 he dallied for the rest of the year in Transalpine Gaul, recruiting amongst the locals, particularly the Averni, who lived in the Cevennes, only crossing the Alps in the spring of 207. This second traversing of the great mountain barrier was much less taxing than the late autumn journey made by Hannibal eleven years earlier, and having arrived in the Po Valley Hasdrubal's followers would have thanked the multifarious gods of their nations for the ease of their passage.

But now the question was, what could they do once arrived? Hasdrubal had recruited amongst the mountain tribes his brother had had to fight his way through; these people now knew Carthaginians arriving in their mountains and valleys had not come to conquer them but were merely in transit to a war far to the south. A happy passage made even more felicitous by the news that 8,000 Ligurians had been enlisted by agents sent ahead. But it was Cisalpine Gaul again where decisive support was anticipated, the need to recruit here causing Hasdrubal to dawdle in besieging Placentia. This place and Cremona had been planted in 218 with the Carthaginian war just begun, when 12,000 Roman citizens were rushed to occupy country won in a Gallic conflict that had only ended in 219. The suppression of this colony would be bound to win over the Boii and Insubres, potential allies who deeply resented the recent Roman intrusion into their territory. These Gauls may have forced the Etruscans to share the area with themselves over the previous four centuries but they had no appetite for the Romans to do the same to them, though their failure to do more to help themselves is something of a mystery during all of Hannibal's war. Even after the disasters Rome suffered in 216 when Placentia and Cremona were abandoned, the local Gauls seem to have failed to take great advantage and not long after, the Romans returned to drive back in those two nails that held up their frontier in the Po Valley, though we do know Modena was besieged by the Boii after Hannibal arrived and seems to have been abandoned, as it required refounding in the next century. But Hasdrubal's delay caused some confusion for his brother looking to coordinate strategy. First, he had traversed the Alps well before Hannibal expected him to or was prepared for, but then stopped for an inexplicably long time outside the walls of Placentia.

Definite word had first arrived from Rome's friends in Massilia that Hasdrubal was heading to the Alps in force and the terror engendered by the news of the coming of this other Barcid was not only great, but reasonably founded; not just because of the threat this new man posed to rock and wreck the Republic in combination with his terrible brother, but because recently other stresses had begun to show in the fabric of Roman control in the Peninsula. While the Republic's successes since the fall of Capua were perceived by some contemporaries as the turning of a corner, of the balance spinning decisively against the Carthaginian cause in Italy, other things had fallen out recently that might have suggested a very different analysis. Most dangerously, in 209, twelve communities in the heartland of the Republic showed signs of failing the cause. Twelve Latin colonies; Ardea, Nepete, Sutrium, Alba, Carseoli, Sora, Suessa, Circeii, Setia, Cales, Narnia and Interamna all refused to stump up, declining to provide any more men or money for the war. These represented over a third of such colonies established over the years and geographically they stretched from north of Rome itself, in a curve around to the east and down into Campania, even including the key military bases of Cales and Nania, and some like Suessa and Carseoli were disturbingly close to Rome itself. The tipping point for these places had arrived for many reasons, but their war-weariness had undoubtedly been intensified when the survivors of the Battle of Herdonia in 210, many of whom were conscripts from these colonies, had been shipped in disgrace to join the remnants of the Cannae punishment legions to rot far away in Sicily for the rest of the war.

On top of this backsliding by these twelve standouts, it looked by 208 that places north of Rome that had seemed safe and steady since Hannibal had left the area in 217 might break away. It was Etruria where the movement was centred. Marcellus had to be diverted to settle the place after he had been made consul for the fifth time and the concern was sufficient to arrange for his army from Apulia to be transferred there if the situation warranted it. In fact just the threat of action seemed to make the troublemakers pull in their horns and Marcellus was able to return to the main front testifying that Etruria now seemed quiet. But it was only a cosmetic tranquillity; the years that Rome had suffered under the flail of Hannibal's ire had begun to work away at the sinews of loyalty in the ancient country to their north. There were plenty of people around who were proud of an earlier generation who had fought against Roman domination, taking up arms against that putative hegemon with Samnites, Gauls and many others. Much of the century might have seen them peaceably conform to the requirements of the Tiber superpower but that did not mean her leaders had forgotten what a history they had had, including the very early years of Rome when the city was, if not controlled by Etruscans, at least largely under their sway. They had known her longer, had given her more culturally and had fought her in more wars than anyone. The epic of Veii, almost two centuries before, had been accomplished against an Etruscan city contesting control of that part of Latium that Rome made the bedrock of her power in central Italy. Many of these people had been expecting Hasdrubal in north Italy for some years and now he was over the Alps, the aspirations of those who wanted out from under Roman control were likely to come to the fore and there would be little question that active agents well-furnished with Punic gold would be exploiting these old political currents too.

So when the news arrived from Gaul the fear in Rome at the prospect of facing another Barcid brother on home soil was palpable, after the disruption and depression brought about by the demise of both consuls the year before. Armies were bulked up from every source. Not only was the levy enforced to the limit (it had to be with decline in military population since the beginning of the war) but the seaside colonies, traditionally exempt because of their naval role, were ordered to furnish soldiers too. It did not make them happy, but grudgingly they complied, except for Ostia and Antium who were exempted, only expected to form militias to defend their own walls. Even slave volunteers were recalled to the colours and other units, particularly missile men, brought back from Spain and Sicily to bolster the effort on the Italian mainland, one of the first occasions when the Romans enlisted foreign auxiliaries as skirmishers to compete with experts recruited by Carthage from the Balearics, Numidia and elsewhere.

It was an odd couple who were delegated to deploy these forces and face the trials and tribulations of the eleventh year of the great war. Marcus Livius Drusus born around 254, had been consul before in 219, but suffered prosecution for peculation when he returned from campaigning in Illyria and had gone into self-imposed exile. In fact he had only just been brought back because of the need for all experienced commanders to turn a hand. He was an eccentric, whose unkempt hair and beard and old clothes were only discarded at the orders of the censors, who declared he would fight the enemy as soon as he found them, either to gain glory by victory or in defeat having the satisfaction that the Roman people who had treated him so badly would suffer, a viewpoint he believed 'if not to my credit, I have at least earned'.[1] Whatever his foibles Livius was thought to be a good fit because his cautious character might temper the impulsiveness of his intended colleague. The Republic's leadership had become chary of gung-ho commanders particularly after the last year's two consuls had got themselves killed in a risky bit of reconnaissance. This other consul for 207 was Gaius Claudius Nero and this impetuous antecedent of the fiddling emperor, who bookended the Julio Claudian dynasty, had had a mixed career up to that point. He had received criticism from Marcellus for failing to get his cavalry into combat at one of the Nola battles, but still had done his bit in the Siege of Capua, keeping a reputation that meant he was sent to Spain to cope with the fallout from the deaths of the two Scipios. There he had done well at first, holding the line at Tarraco and along the Ebro, even trapping Hasdrubal's army in a canyon, but then had allowed himself to be humbugged, with the Carthaginian distracting him by days of surrender talks while secretly extricating his men in small groups. But being duped there had hardly tarnished Nero's reputation, unless a hint by Cassius Dio is taken seriously.[2] He had then held high command under Marcellus at the three-day Battle of Canusium and now this crisis year saw him reach the summit, an experienced and able officer elected as a commander-in-chief.

The rub with these two was that they hated each other. Not only had Nero been a witness against Livius when he was arraigned after the Illyrian War, but feelings were aggravated because he was convinced Nero looked down on him because of his earlier disgrace. So it was perhaps with some relief, though they had at least formally been reconciled, that the decision was taken that Livius should face Hasdrubal in the north while Nero should try and occupy the older Barca brother in the south. Not that these main deployments were the only military efforts at the outset of the fighting season when the Romans understood the hour of decision was on them. The usual arrangements were made in the islands of Sardinia, Sicily, in Greece and Spain, while soldiers were also sent to Liguria to try and occupy the 8,000 locals who were preparing to join Hasdrubal when he arrived in Italy. Hannibal was going to have to face seven legions and their allied auxiliaries in the south of Italy as the Republic made an effort almost as great as for any year since the war began. Well over 70,000 men would be spread in field armies over Campania, Lucania, Sallentini and Bruttium ready to confront whatever forces the Carthaginians could muster.

There are hints that Hannibal had gone north early in the year hoping to be well placed when he got word from his brother, perhaps even reaching as far north as Larinum in Apulia, well above his old post near Canusium. It may have been that both Hannibal's activity there in 209 and indeed his attempt to retake Salapia after Marcellus' death, were an effort to ensure the road north he would need to use to join a brother, expected at any time, would not be closed to him. This was the furthest north he had been since Cannae and must suggest he had high hopes of news that Hasdrubal was coming the other way. But if this was eager stuff, looking to make the other half of a pincer, there is another version of events where, even though the campaigning season had hardly begun, he had suffered something of a setback. If one account is to be believed, Hannibal had been manoeuvring around the borders of Tarentum and Sallentini country, down towards the extreme heel of the Italian boot. There a Roman officer called Tubulus waylaid his mobile army when they were on the line of march. This man had ordered his soldiers to drop all their paraphernalia and marched them light shod to get one over on his usually vigilant foe. Assertions are made that

4,000 of Hannibal's men were killed and nine standards taken, though this seems likely to be exaggeration, considering the very sizeable army Hannibal was able to field later in the season and anyway this was open flat country where ambushing a wary man like the Carthaginian general would surely have been very difficult. But perhaps some reverse did occur, even if the details are improbable, as when soon after Quintus Claudius mobilized his Salintinian garrisons from winter quarters and joined Tubulus, in the face of the two of them Hannibal withdrew, fading back to Bruttium to circumvent an encounter, even marching passed Tarentum in the dark, to avoid being harassed by the Romans ensconced there.

With the enemy now pushed away from the crucial roads between Tarentum and their main bases in Campania and Samnium the Roman forces were free to reorganize themselves for the new campaigning season. Tubulus marched north to Venusia where he joined Nero, just arrived at the Lucanian encampment to head up the task of confronting the main enemy in the south. The consul took his pick of the legions gathered there; 40,000 infantry and 2,500 cavalry in all, while Tubulus marched the remainder off to Capua to beef up the occupying army of the proconsul Fulvius, that capable officer who with Appius Claudius had captured the place four years before and now continued in charge. The Carthaginian leader, undaunted by whatever might have happened around Tarentum, now prepared to coordinate his movement with his brother once he received detailed news of his intentions. After filling out his field army with what garrisons could be spared from Bruttium, the next goal was Grumentum in the rugged centre of Lucania. This place had been occupied by the Romans since the end of the Samnite Wars and is claimed as the site of a defeat of Hanno by Longinus in 215. The road from near Metapontum north was hard enough, through deep beautiful green valleys dappled with stands of oaks, chestnuts, pine and cypress, where every village was perched on one of the high hills through which the road ran, with distant vistas of high mountains splashed white with pockets of lingering winter snow. These small communities, ordinary villages in a wonderful landscape, would be protected by rough walls to keep out brigands and wild animals while larger towns had proper fortifications that would have needed serious attention to overcome. But the consolation was that most of these Lucanian places were no friends of Rome and many could be depended on for supplies and encouragement.

But where he was going had now become a frontier zone and his intent was to bring back over not only Grumentum, but other places in the area

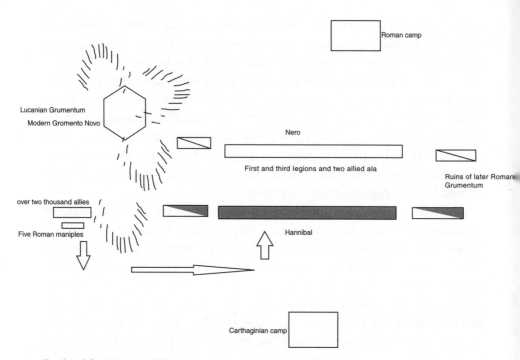

Battle of Grumentum 207.

that, for fear of Roman reprisals, had left the Punic camp when they were no longer able to offer adequate protection. This had become the crucial challenge since Roman offensive action had not only forced the recapture of Campania, but cut deep into Samnium, Apulia and Lucania pushing far down the road south. In these regions it was extremely difficult for Hannibal to maintain effective security even for those communities that, given the choice, would have never sided with his enemies. The people in these places hated the Republic's domination of a peninsula where for centuries they had kept a treasured independence but, with Roman armies closing in, many even here were bound to reconsider their options. So now Hannibal, while awaiting word from the north, was back trying to reverse the effect.

But while he had been on the move, Nero had been preparing too. And receiving word where his enemy was, he lost no time in stepping out with his men in marching order to find them. Leaving Venusia, an army encampment that had been Rome's military bridgehead in the south for some time, his legions, beginning their journey under the shadow of Mount Vulture, started towards a destination near eighty miles as the crow flies and much more on the ground. Nero was careful in this difficult country, very wooded where it was difficult to find the way and ideal for an ambush. So he sent scouts and spies to drive ahead and ensure the ridgelines and valleys he had to traverse were not the site of the kind of traps for which the Carthaginians were justly famous. Roman military intelligence had improved mightily after years of painful tutelage at the hands of Hannibal and it was now bearing fruit, able to make some sense of information that might arrive as a mix of rumour, mangled reports and fabrication. Their army arrived from the north-west, travelling the road through empty, steep fairy-tale hills and getting to within a mile and a half of the enemy camp without mishap, and dug themselves in. The men showed all the enthusiasm that might be expected to get stout defences constructed, so close to a deadly foe who had shattered so many Roman armies in the past few years.

The Carthaginians were encamped only 500yds from the walls of Grumentum and with just a short distance between the bivouacs of the two armies skirmishing became inevitable. For a few days Roman light troops contested with Balearic slingers and Numidian javelin men but when Hannibal drew up his main line of heavy infantry and offered battle Nero stayed put, happy to keep his enemy where he could see him and hopeful of finding a way to gain an advantage. The country between the two encampments was mainly clear and treeless, offering little cover for either side. But on the right of this plain Nero noticed some hills where the town of Novo Grumentum stands today, and he decided to utilize these to try and play a trick of his own. So under cover of night he sent several thousand allies supported by five maniples of Roman infantry to take up a position on the reverse of these hills and wait there until the right moment. The Roman commander and his military tribunes with this ambush prepared, at dawn led out their army. Over slightly rising ground their road wound through hayfields before deploying in sight of an enemy who were expected to be eager to pick up the gage having themselves offered battle on an earlier occasion. Indeed the Carthaginians' enthusiasm was such that in response they lost much of their order, with the cavalry and infantry chasing each other through their camp gates to get into battle formation. This was slapdash stuff and Hannibal himself seems to have been well behindhand, not even out of the camp gate when the Romans' first line charged into the ranks of an enemy they were pleased to see in such marked disarray.

By the time Hannibal reached his frontline men and enforced some symmetry, the Roman 3rd Legion, under a man with the unusual name of Aurunculeius and the First Legion on their right, were either already engaged or moving up to attack. And supporting them we are told was the cavalry of the 3rd Legion on the left and perhaps we can assume more cavalry on the other flank as well, who were ordered to charge with all the impetus they could muster to take advantage of an enemy who are graphically described 'as a mob like that, scattered all over the place more like grazing cattle than an army'.[3] In the face of this eruption of armoured warriors, both Roman and allied, powering up towards them, who had already discharged their pila and were coming on with swords bared, it took all Hannibal's powers of command to prevent more confusion in his ranks, particularly as Roman cavalry were now dashing towards them across the ground where now the broken stones of the later Roman town of Grumentum litter the ground. Still Hannibal's men were tried and tested in a hundred fights and even under extreme enemy pressure their officers were able to badger them into some sort of battle line. But just as they managed to stiffen the resolve of his depleted number of veteran Spaniards and Africans buttressed by Italian recruits, and it looked like they would hold their own, the military tribune and the prefect of allies placed behind the hill sprung their trap. The Carthaginian army was deployed with its left anchored on the slope of the hill behind which this enemy were hidden and while this position looked solid against the Romans coming up the slightly inclining ground in their front, when the ambush troops appeared around the hill and came hurtling down on their left rear, it was different.

The Romans had planned to ensure the enemy were well embattled before the ambush was sprung and in this they had succeeded. The Carthaginian reserves had already been employed as these several thousand yelling men erupted unexpectedly in their backs. It was too much as they threatened to cut Hannibal's soldiers off from the shelter of their camp. The battle all along the line had anyway not being going well for the Carthaginians and now this was the final straw. The men broke and ran with only the proximity of their encampment preventing a complete disaster. With 8,000 killed and 700 prisoners recorded, as well as four elephants dead and two taken prisoner, all this for just 500 Roman and allied casualties. Nero was up and ready the next day to fight again but Hannibal was not at all prepared for another such bloody encounter; he could not afford to lose the men, and so declined combat allowing the Romans carte blanche to recover the corpses of their own fallen warriors and strip the enemy slain as well.

Now the Carthaginians' thoughts turned only on how to get away. After several days Hannibal made his move. It was difficult to prepare his column of march in secret, to avoid alerting the enemy, as his sumpter animals' kicked as loads were packed and the elephants lumbered clumsily into line. But it was done, as Hannibal, astride his horse encircled by his picked veteran guard gave the signal to march, leaving fires burning and a few Numidians to walk the walls of their camp defences until the very last minute. These brave men kept up the pretence long enough for their comrades to put good distance between them and any possible chasing pack, finally getting out themselves, just before the cautious Romans, still wary of a trick, burst through the camp gates. By which time Hannibal and his army were hard down the road to Apulia, taking much the same route that Nero had come down the other way on his long march to Grumentum. The Carthaginians reached the environs of the old Roman base of Venusia before Nero caught up, where the arrival of his hard-marching soldiery brought on a running encounter that may have cost Hannibal upwards of another 2,000 men. This bloodletting was enough and Hannibal again withdrew under cover of darkness, moving back to Metapontum to recoup his strength with the help of Hanno, the local commander, who had been raising fresh troops in Bruttium. But not staying long, with this infusion of new blood he once again took the old road back towards Venusia.

Nero had shadowed his enemy's line of march after the battle knowing their vital role was to stop Hannibal from getting north to join his brother. He did not however neglect other duties and while down near Metapontum keeping close watch on the Carthaginians, he also sent to Quintus Fulvius, ordering him to come over from Capua to protect the gains made in Lucania. The consul did not remain long near Metapontum as his scouts reported that the enemy had been seen on the road north again. And he was still on their heels when Hannibal changed direction at Venusia and struck out over the Apennine tops in the direction of the Apulian plains. Nero keeping close, when Hannibal reached Canusium and camped near that town, the Roman commander moved there too, camping himself and blocking the road north that Hannibal would need to take to reach his brother. This now looked like a standoff in this rolling country, but in fact it was only the prologue to dramatic activity, as something happened that decided Nero to make the difference against an old opponent from Spain who had now arrived in Cisalpine Gaul.

Hasdrubal had swung east after he finally decided the siege of Placentia was not worth the candle, though this was no new dawn for this foundation, as within ten years it would be trashed, burned and its population sold into bondage by still-resentful Gauls and Ligurians, Insubres, Cenomani, Boii Celines and Ilvates claimed as numbering 40,000 under one of Hasdrubal's lieutenants called Hamilcar.[4] Keeping the Apennines on his right he sent couriers south to reach his brother so they might synchronize their movements. The intention was for the two to meet in Umbria in the heart of Roman Italy and together deliver a decisive blow. The six Gauls and Numidian horsemen dispatched unfortunately, but hardly surprisingly considering the length of the trip through enemy territory, ended up in difficulty and were captured almost at journey's end. They were scooped up by Roman foragers after mistaking the road to Tarentum as the one to Hannibal's base at Metapontum. Though all this is very questionable as it seems Hasdrubal made no effort to reach Umbria and also must have anticipated that it was very likely his messengers would be intercepted. It is surely possible that this was all a ploy and expecting them to be intercepted the Carthaginian hoped this would encourage his enemies to dissipate their forces in covering the routes to the west and so allow him to head down the Adriatic coast road and reach his brother. But whatever the intention, when the information these messengers carried was rushed by Samnite cavalry escort to Nero holding the line near Canusium, it suggested to the Roman commander that if he acted quickly he could make use of interior lines to strike a decisive blow against the Republic's most recent adversary. After first sending to the Senate to rush troops to Narnia in case the invaders actually did head that way, the consul decided to leave most of his forces encamped to fasten Hannibal in Apulia, while he took 6,000 infantry and 1,000 horse, the best in the army, to reinforce his colleague fighting Hasdrubal in the north.

He slipped this elite force out of camp at night, even putting it about amongst his own men that he was going to seize a nearby Lucanian town, but really rushing them on the road directly north. Something of the energy of Nero rubbed off on his soldiers and they marched as they had never done before. The first stage was easy through smooth terrain, but once into what is modern Marche, the serrated outline of snow-capped mountains showing dazzling white against a blue sky and reaching near 9,000ft were visible in the distance on their left, indicating that hard and testing topography was never far away in Italy. So when the road became up and down as the

Apennine foothills fell more directly into the sea the soldiers appreciated the organization of supply and the provision of transport by locals that their commander had required from the people along the route. But still the performance was extraordinary, 250 odd miles of eating road dust in seven days, with crowds lining parts of the route letting the soldiers in the column know how decisive the battle they were hurrying to fight would be, and with their lighter baggage carried in the wagons these enthusiasts provided. The consuls had been in touch while the men marched and agreed the new arrivals would enter Livius' camp in the dark so the enemy would not be aware of their coming.

Hannibal's brother had known all along that he could not delay forever besieging Placentia and with the campaigning season well underway he had pushed along the ancient route, on through to the Adriatic, before turning to follow the coast south. Encamping at Sena, where modern Senigallia now stands, a seaside town down the coast from Fanum where the Apennines nearly reach the sea. He had come a long way to get to this way station on the Flaminian Way but this was only the first stage and if the intercepted missive to Hannibal was genuine it showed an intention to cross the Apennines, that he meant to rendezvous with his brother north of Rome itself. But in fact he had to remain by the sea, facing an enemy who blocked his path, posted in two stout camps, one under Livius the consul and the other commanded by the praetor Porcius Licinus. The Romans had 'used every manoeuvre known to warfare in an attempt to hold him up, keeping to the high ground, blocking narrow passes to stop his getting through, and harassing his columns by attacks on flank and rear'.[5] Now the two sides were posted close enough together to suggest a battle was imminent.

Though the arrival of Nero on the scene actually stalled the incipient encounter as Hasdrubal himself noticed the differences in the enemy's appearance, old shields not seen before and stringy horses were suggestive, but it was when it was reported that the trumpet call for the consul was sounded twice, that the Carthaginian commander was convinced. Realizing his opponent had been reinforced he decided to withdraw north, to cross the Metaurus River that flowed into the sea fifteen miles north of Sena. But all was confusion and everything went wrong. Instead of slipping away to find another route to his proposed rendezvous in Umbria, the locals pressed as guides, riding with Hasdrubal at the head of the marching column, slipped their minders and deserted; 'one of them settled himself in a hiding-place he had previously determined upon, while the other swam across the river

Metaurus, using a shallow place known to him' and the army could not find a way across the waterway.[6] They were only able to press on westwards following the river's twisting course inland as the Romans pressed them not far behind. A day and nights' hard marching brought them up with Hasdrubal's army that now found itself brought to bay with its back to the high-banked river.

Cavalry under Nero and light infantry led by the praetor pinned the wearied and disordered invaders in place while Livius brought up his heavy columns ensuring that finally a decisive encounter would ensue. Knowing he had to fight, and hardly able to begin to entrench a camp in the face of an already deployed enemy, Hasdrubal ordered his regiments as best he could, taking his own place just behind his ten elephants drawn up in front of his right and centre where the Iberians and Ligurians were placed in a particularly deep formation, making a very short battle line. Once ordered Hasdrubal, confident his own left was not in danger, exhibited his usual aggression throwing his troops forward into an assault against the left of the Roman line. There Livius was in command with the praetor Licinius holding the centre and their soldiers pressed forward too in good order, so when the sides met they fought hard 'with great courage' with little to choose between them.

On the other wing things were very different indeed; there the Roman right led by Nero could not even reach the opponents facing them. There was difficult terrain, a ravine or the spur of a hill, to their front separating them from the Gauls who comprised the enemy left and were defending in advance of the half started camp or at least those of them that were not in a drunken stupor collapsed on their litters. While this might have seemed a splendid defensive position it had great disadvantages. Though for the Romans it meant a direct attack was impractical, it also meant they themselves were little threatened by the men opposite. Nero, his impatience growing in these circumstances, determined to break the deadlock. Taking advantage of the fact the enemy opposite could not get at him, he detailed some of his best soldiers to prepare to move out and join the fight on Livius' wing. With these veterans falling in behind, he hurried around the rear of the whole battle line, materializing on the right side of the enemy. There the new arrivals found a disorderly but bitter combat in progress, with the elephants exposed to missile fire from all directions, causing mayhem and panic on both sides. So the Iberians were already shaken when Nero and his men probed for their rear and began wading into the fray in a slashing attack.

The tide started to turn as soon as Hasdrubal's men found their flank and rear threatened by men they expected to be occupied by their comrades on the far sector of the field. They fought on, but almost encircled even these formidable warriors were bound to go under in the end. By the time the sun had reached its zenith the depths of their endurance had been almost reached and the elephants deployed in support across the centre, in front of the Ligurians, had now been eliminated as an effective force

> Six of the elephants were killed with the men on them, four forced their way through the lines and were afterwards captured, having been abandoned by their Indian drivers.[7]

But pusillanimity was not a complaint that could be levelled at their commander. Hasdrubal was abandoning no one. He continued to rally broken units and encouraged those who still stood solid against the enemy assaults. Yet even these efforts could only stave off the inevitable for a while, few battle lines could hold when hit in both front and flank. And when it became clear all hope was snuffed out, he resolved to die sword in hand rather than suffer the taint of capture that would only anyway gain him a few extra months of life to ride in his conqueror's triumph before dying strangled in the dark dungeon of the Tullianum. With his face flushed with determination the Carthaginian commander trailed a kite's tail of staff men, friends, guards and servitors as he plunged towards the hottest part of the battle. How many would have completed the fatal charge with their leader is not known but no doubt some would, old comrades from his Spanish campaigns who like him preferred death to being an ornament in a Roman victory parade.

When the dust cleared on this Roman triumph casualties had been high and the straggling even higher, no less than 10,000 of Hasdrubal's men were killed with him, though an exaggerated account boosts the losses to 63,000, certainly greater numbers than in the whole army at the commencement of the battle. While some Carthaginian officers were captured, not following their leader's example, apart from these, few prisoners were taken. We also learn some of the Gauls were drunk and incapable or sleeping their debauch off, when the Romans, looking for booty in the enemy camp, killed them with no trouble at all. The next day the tally of casualties could have been raised further when it became apparent a speedy pursuit might overtake mobs of disorganized and dispirited Ligurians and Gauls who had survived the battle. But Livius decided to call a halt to the killing so these desperate men might take back word to their people of what happened to those who dared to join the enemies of Rome.

More formal messengers sped to Rome with the news of a great victory won at the cost of only 2,000 Roman and allied lives. And if it was horror and despair on the Carthaginian side, in Rome it was all joy; 'every temple-court was decked, and every shrine full of sacrificial cakes and victims', the city accountants particularly felt the joy, when more than 300 talents, booty taken in the enemy's train, were dispatched from the battlefield and paid into the treasury. The three days of public thanksgiving and the triumphs celebrated all shout out that this victory had been something special, a decisive success in the open field by a Roman army against a major Carthaginian enemy. This must again make us very careful in accepting the many claims made about Hannibal and his lieutenants being defeated with losses of many thousands of men. If he had really been badly handled at Nola, Nuceria, Canusium and Grumentum, a city used to such regular success just would not have reacted so extravagantly to the Metaurus. After all, the reasonable figures the histories give for Hasdrubal's losses were not much greater than the claims made in some of these earlier affairs, though of course the enemy commander himself was killed.

The man who had contributed so much to this achievement did not allow himself time to revel in his success, but aware of the risks he had run by leaving the rest of his army to face Hannibal without him, Nero had those soldiers he had brought from Apulia step out and straight back south again. It only took six days this time, showing what he could get out of his men when he needed to. Returning, to his relief he found Quintus Catius still encamped near Canusium and unscathed at the hands of an enemy who had attempted little in the way of offensive action while he had been gone. Nero had returned with Hasdrubal's severed head to his old army and he wasted little time in delivering it where it would have the most satisfactory impact. The grisly trophy was deposited outside Hannibal's outposts and just in case this was not sufficiently informative, the Romans also released a couple of African prisoners, taken at the Metaurus River, to give first-hand details of the defeat to their army. Now Hannibal learnt there would be no army of Spanish veterans and brave Gauls and Ligurians coming to reinforce him and make a conjoined Carthaginian army of Italy capable of taking on anything the Romans might field. Instead there was the sight of his brother's severed head and definitive news that his army had been eliminated.

Sufficient a setback for a claim to be made that even Hannibal now finally accepted the war he was waging would end in defeat for Carthage. With supply lines stretched and with Apulia and much of northern Lucania lost to him Hannibal withdrew to a Bruttian stronghold from which he would hardly ever emerge again.

The question remains: why did Hannibal do nothing in the couple of weeks Nero was absent? One answer only can make sense of this, that without information as to Hasdrubal's plans, to march blindly north with a large enemy army behind, his communications would have been just too risky. And to have tried to eliminate that host by attacking Quintus Catius' camp chanced the crippling of his own army that he needed to keep in prime condition if he and his brother were to make the most of their conjunction. But there is no question that the Carthaginian's apparent torpor does not compare well with the extraordinary energy of the man who had faced him in Apulia. If he really had said after Fabius had taken Tarentum, that the Romans had found their own Hannibal, surely this accolade should much more properly be applied to Nero after what he had just achieved.

This man had certainly lived up to the concerns his peers felt about his impetuosity, but he had done so much more. It should never be underestimated what he had accomplished when he took his best troops to help a consul who was his personal enemy, then in the middle of battle performing a tactical tour de force, screening the men in front of him and taking his soldiers round behind, to attack Hasdrubal on his flank and win the battle. In leaving his army under a subordinate's command in the face of Hannibal, who had just been giving him so much trouble at Grumentum, and taking his men on a huge and arduous march, he risked his reputation and career in a very un-Roman way. It was not just the imagination or cunning or the preparedness to gamble, but that he should risk all to help a man who had been and indeed continued to be a bitter personal enemy and political rival. Only three years later, when both Livius and Nero were elected censor, they continued their contentious feuding, each stripping the other of their publicly funded horses for one charge or another and degrading whole tribes of voters just because their enemy belonged to them. Making even more extraordinary Nero's heroic seconding of his hated rival in the year 207. Altruistic patriotism that if not unheard of was very rare indeed and this behaviour, combined with ploys like the ambush at Grumentum and trapping Hasdrubal's army in Spain, makes a convincing case for Nero as the pre-eminent commander amongst those talented opponents that Hannibal faced in his fifteen years in Italy.

Yet if after this man's triumph one side acted like they had won the lottery and the other that the crack of doom was sounding, the behaviour of neither in the year to come exactly fits. It was almost as if the Republic, so relieved by the evaporation of an awful threat, after trumpeting the Metaurus as the greatest success over their enemy ever achieved, just relaxed and decided they did not have to follow up their advantage with any urgency. But if it was not military chops they seemed to be too bothered about pursuing, at least other very practical stuff was not left undone. In the period after the victory there was a larger context and the Romans cleared the decks east and west. The Macedonian War was wound down with fighting virtually ending in 207 and a peace signed in a hilltop town in Molossia in 205, while in Iberia Scipio defeated the last Carthaginian army standing, before being tested by troublesome locals and mutiny amongst his own men. Apart from foreign affairs the Romans also attempted economic regeneration. An effort was made to get people back on the land around Rome and in Latium. As well as this endeavour to kick-start food production in the centre of Italy, up in Cisalpine Gaul too pains were taken, where the depopulated colonies had their dispersed citizens repatriated while a praetor took his army up to protect the returnees. This was not a universal success, the disruption of years of war could not be so easily overcome by senatorial diktat when 'the free farmers had nearly all been wiped out in the war; slaves were scarce; cattle had been carried off and farmhouse destroyed or burned'.[8]

Over the next two years the Roman authorities also resolved to reimburse the senators and equites who had handed over the family jewels and plate to fund the war. Equally they decided the time had come to deal with the twelve colonies who had ducked out of their responsibility to fork out money and men years before. But if after this there was some little offensive intent it was hardly robust, as the new consuls Metellus and Philo, heading up Nero and Quintus Claudius' southern armies, overhauled to full strength by recruits, decided to try their luck against the western margin of the enemy's Bruttium fastness. Consentia, the largest market town in the region, was set in a wide bowl of country amongst rugged highlands, that while they made it very defensible also meant it was pretty isolated, turned out to be the target. The invaders' ambition showed limited when they arrived in enemy country, certainly they wrecked the agricultural land far and wide, taking prisoner those too slow to get behind the city walls. But there was no indication there was ever any ambition to take the place. Indeed plunder seemed the main concern of those involved and when leaving the district their attention was so fixed on getting their wagonloads and pack animals laden with loot away, that they had little thought of defence. The two-consul army must have amounted to a very large force but still they found themselves roughed up by just a body of local Bruttians supported by a few Numidian javelineers as they marched through a narrow pass, men and animals struggling in the press, caught crammed into narrow spaces with little room for tactical manoeuvre. In defiles their attackers knew well, the struggling mass strung out along the rocky roads in column of march found the enemy's missiles raining down on them. It was no disaster, but that they did not easily swat off these gadflies is telling, though we do learn that the same army moved north to Lucania to occupy a country where all the people were reverting to old allegiances now Hannibal could not protect them. Nor was Lucania the only region in which this occurred, but that the Romans were able to spread back down into places they had been excluded from for years was not the result of military activity but principally because the enemy had evacuated them.

Yet if there had been little to excite the Roman crowd from the doings of their armies in Italy after the victories of 207, for those who noticed such matters it was going to be different back home. As a young hero returned from his triumphs in Iberia, Scipio had stepped off the boat at Ostia and gone directly to report to the city fathers at the Temple of Bellona, which stood just outside the city, below the Capitoline Hill and across from Tiber island near where the theatre of Marcellus is now exposed in the centre of modern Rome. Collecting at dawn when the auspices were taken, there were up to 300 senators present, most of whom had been one sort of magistrate or another in their past, proud in rings, special maroon shoes and with flashes of purple on their tunics and togas, that bit broader than that paraded by the equites, the business class occupying the social rung below them. It was autumn in 206 in a meeting that would have been packed to see the conquering hero returning home and where the weather would still have been warm enough for the multiply-folded robes worn by the attendees to have felt uncomfortably heavy. The young commander who had come to meet them had had an extraordinary career in his short life, one that had shown how a crisis could bring about a preparedness to consider real constitutional stretches even in the tradition bound Republic. Born around 235 to one of the great patrician families, who could count thirty consuls in their bloodline and who reputedly traced their families back through the mists of time to when deities meddled in the lives of Greeks and Trojans. Some said he had saved his father's life, at that time the consul leading the Republic's armies in the first clash with Hannibal, when he was only 17 or 18, already a boy whose life seemed to promise a great career ahead. It wasn't long in coming; covering himself in glory in the aftermath of Cannae, claimed as the man who put the backbone into survivors contemplating fleeing Italy in the face of an apparently unstoppable enemy. And in 213, elected as aedile or quaestor, it is not exactly clear which, two years before he reached the required minimum age of 25. But this was but a prolegomenon, a curtain raiser, for two years later when he was given command of the army reconstituted in Spain after the death in battle of his father and uncle who had struggled there since almost the beginning of the war, a dramatic appointment of a son intent on revenging his father that came about at a time when senatorial politics were changing. For half a decade the Fabii had dominated, providing as they did the required leadership in desperate time. But since 212 others who were far from Fabii loyalists had won the consulship and now with survival, if not success, seemingly guaranteed by triumphs like that at Capua, the normal competition for places became once more the dominant senatorial motif.

Wagonloads of gold and silver preceded his arrival and with these riches to bolster a depleted treasury housed at the Temple of Saturn, and the news of how he had defeated four Carthaginian armies in Spain it might have seemed to warrant a triumph. But it was refused on the grounds he had not had official consular imperium when he went to Spain. Still, the new hero's record was enough to ensure that bedecked in his specially whitened candidate's toga, he received the almost immediate consolation of being voted in as consul for the following year on a huge turnout, showing that the citizens across the classes had the expectation that he was the man to do to the rest of the armies of Carthage what he had done to those in Spain and finish the war with the enemy's unconditional surrender. Filling the other billet, alongside Crassus in the consular contest, Scipio lost no time in putting to the Senate the proposal to use his new province of Sicily to prepare for the invasion of Africa. He had come back home with a plan, that he had been preparing for some time, to finish off the enemy. Indeed he had even visited King Syphax of Numidia in Africa in 206 to try and win allies for the time when he brought his army of invasion onto African shores. But despite that he faced no opposition from his colleague, Crassus, who as Pontifex Maximus (the most prestigious post in the Roman religious hierarchy) was anyway forbidden from leaving Italy because of his sacred duties, still the reception was not universally warm amongst the rest of his peers. It is not difficult to imagine the resentment of men who had seen this sprig achieve both the kind of victories none of them seemed capable of and won the consulship at an age when he was hardly entitled to step on the lowest rung of the '*cursus honorum*'. The stakes had become extremely high in the eyes of many; more victories in Africa might give this man and his people a position in the state that no one else could even attempt to match.

When the Senate met next, on the Capitoline Hill, the spokesman who turned out for this tendency was none other than Fabius Maximus, the greatest Roman of the age. He was old now and with Marcellus dead none could match a reputation that included virtually saving his homeland after the disasters of 217 and 216 and occupying the consular chair an extraordinary five times. These members of the Roman elite knew the requirement for public display, to reinforce a reputation they wanted to bring down the generations. So any man wearing his purple bordered toga who sat on the consul's seat with twelve lictors at his bidding was inevitably going to be something of an egotist from the off. Fabius was undoubtedly expecting to be one of the best remembered men in Rome's long history and the idea of another's reputation even coming close to his was difficult for him to stomach. So the old 'delayer' now put all his political heft behind the opposition to Scipio being allowed to carry out his plan to end the war by invading Africa.

From the beginning he made it clear that he considered that both senatorial and Roman traditions had been affronted by the way that Scipio and many others had somehow assumed that Africa would be his field of endeavour, despite neither the Senate nor the people having debated or decided this. Though still he was aware if he was not careful he could end up looking petty and envious as he martialled his arguments against the man of the hour. The old man knew he was risking being seen as 'a captious and malicious man, or one whose old age had robbed him utterly of courage and confidence, so that he was immoderately in awe of Hannibal'.[9]

But he resented the kudos of the younger man in a way that is perhaps not surprising in one whose days of glory were well behind him. It was a faction fight compounded by a generation gap that was both perhaps very human and totally inevitable. To counter the notion that his response was personal he played on his seniority for all his worth, pouring scorn on any suggestion that he might be jealous of the new hero, who was younger than his own son. Then he tried to dig in the knife, playing down Scipio's achievements in Iberia, claiming that his greatest triumph of taking Cathago Novo was done with the enemy armies making no real attempt to defend it. Some of this stuff resonated, as a cloud lingered from before, it after all had been on Scipio's watch in Spain that Hasdrubal had actually started on the march into the Italian Peninsula to threaten Rome. He had been allowed to escape east over the Pyrenees and this had never happened when the Romans were commanded by any of the men who predated the young general.

Fabius also stressed the dangers of invading an enemy's country, that the Carthaginians defending their own turf would be a much tougher prospect than even they had been in Italy. Anguishing over the monies that would be required to fund two great armies, one at home and one abroad, and even referencing Athens' disastrous attack on Syracuse 200 years before, as well as their own Regulus' failed incursion into Africa in the First Punic War, highlighting the perils of depending on new allies in Africa, who might be more phantom than real and that Scipio could find like his father and uncle did in Spain that it was fatally dangerous to put much faith in such local auxiliaries. If this was a solid argument Fabius showed he was prepared to get personal too. He first claimed Scipio had behaved improperly by leaving Spain and visiting King Syphax in Numidia to win him to the Roman cause, acting like 'a king or tyrant' by leaving the province where he had authority without senatorial approval. According to his biographer he even suggested that Scipio might be running from a confrontation with Hannibal by going to Africa, though disingenuously he also assured his audience that he had no wish to deny the young general the chance to win glory but that there was plenty of honour to be gained by taking on Hannibal 'the heart and seat of the war' in Italy and so compound his fame for throwing the Carthaginians out of Spain by doing the same in his home country.

Yet sufficiently aware he might not be able ultimately to thwart Scipio's plans Fabius was at least determined to throw obstacles in his path. Contending that any invasion of Africa was bound to leave Rome itself vulnerable, with her arms directed abroad, the danger would be that Hannibal reinforced by another brother Mago, who was thought to be on his way to Italy, would once more start destroying Roman armies in the Peninsula. He hoped to put the brake on any rush to join the invasion army by warning that these recruits would be leaving wives, parents and their home itself potentially at the mercy of a rampant Hannibal. That it could only be safe if the troops Scipio led against Carthage consisted just of those he had brought from Spain or men already in Sicily who could be spared from their duties there. There was real feeling here, but not just a distaste spawned from family and generational resentment, but policy too. Fabius and his supporters found it difficult to look with equanimity on proposals that flew in the face of their own preferences. They largely saw an Italian future for Rome, certainly one that included the Po Valley, colonized by Roman farmers, and most immediately one where Hannibal was prised out of his Bruttium stronghold as soon as was humanly possible, but not one that included Roman armies defending provinces in Spain and Africa. There was always something of the 'little Italyer' about Fabius Maximus, he had even argued against going to war over Saguntum in the first place and this was brought more and more to the fore with the return of Scipio and his demands for an African war.

But the hand of the man he was traducing was extremely strong, even beyond a claimed personal relationship with the top deities, he was also the scion of a great patrician family with vast traditional clout in the Senate and the city and on top of this his five years of triumph in Spain gave him credit across the orders that it is difficult to overestimate. He was also thorough in mobilizing support, even bringing representatives from Saguntum, in defence of which place the Romans had claimed they began the war, to the Senate to praise this man who had restored them to their homes and made them safe from dangerous neighbours. He had shown in the past that he knew how to woo the people, during his first stint in office when he not only organized substantial games to entertain the populace but handed out a dole of oil, paid for out of his own pocket, to all the city districts. The full extent of this popularity is illustrated a year or so after his winning the consulship, when, following a reading of the Sibylline books, it was decided a sacred stone, representing Cybele, an Asian mother goddess, needed to be brought to Rome. Envoys went to the Delphic oracle asking for advice on the process, where they were told that the stone must be received on arrival by 'the best man in the city'. In the end a young cousin of Scipio received this honour and it is difficult to credit the distinction to anything except his connection to the man who was by then in Sicily preparing for the final push against the Carthaginians' enemy. Nor was his popularity just restricted to the capital, he had a great name with the citizenry in the rest of Italy and the allies too, which became very apparent as he prepared his military campaign. Though obstacles may have been put in the way of his levying troops and naval support in the normal way, sufficient was produced voluntarily, by both inland and coastal allied towns and colonies, stumping up extra to fill out his legions and build the warships and transports he needed.

When he pressed his case with the Senate, Scipio made no bones about his desire to do great things and make a name that might even surpass that of Fabius. This was the Roman way and he made no apology of desiring to become as great a figure as possible in his country's history as this was the motivation that would make him serve Rome's interest so well. He dealt with the details of Fabius' case, arguing that invading Africa would be the most effective method of ensuring Hannibal left Italy. He drew on history too, contending that Regulus' experience supported his strategy, as that general had found it fairly easy to establish himself on enemy soil and it was only when it came to the final battle that things fell apart. He also reminded his audience that well before this Roman invasion, Agathocles, the tyrant of Syracuse, had shown that Carthage's soft underbelly was indeed her African territories, where she had no strong home army or dependable friends such as had served Rome so well, that indeed her allies were an Achilles heel who would fall away and support the invader once he would show himself with his legions in their neighbourhood. Finally the young commander showed he was prepared not to be over subtle, that if his plans continued to be blocked in the Senate he would use his credit with the citizenry by taking his plans for approval to the popular assemblies. In the end a form of words allowed the consul to have Sicily as his province from where he could invade Africa if 'he judged it to be in the public interest'. So arguably the most significant decision of the war was botched together that would allow Scipio to proceed along the road that would earn him the sobriquet of Africanus.

Chapter 10

Holding and Hoping

In actual fact, however, so far did Pleminius surpass Hamilcar, commandant of the garrison, so far did the Roman soldiers in the garrison surpass the Carthaginians in villainy and greed that they seemed to be competing not in arms but in vices. Of all the things that make the power of the stronger odious to the helpless man not one was overlooked by commander and soldiers in dealing with the townspeople. Unutterable insults were practised upon their own persons, upon their children, upon their wives. It goes without saying that their avarice did not refrain from despoiling even sacred things. And not only were other temples desecrated, but also the treasure chambers of Proserpina, untouched in every age except that they were said to have been despoiled by Pyrrhus, who met with a signal punishment and restored the plunder gained by his sacrilege.

Livy, *The History of Rome*, Book 29.9.

In the mid second century a historian, standing between six and seven miles south-east of Croton on the promontory of Lacinium, modern Cape Colonne, saw a column placed in position at the Temple of Hera some forty years before. That man was Polybius, a Greek from Achaea and the man who had erected it was Hannibal. As a serious chronicler of the rise of Rome to world dominance, the Greek was not content with a small patch to work; he wanted to transfer Platonic concepts of unity in art and literature to history, to tell the story of the whole world of the Mediterranean basin and beyond. And he prided himself on going to all those places where great events had taken place. For Polybius you had to see the ground, he had crossed the Alps to try and discover the route taken by Hannibal, travelled in Iberia and even explored the Atlantic coast of Africa and Spain; 'I underwent the dangers and hardships of making journeys through Africa, Spain and Gaul and voyages on the sea which adjoins these countries on their western side.'[1] He was even present at the sack of Carthage at the end of the Third

Punic War. Son of an important Achaean magistrate, he had suffered years of exile in Rome from when he was in his thirties and in that time he became an intimate of a great patrician family, descendants of Scipio Africanus, a position that allowed him access not only to the records of the Republic and the texts of her historians but an introduction to members of the Tiber town elite. Like Laelius, Scipio Africanus' very competent lieutenant, who a century and a half later Cicero could only imagine as he had him sound off about friendship in one of his philosophical treatise,[2] or others involved like the old King Masinissa of Numidia, people who either had personal recollections of what had occurred in the great war against Hannibal or who were aware of the family traditions of great actors themselves long dead.

Where today only one lonely Doric column stands 27ft high within formidable foundations, then a monument stood in an extensive wealthy precinct that recorded the events of Hannibal's campaigns, the numbers of the soldiers deployed by Carthage in the epic struggle and as Polybius says, its provenance and veracity was such 'holding it to be an entirely trustworthy authority for such facts, I did not hesitate to follow it.'[3]

He accepts the truth of the assertion on it, that after a march from New Carthage of five months and fifteen days, Hannibal arrived in the country of the Gallic Insubres in the Po Valley, with 12,000 African, 8,000 Iberian infantry and no more than 6,000 cavalry. So through him again we hear the genuine if feeble voice of the Carthaginian version to go with other echoes when the two Greeks who accompanied Hannibal's army of invasion are referenced by our histories. Still it is little enough when compared with the avalanche of information that comes from the pens of their enemies. Livy knew of this hard evidence too and confirms it was in the summer of 205 when the Carthaginian general put up a 'great record of his achievements in a Punic and Greek inscription',[4] appreciating it as one of the few tangible reminders even in his age, along with a tumulus built to cover Hannibal's remains in Bithynia reported by Pliny the Elder, of the man who had given the Roman Republic one of its greatest scares in a long and taxing history of conflict.

It is perhaps no surprise it was not long after the Metaurus disaster and at a time when famine and disease were wrecking the fighting potential of the forces holed up in his Bruttium fragment that the urge came to Hannibal to record what he had done since leaving Spain. It is likely he now realized that his strategy had in the end not borne fruit and he was a man who prided himself on having a clear view of what was happening. Not for him fantasies of one more victory against a Roman army turning the tide. Looking back he could not unreasonably have calculated that nobody could have done more than he had, nobody could have hit the Republic with more trip-hammer blows, but finally the strategy of detaching sufficient of his enemy's dependants and allies to bring her to her knees had not come off. He might have ranged loose in Cisalpine Gaul, Italy and Magna Graecia for over sixteen years and still no Roman general cared much to face him in battle whatever the odds in their favour, yet still this did not amount to success. The reality was that he was contained in a pocket of territory in Bruttium and coastal Lucania and a war directed by Scipio, the conqueror of his compatriots in Spain, looked set to pass him by.

The region from where Hannibal still showed a defiant face to the Republic, whose resources had just been too great for even his talents to overcome, had had an action-packed history of its own in the past few centuries. Adventurous Greeks who did not have the assets to live the good life at home, and often led by disgruntled bigwigs, drew up their boats to land on the south Italian coast where river valleys offered wide open acres or a substantial coastal plain between the mountains and the sea, allowed agriculture to flourish. Sometime in the eighth century Achaean colonists from the northern Peloponnese and other Greeks, even some few from Laconia, settled places like Croton, Sybaris, and Tarentum. Often utilizing older prehistoric sites, these places in the fullness of time, not infrequently dispatched colonies of their own. Heraclea was founded from Tarentum, Sybaris set up far away Poseidonia on the Tyrrhenian Sea, while Locris founded Hipponion. The interior of Bruttium and coastal Lucania where most of these places were planted might be underpopulated and underdeveloped but still the indigenous people resented the intrusion, setting up a tension that lasted well into the time of the Second Punic War. For them there was little consolation that the region soon became as much a part of the greater Greek world as any place in the Aegean or Ionian seas, producing Olympic champions by the bushel, amongst the most famous a celebrity wrestler from Croton named Milo.

Rhegium on the very toe of the Italian boot had been settled by people from Chalcis in Euboea in 730 or 743 and a tyrant based there called Anaxilas, another Olympic winner, made himself king of the crossing at the very beginning of the fifth century, when he captured the town on the Sicily side and renamed it Messene from his own place of origin in the Peloponnese. But this man was only the first of many, particularly from Syracuse, who, trying to win control of the strategic passage, attempted to build a hegemony around this coast dotted with Greek communities. Dionysius I, the tyrant of Syracuse, might have spent the most of his long reign fighting Carthage but he always had an eye on controlling the key straits between Sicily and Italy. In this struggle he had to fight it out with Rhegium, often allying both with Locris, a local Greek rival and 'barbarian' Lucanians. He ended disputing with a league of cities led by Croton that came to his enemy's assistance, a contest that lasted through the early 380s only ending with the Italian Greek confederation being decisively beaten in battle at Eleporus between Croton and Caulonia. The result for Rhegium was destruction, after a long and brutal siege, that saw her walls torn down and her people enslaved or dispersed. The straits and the toe of Italy were now a Syracusan holding and even after Dionysius' ineffective son took over and despite tiresomely convoluted politicking at home, the Sicilian city's influence remained strong in Magna Gracie. Dionysius II was even able to find an exile's home in Thurii when family control at Syracuse fell apart in the middle years of the fourth century. Thirty-odd years later another hard man called Agathocles took over as autocrat of Syracuse and tried his hand at establishing a south Italian empire. The short trip across the channel at Messene was no big deal for a man who was prepared to invade Africa to get at Carthaginian enemies who were at the time actually besieging his home city and base.

Nor was it just from the south that interest was shown; at the end of the fifth century the area inevitably became entangled in the great Peloponnesian War with Athens long dominating the straits, though as with so much in Greek politics, if Athens had her friends there they had enemies too, both within and without the communities involved. Thurii in particular often swung between the sides, sometimes hooked up with the Athenians; they helped General Demetrius when he was on his way to the Siege of Syracuse, even providing troops, but sometimes with their enemies. Indeed the Athenian commander Alcibiades sheltered there after escaping his compatriots' clutches while being taken home for trial, accused of sacrilege by wholesale vandalizing of images of household deities, before the campaign against Syracuse began. But apart from the involvement of the great Greek Republic the fourth and early third century saw the region impacted from the east by a blue-blooded sequence that not infrequently ended fatally for those involved. First down this royal road was a king of Sparta. The bellicose people of Laconia were always the first stop for the Tarentines looking for imported military muscle, because of the connection as home of her original colonists. Archidamus

III had done much in an adventurous life before turning up in Italy; he had defended his home city against the great Theban, General Epaminondas in 360s, gone a-roving in the 340s to fight in Crete before in 342 answering the call of Tarentum to help them against local enemies, Lucanians and others. A response that had been initially put on hold by his Cretan entanglement but that only ended with him, as the first casualty in this graveyard of Hellenic kings, dying in combat under the walls of Manduria in 338.

Hardly had this adventurer fallen, than a mere four years later another professional warrior from over the Adriatic got involved. This one had real pedigree; brother of Olympias, the wife of Philip II of Macedon, so uncle of not only Alexander III, but of Pyrrhus of Epirus too and himself king of that country from 350 to 331. This Alexander the Molossian, named from the leading tribe in the Epirote federation, had an upbringing at the Macedonian court at Pella that had instilled in him an aggressive streak little short of his nephews, and exactly as the future Alexander the Great set off east to conquer that world, he crossed the sea to Italy with another invitation from Tarentum in his sleeve, to do what the Spartan king had failed to do. And he started well, battling Samnites, Lucanians and Bruttians even getting as far as the neighbourhood of Paestum on the Tyrrhenian coast and making diplomatic contact with a Rome that was then ten years into a generation-long struggle with the Samnites. He looked to be achieving much, taking Heraclea from the Lucanians, Terina, Consentia and the pirate port of Sipontum from the Bruttians, before, like his predecessor, he came to a sticky end.

The dates are difficult but probably in 331 Alexander found himself mired down on the Lucanian, Bruttium border at a place called Pandosia. Things had become very difficult for him with his sponsors in Tarentum now lukewarm. Strabo even notes that Alexander tried to transfer a Panhellenic festival from Heraclea to Thurii out of enmity to his old employer. Accompanied by a couple of hundred Lucanian exiles he had encamped his forces on three hills looking to harass his enemies from these strongpoints. But heavy rain flooded the country and turned his army into a fissiparous outfit, divided into three parts, who could only communicate with each other with great difficulty. The king could only watch the outlying groups as they were overcome individually and with Alexander and the last corps standing firm the enemy took to blockading them while the Lucanians with him began looking to their own safety and intrigued to sell him out. So Alexander tried to fight his way free 'cutting down the Lucanian general in a hand-to-hand encounter' but only to find himself exhausted with those of his followers who had kept up with him at a river called the Acheron, the very name of a stream in Epirus that an oracle had warned him to avoid. Trying to fly his fate he pushed his horse into the shallow water of a ford, sword in hand, when one of the exiles pieced him from behind with a flighted javelin. Another royal *condottieri* had died, his body carried downstream to be discovered by enemies who mutilated it. Cutting it in half, one part was sent to Consentia, while another was abused until a woman rescued it, in hope of swapping the remains for her husband and children held by some of Alexander's men as prisoner. While his nephew was founding Alexandria in Egypt this man was dying mired in other people's troubles and misled by the misinterpretation of an oracle.

It was a Sparta then Epirote, then Sparta, then Epirote sequence, with the latest in the series being a king in exile from Laconia where his nephew had been chosen to replace him on the throne. This Cleonymus son of Cleomenes II was considered even too violent for this ferocious people and departed to try his hand as a hired gun for Tarentum in 303 or 302. But after intimidating that city's Lucanian enemies and capturing Metapontum he shipped over and took possession of Corfu, a series of triumphs that ended when, while returning to Italy, his ships were severely knocked about in a storm. A second round saw him take Thurii as a potential base; he also had fallen out with the Tarentines by then, before the Romans, new players in the region, drove him out. Privateering in the north Adriatic then kept him busy until returning to Greece, where at one stage he even convinced Pyrrhus of Epirus to help him win the throne of Sparta. So Pyrrhus, who became in the 270s the fourth royal intruder in Magna Gracie, had known his predecessor well, perhaps even gaining sufficient inspiration from his accounts to risk a personal involvement that turned out a swansong for a south Italian Greek world, that after his departure swiftly succumbed to the power of Rome.

Hannibal, the man who had allowed these Greeks to dream again of past liberty, was now bottled up in this much fought over patchwork, though it was not complete passivity at this time. The fissures in Carthaginian hegemony in southern Italy had been apparent and deep for some while, but even reduced to hunkering down in their fastness, nobody in Hannibal's headquarters was throwing in the towel yet. It was possible to still hope despite the long-term plan of decisive support arriving from Spain being a busted flush. Yet equally nobody was assuming that just their commander's genius would be enough and the more farsighted must now have begun thinking of an exit strategy. Though for many it was not just the prospect of defeat in Italy that concerned; plenty of the officers and men in Hannibal's army had, like him, grown to manhood in Iberia rather than Africa and now that country was no longer a secure refuge since Scipio's victories and indeed might be completely closed to them. So if they had to withdraw from Bruttium it would be to defend a city none had seen for many years and some had hardly known at all in their nomadic lives.

Whatever his lieutenants contemplated at this time Hannibal kept alert, he still had his agents gathering news on the enemy's intentions. Spies in Rome picked up gossip from a Senate that had little idea of national security while travellers, traders and deserters too would have fleshed out the files of his intelligence staff. The great Carthaginian had always prided himself on knowing his Romans from as early as the Trebbia when his appreciation of the commanding Roman general's character part-moulded his battle tactics. So now surely he would have heard reports of what Scipio intended in the coming campaigning season and the resistance his intentions had aroused. But because hindsight makes the strategy of taking the war to Africa seem inevitable, it is easy to assume that Rome's enemy would have expected this too. Yet that we know what happened, should not make us imagine this was a given from the start. While Scipio envisaged a decisive assault on the Carthaginian homeland many people surely saw him as the man to deal with the cancer of Hannibal's presence in the body of Italy. And it was probable that it was in that man's mind too that he would be the target of the new Roman hero, that an ultimate showdown could occur somewhere in his Bruttium refuge.

But it was in fact Licinius Crassus, Scipio's consular colleague, who was allocated the south Italian front, to chase down Hannibal and his army that since the disaster on Metaurus had faded back far from Campania, Samnium and Apulia. A descendant of this man would in 130 years' time gain renown in the same area, eradicating the threat of Spartacus and his slave army that had been terrorizing Roman Italy for several years. This later Crassus showed great energy building a defensive wall down near Rhegium to entrap his enemy in the furthest part of Italy's toe. And success in this campaign would lead to his sharing supreme power in the Roman world with Caesar and Pompey in the first Triumvirate before being defeated and killed in an ill-fated attempt to invade the Parthian Empire. His namesake and antecedent however never made this kind of impact in 205 when he was delegated to cross swords with the Carthaginian enemy. In fact it never came to blows at all; we learn that both the invading Romans and the defenders in the deep south were struck by an epidemic that not only killed or debilitated a large number of combatants on both sides but also, striking the agricultural workforce, brought famine in its wake in a region that anyway never produced a great surplus of food, 'and even if the whole of that country had been in cultivation it would have afforded but meagre support for so large an army. But as it was, a large part of the population had been diverted from the tillage of the soil by the war and by their traditional and innate love of brigandage.'[5]

So apart from devastating germs and men with empty bellies Hannibal had little to directly contend with in the campaigning season of 205. There was apparently going to be no explicit threat from Rome's consular armies in that pestiferous time to this region around the instep of the Italian boot that he had run for most of a decade. Croton, Thurii, and Locri were key Greek cities here on the Ionian literal and these and their like had been on his side since, if not immediately after Cannae, at least once Hanno and Mago had made their presence felt in the region, with laggards joining after the Carthaginian takeover of Tarentum in 213. These places were worth having, the repositories of wealth and culture, basking in a climate so mild that even in December and January the temperature stayed between 50–60 degrees. Rising behind were the high, green and rugged mountains of Bruttium that after filling the Italian toe fell down almost directly west into the sea on the Tyrrhenian side. Here lived Italian tribes, hardy warrior people normally eager to pick up the proffered wages when Hannibal's recruiting sergeants circulated around their communities. And for the Greeks in the region this was an advantage, enlisting amongst these Bruttians siphoned off exactly the kind of adventurous young men who otherwise would have been tempted to raid the affluent communities along the coast. On that west coast the Carthaginians or their friends controlled towns like Clampetia and Taurianum, though these could only easily be reached by sea and Punic weakness on that element meant their strategic importance was limited. The same was true of inland places like Pandosia or Consentia nestling almost 1,000ft up at the junction of the two rivers, Busento and Crathis, in large fertile bowls of land set amongst the high mountains, Bruttium towns that had also come over to the Carthaginians as soon as the victorious invaders arrived in their neighbourhood and remained stalwart to near the end. But they were isolated and if this made getting at them difficult for the Romans it equally meant they were of lesser military significance on the grand stage.

The Carthaginians' southern holdings had begun contracting from 209 when Tarentum had fallen to Fabius. This had given the Romans, who had always kept control of Brundisium, sway over the whole of Italy's heel which, well held by strong armies, meant Hannibal now always had to worry about a threat from that direction. The taking of Syracuse and the defeat of the Carthaginian armies in Sicily had changed the dynamic there as well, meaning an eye had to be kept on the short crossing from Messene where enemy invaders might materialize at any time. The waters along the straits might be risky with dangerous currents and tides but it was only nine miles across at its broadest and just two at its narrowest. After Hasdrubal's defeat on the Metaurus in 207 contraction sped up, as those places Hannibal had controlled in Lucania, including Metapontum, were abandoned with their garrisons and inhabitants pulled back into Bruttium.

But while these changes had occurred there had been one constant and it would be from there a peril threatened. Rhegium had remained over all the years of the Hannibal war the one Roman holdout in Carthaginian south. This city four miles south of Cape Caenys, where the straits of Massine are at their narrowest and Sicily is easily seen, sits on a coastal plain hardly a mile from the foothills of the steep rising ridges of the Aspromonte Mountains, where very rugged country rises to thousands of feet in hardly any distance at all. Remaining out of Carthaginian hands it became the bolthole for those people from all the towns around who had not thrown in their lot with the invaders but preferred exile, supporting a Roman hegemon that they considered still best suited their class and family interest. Hanno early on in 215 had tried to take the place, even before he rolled up the likes of Locri and Croton, but the siege was aborted when the defenders were reinforced by troops shipped in from Messene in Sicily.

This tough nut even claimed the attention of Hannibal himself in 211 when, after failing to draw off the armies at Capua by his gambit of threatening Rome, he force-marched all the way down to this holdout on Italy's toe in an attempt to surprise the defenders. The coup had imagination but came to nothing and indeed in the very next year the place's capacity for both defence and offence was upgraded by some arrivals from Sicily. This very motley crew were bandits, refugees and insolvent debtors whose lives had been shattered by the long war on the island, reprobates who had landed up at Agathyrna in Sicily, their desperation increased by the knowledge they would certainly receive death sentences if the authorities decided to prosecute them. The consul Laevinus, in charge on the island since 210, knew a tough and resourceful lot when he saw them and judging they would be bound to cause him trouble if they stayed put, decided to transport them to Rhegium. There they could boost the capacity of the garrison to do damage to the Carthaginians and their friends in Bruttium who had for years been enjoying the independence from Rome that Hannibal's successes allowed. There were 4,000 of them, a significant enough addition to the command, allowing an increase on the occasional forays made in the past. Now the Romans could not only be much more confident in their capacity to hold the town but could increase their efforts to harry their many enemies in the region.

Tit for tat raiding was the pattern of years between Rhegium and Locri, the nearest major enemy. It is contended that Hannibal's Numidians had shown the way to the local Bruttians in a life of pillage, but the reality was they needed little encouragement and their Roman rivals had not been laggard in taking up the practice either, particularly since the new arrivals from Sicily had added extra enthusiasm and aptitude to these enterprises. Locri itself, where the extensive defensive walls can still be imagined from the foundations that remain today, would have overawed people at the time. This place continued to be a very tough competitor so when an opportunity arose, the command at Rhegium decided to pull out all the stops. What happened was that sometime early in 205 raiders out of Rhegium had a windfall when they came across a number of Locrians outside the city walls and whisked them back to their base. A number of these unfortunates were workmen who had been engaged in refurbishing the defences of one of the place's two citadels. And it turned out when some Locrian aristocrats, long exiled at Rhegium, visited them in prison and quizzed them about what had been going on back home they found they were willing to sell out their Carthaginian employers. The ransom for these men was quickly organized and a system of signals agreed so that once they were back working on the citadel defences they could facilitate the ingress of an attacking force that was rapidly being prepared .

The Locrian blue bloods then travelled from Rhegium to Syracuse to meet Scipio and the young general found them in his antechamber selling an attractive opportunity. Even if it seemed to deflect from his main push, to train his forces and settle Sicily as a solid base before invading Africa, still this opportunity to do a bit of useful housekeeping on the mainland was welcome enough. The chance to take a swipe directly at Hannibal in Bruttium was always going to be attractive after the censure Scipio had got for concentrating on his idea of Africa to the detriment of the effort against the Carthaginian presence on the Peninsula. So he ordered an officer named Quintus Pleminius to draw 3,000 men from the Rhegium garrison and assist the Locrian exiles in making their attempt against the citadel, where the bought workmen where labouring and living. The campaign itself unfolded as the men from Rhegium and their allies after a few days' march approached the walls of the town. It would have been a short but difficult journey whether they took the direct route through the Aspromonte Mountains or even along the coast where the mountains falling almost straight into the sea made travel far from easy. But these men were well-prepared, even being equipped with ladders specially made on the specifications supplied by the workmen, to reach the top of the fortress they were intending to attack.

Once on hand and alerted by prearranged fire signals the invaders were up and over the walls before the alarm was given, their own bespoke ladders being supplemented by others lowered by the fifth column in the citadel. Bustling in around midnight with a scintillation of stars overhead in the night sky, they killed many of the sleeping guards before the rest stirred. Though once Hamilcar, the Carthaginian commander, was woken and on the scene he soon got some order into the defenders. But by then the garrison was deeply unnerved by the racket raised by the assailants still below the walls and disorientated by the darkness. So believing they were being attacked by a much larger force than they really were, they decided the best policy was to retreat to the other citadel where they were still in control, withdrawing by moonlight in decent order.

Now it was a war between the two forts with skirmishing a-plenty in the narrow and nocturnal streets. The destruction must have been great, a warning for the Locrians that the introduction of these Roman raiders was not going to be without its drawbacks for their city. Both sides now looked round desperately for support as this local spat sucked in the major players. Hannibal had been contacted by Hamilcar and came down from Croton, stopping at the River Bulotus to send scouts forward to discover the latest situation before the crossing proceeded smoothly. Once he had a clear idea of what was happening orders were dispatched to his garrison commander charging that first thing the next day he must fall on the enemy from his stronghold in the town, while Hannibal brought his men up to attack from the outside. This cooperation between the two bodies of troops was key, but on approaching things began to go wrong. Hannibal realized he could only easily enter by going in through the citadel, but doing this would mean his men would have little room to deploy once inside the walls. The alternative of assaulting elsewhere along the city ramparts was even more problematic as scaling ladders had not yet been brought up. So instead he decided to try and intimidate the defenders. He 'paraded his army close to the walls' and ordered his Numidian horse to ride round the town to both threaten the garrison and explore for weak spots that his men, once prepared, might utilize.

But not long after, it appears missiles from an engine on the fortifications drove the attackers away to take up a position out of range. While this disorganized stuff was underway the defenders' morale was boosted as they received information that Scipio himself was on his way with a considerable army and that these reinforcements would soon be disembarking at the town port. He had shipped over the straits from Messene, leaving his brother Lucius in charge on the Sicilian shore and sailing with all the soldiers he had to hand, when he heard that Hannibal might be making an appearance. They beached early enough that they could disembark and enter the city before darkness fell. The very next day it came extremely close to a direct clash between Hannibal and Scipio, an event that would only occur in Africa a few years later on the battlefield of Zama. The Carthaginian, unaware of the increased strength of his enemy, was intent on a proper escalade now the paraphernalia, ladders, sheds and rams, his men needed were ready and Hamilcar again primed to cooperate in the attack. But on approaching the city walls, the gates swung wide and the Roman army, the men from Rhegium and Scipio's too, deployed out in serried ranks in double quick time. The arrival of these tough-looking men adept at swift manoeuvre apparently totally unnerved the Carthaginians and they precipitously withdrew to their defended camp receiving 200 casualties in the process.

When night came Hannibal decided he was too exposed even in his defended camp and while the step off of his own soldiers back on the road to Croton was ordered, he let the men in the citadel know that they must shift for themselves the best they could. This turned out to be organizing their evacuation as soon as possible with Hamilcar, after distracting the enemy by setting fire to the house his men occupied, piloted his Numidians and Spaniards north up the coast in the footsteps of his leader, moving so fast they soon overtook him on the road. The story being clearly peddled here is that Hannibal was intimidated by the very presence of Scipio and while this may have appealed to the Roman tradition it is not really likely. In truth on this second day when the Romans came out to face him it became clear he was considerably outnumbered and had no chance if he stayed to fight.

The initial assault force from Rhegium had alone consisted of 3,000 men and more and adding to these the decent numbers Scipio himself must have brought over from Messene would have made a considerable army, while Hannibal, rushing to help Hamilcar, had come with only a few Numidians and those of his infantry he could get on the road in double quick time. So it was not an intimidated but a prudent general who declined battle against crippling odds. Locri was important but not so important he could risk the precious men he had with him, who could be much better employed in making his bastion around Croton more secure.

A postscript to these events is instructive, even if much could be an elaboration 200 years after the event. What is apparent is the friends of Rome at Locri had little chance of revelling in their liberation before they found the people who had won the day saw them more as foreign enemies to be plundered than old friends to be cosseted. And more than this the particular individuals whose power they had come under were an awful lot. Quintus Pleminius, given command over the town by Scipio after its recapture, turned out a rebarbative man who not only brutalized the population, but fell out with his military tribunes and the troops, with divided loyalty, ended up fighting each other over the loot extracted from the citizenry. Atrocities resulted, with first the military tribunes being scourged and then Pleminius suffering violent disfigurement when he fell into his rivals' control. In all this Pleminius justified a vicious reputation as aping the sea monsters of the narrows between Italy and Sicily, by looting the Temple of Proserpine, a goddess so protective of her wealth that when Pyrrhus of Epirus stripped the shrine and loaded his ill-gotten gains aboard his ships, he found his fleet was wrecked and the gold cast back on the coast to be returned to the deity's treasury. Indeed it was claimed that Pleminius' desecration had been the direct cause of the bloody infighting between the Roman factions after the goddess had driven all those involved mad.

Rancorous personal rivalry was pretty much a Roman way of life, and the tendency of their officers to indulge in competition while the enemy were still at the gate is well-attested throughout and '*inimicitiae*' or enmity was part of the lifeblood of political life.[6] It was accepted indeed, almost demanded, that payback would be a dominant motivation. These were not a turn-the-other-cheek people and a failure to use all one's influence and power to hit at an enemy would be seen as weakness and could badly affect a person's reputation. It was carried down generations too; sons taking on the feuds of their fathers, and even those of important clients too, were required to sustain the family name. But this brew ha-ha down south had taken things to a new level. The general and the military tribunes had turned their personal vendettas into a blood feud, arranging the most extreme physical assaults and their behaviour, both towards each other, and towards locals who had helped them to success, had been shocking even for a people, whose anyway thin humanity, had been further worn down over thirteen years of desperate war.

Much may be exaggeration but the tableau is vivid of desperate folk from Locri who had travelled to Rome, really hamming it up when they got to the Comitium in front of the Senate and found themselves in the presence of the consuls, dressed in rags with olive branches in hand with fillets on their brows and prostrating themselves with 'pitiful cries and floods of tears'. They came with complaints about what had been done to them. The man involved in plundering the Locrians would get his due desserts in the fullness of time. Indeed there are a number of accounts of what happened to the disagreeable Pleminius. One claims that he attempted to flee to Neapolis but was caught on the road, while another has Scipio arresting him and handing him over to the commission sent to investigate the citizens' complaints. His end may have come at Rome, dying in prison before he could be tried, and after dabbling in arson and attempting a prison break. But if the man on the spot had to answer for what he had done it could be claimed that he was just an underling, whose commander-in-chief bore some responsibility for what had gone on. This was Scipio and though not present when the outrages at Locri took place he had enemies back home who intended to make every effort to taint him with responsibility.

Tensions between the factions within Roman political classes, particularly those supporting Scipio and those backing Fabius, were being sustained as viciously as ever. The arguments highlighted in late 206, when Scipio had returned from Spain over his strategy of attacking Carthage, had not gone away. And the Fabians remained as determined to clip the wings of the conqueror of Spain and were prepared to use any weapons that came to hand. The representatives from Locri had not wanted to involve the young general in their complaints, not desiring to make an enemy of this powerful man, but they found that when he questioned them, Fabius for one was looking to use their issues as a stick with which to beat his rival. In fact the old man's first questions were about whether they had gone to Scipio with their grievances and if so what his response had been. The delegates explained they had felt he would be too busy with his preparations to invade

Africa and also that having backed the chain of command by supporting Pleminius over the tribunes, that that man's influence would ensure they would not be given a fair hearing. There was no intended criticism of Scipio here, no claim he was involved in their ruin, but their interrogator would not let it go at that.

When the supplicants left the senators' presence Fabius expanded on how not only should Pleminius receive dire punishment and the temple gods placated with recompense and more, but that Scipio who had been in overall charge must be brought to book too. That it should not be just the underlings who should suffer but that the man in overall charge of the campaign must shoulder his share of responsibility. Those who remained deeply disturbed both by the extraordinary success Scipio had won at such a young age and the policy of taking on the Carthaginians in their own backyard had by no means accepted as a 'fait accompli' that he should be left undisturbed in Sicily preparing for his invasion of Africa. Now the behaviour of the officer he left in charge at Locri had given them another opening and while the details of the debate are open to question, like so many such set pieces in our ancient histories, the senatorial discussions reported point up the thinking of plenty in that body. Fabius led the charge, deriding Scipio as incapable of properly leading a Roman army, claiming that his condoning of Pleminius' action was typical of a man who had let the troops get out of hand in Spain, allowing such indiscipline that it eventually led to mutiny, that things were so lax not just amongst his men but the officers too, who it was claimed were wallowing in the fleshpots of Syracuse and had forgotten all about Hannibal and Carthage. And that apart from that Scipio had exceeded the mandate of his command by entering Bruttium the province of his consular colleague, Crassus.

It apparently took days for everyone to have their say and for many it turned out it was Scipio's grecophile leanings that seemed to cause the most affront. He certainly opened himself up to this kind of thing over the years, advertising that he knew his Herodotus and Xenophon. Even aping Agesilaus, the Spartan king in his Asian war in the 390s, when he exploited the local gentry in Sicily to equip and train 300 cavalrymen, so they themselves could avoid the call-up to fight in Africa. And in advance of the Battle of Zama in 202 he would clearly reference Xerxes' actions before invading Europe when, on capturing some Carthaginian spies near his army, he invited them in to take a detailed look at his army's strength before returning them unharmed, assuming that their reports would unnerve his enemy. Not that he was alone; plenty of other prominent men were philhellenes too but they had not become the greatest warrior in Rome while hardly 30, so were not such targets for xenophobes of the old school, whose accusation told across the classes of a population still deeply hidebound and traditionalist. Cato the Elder, who would make a name in later years for hounding Scipio Africanus and generally harassing elite grecophiles, was also vocal, offering appropriate intellectual mood music, bitter from his time under Scipio in Sicily when as quaestor they fell out over his claiming that the general was too generous to his troops. In all the world cultural indebtedness usually meant ambivalence and resentment and it was certainly the dominant leitmotif in Roman Greek relations. However much they plagiarized their literature or cannibalized their rhetorical tradition, however de rigueur it was to buy an expensive Greek slave to educate one's children, it did not stop the predominant feeling that Greeks were slippery and somehow unmanly and the desire to embrace all things Hellenic could easily be interpreted as being anti Roman.

Quintus Metellus, who had been not only consul in 206 but dictator in the months just gone, given the top job to take care of the elections, and who is reported being the one to personally put the manacles on Pleminius on the road to Napoli too, tried to deflect feeling against Scipio, reminding them of his service done in Spain and that now they were depending on him to end the war. He agreed the Locri situation had to be addressed, but arguing that there was no evidence that the young commander had been involved, rejected the idea he should be withdrawn before it was discovered if he had been at all culpable. His solution was eventually approved in the Senate: to send a ten-man commission the next year to investigate both what happened at Locri and the other allegations against the young general. But if Pleminius was made to pay, his commander-in-chief eventually came off scot-free, as whatever the concerns of the ten-man commission they were trumped when they saw the efficient and eager army and fleet going through their evolutions in and around Syracuse harbour in preparation for a descent on the Libyan coast. But if Scipio was exonerated on this occasion, there had been a real sword of Damocles hovering over his head, with the threat of arrest if he had not convinced the ten-man board, showing that those who had opposed him and his African plans had not gone away and were still looking for any slip-up to try and derail his plans.

Chapter 11

Endgame

Of all that befell the Romans and Carthaginians, good or bad, the
cause was one man and one mind – Hannibal. For it is notorious that
he managed the Italian campaigns in person, and the Spanish by the
agency of the elder of his brothers, Hasdrubal, and subsequently by
that of Mago, the leaders who killed the two Roman generals in Spain
about the same time. Again, he conducted the Sicilian campaign at first
through Hippocrates and afterwards through Myttonus the Libyan. So
also in Greece and Illyria: and, by brandishing before their faces the
dangers arising from these latter places, he was enabled to distract the
attention of the Romans, thanks to his understanding with Philip. So
great and wonderful is the influence of a Man, and a mind duly fitted
by original constitution for any undertaking within the reach of human
powers.

Polybius, *Histories*, Book 9. 22.

The armies of Rome in the few years past had been pushing out
from Tarentum and down along the instep of the Italian boot,
where a wide coastal plain was dotted with other Greek towns like
Metapontum and Heraclea before the mountains came in to curtail but not
rule out settlement. Attempts had been made to suck up places even further
along this coast from earlier in the conflict; Caulonia particularly had been a
target of a Roman fightback. Even before, this town positioned between the
mouth of the Assi and Stilaro rivers, where ruined columns, now underwater,
remember the probably Achaean foundation, suffered much in its short life.
It may have been subject to Croton in its early years but by the end of the
fifth century as an Athenian ally it experienced attack by Syracuse and was
burned down during the Peloponnesian War, before being later taken over
by Dionysius I, who destroyed the buildings, shipped its people to his home
city and presented its territory to his Locrian allies. Refounded it was razed
two more times, the last occasion in the Pyrrhus War, and was eventually

destroyed by the Romans in 200, when the population was moved upriver to another settlement in the hills. So it was a place that had suffered plenty before it was assaulted in 209, when orders from Rome activated the men in Rhegium. The commander there, who had been boosted by a number of Bruttium deserters of the Punic cause, hurried to wreck all the enemy farmland they could reach before making a concerted attack on Caulonia itself. On this occasion when Hannibal responded he found the motley lot troubling his allies were no great challenge, forcing them with hardly a fight to raise the siege and retire to some 'high ground' where he compelled their surrender after besieging them in their unsound refuge.

Yet if the Carthaginians had sustained themselves against this local offensive, by the year 204 the Romans had gained mastery as far down as the wide acres around the valley of the Crathis and Sybaris rivers, where the riches garnered had made the first Greek settlement there notorious. The very name became synonymous with a life of luxury. Sybaris town, settled from 720 BC by people from Achaea and Troezen, became so prosperous its elite were famed for their indulgent and opulent lifestyle. But riches invite envy and in 510/509 the city was destroyed by a coalition of neighbours led by Croton. After several failed attempts at refoundation, Thurii had risen out of the desolation very nearby, as a successor city sponsored as a Panhellenic enterprise by the great Pericles in 446, with celebrities like Herodotus the historian and Lysias the rhetorician, and later hero of Athens' fight against her thirty tyrants, living there at times. Battered by the Bruttians in the middle fourth century and fighting with the Tarentines over the rich meadows of the Siritis well to the north, these contests eventually brought Rome in and provided a *casus belli* for that people's assault on Tarentum in 282. This town had been one of many that cleaved to Hannibal either straight after Cannae or perhaps when Tarentum was won by the Carthaginians in 313. The community had remained a Punic stronghold, even receiving a population boost when the Carthaginian-inclined folk from Atella, who had survived the return of the Romans, were relocated there. Though like Caulonia it became a target for the Romans as soon as control of Sicily gave a good base for the attempt and in 204, under threat, 3,500 of the most prosperous citizens were relocated to Croton, with their ox-carts loaded with what goods they could carry rumbling along the road south, and the place given over to Hannibal's troops to plunder, accumulating treasure that was not only a valuable addition to army funds, but ensured the Romans would find as little as possible for their own use when they arrived.

Publius Sempronius Tuditanus would be the last real opponent Hannibal would face on Italian soil and the first since Nero to offer him a real test. This Roman was an impressive character, reputed if almost contemporary sources distilled through the historian Coelius Antipater are credited, for cutting his way out with 600 men from the charnel house that was Cannae to find refuge at Canusium, who we also find elected as curule aedile, two years later, and then given Ariminum as a praetor level command the year after that. It is also noticed that both he and his colleague Marcus Cornelius Cethegus, when they became censors in 209, were generally regarded as young and inexperienced having still not served as consuls, suggesting a real military reputation to warrant such early attainment of high office, during which stint as censor he was famous for overruling his colleague to make Fabius the new 'princeps senatus', indicating a political connection with the 'delayer'. Most recently in the year before he reached the pinnacle as consul he had done well in Greece, showing real capacity and energy in freeing up this front by arranging a general peace.

This commander in 204, after his posting to Bruttium, needed to raise almost a new army to replace the diseased remnant who had survived the plague that devastated both sides the year before. Things had been so bad in the Roman camp that it had been proposed that the affected legions should be disbanded, though the men under the previous consul, Publius Licinius Crassus, had been kept in sufficiently good shape that his command was extended to ensure some continuity where a still dangerous Hannibal ranged untamed. By the summer two legions had been raised and Sempronius was feeling secure enough to act, knowing Titus Quinctius Flamininus, the later victor over Philip of Macedon, was still holding Tarentum solid as indeed he had the year before. With two armies eventually scraped together, an advanced base was established probably at Thurii, from where the soldiers prepared to march. This area had suffered like so many places in the war with agricultural productivity well down, but still the men would have been sufficiently supplied from this naturally fertile region as they took to the road.

Hannibal would have expected his enemy's coming and despite the decrease in the amount of real estate he controlled, still the Carthaginian general never lacked confidence. What exactly he had to fight the new consul off with at this time is difficult to estimate, yet there is some evidence on the make-up of Hannibal's army at this butt end of the Italian War. He certainly still had some Numidians and African troops, as Hamilcar had brought just such veterans with him when he evacuated the garrison of Locris in 205 to join his commander-in-chief at Croton, while some few of their comrades might have been Spaniards and Gauls and a number of Balearic slingers no doubt remained as well, though presumably like the rest they would have suffered heavy attrition since they arrived in the Peninsula. There would also have been those Campanians, Samnites, Lucanians, Apulians and Roman deserters who had been recruited since the great victories of the first years and had survived the campaigning that followed. People who had no confidence at all in the possibility of anything except instant death at the hands of the Romans if they tried to return to home communities that had either by negotiation or assault been brought back into the Republic's fold. But one thing is clear though, if these accounted for some of the best men, much of the army's ranks were filled with tough warriors recruited locally in Bruttium over the last few years.

Any essaying of absolute numbers can only be based on guesswork, yet guesswork predicated on some evidence. When Hannibal returned to Africa he took with him between 12,000 and 20,000 of the best men from his Italian corps, but these were far from being the whole of those who had been fighting in Carthaginian ranks in 204 and 203. Many who were prepared to fight for Hannibal in Italy would not have agreed to leave their homeland with a strong prospect of dying on foreign shores. And anyway the fleet scraped together to evacuate Hannibal's army of Italy was far from roomy enough for everybody. We know valuable horses and other transport animals were put down because there were no places for them, so there undoubtedly would have been men he wanted to take but for whom room just could not be found on board ship. Equally some garrisons had to be left to hold the towns Hannibal still controlled, that might be useful if he was able to come back later or at worst would ensure a diversion of Roman military resources to deal with them. All this must have meant he could have mustered at least double the 12,000–20,000 that left, suggesting the great Carthaginian had something towards 30,000 men to draw on as a mobile force against the enemy coming down against him from Thurii. This would mean he could field in battle the numbers of a two legion consular army or more, and moreover many of these men had had years of experience of victory against the Romans in battle and their already keen edge was now honed by desperation. Every man under arms knew there was no hope of mercy from the foe they were facing if they allowed themselves to be defeated.

The Bruttians who made up so many of his men were going to be very useful to Hannibal in the fighting to come. They might be derided as little better than brigands by some sources but they excelled in irregular fighting and their commander intended just this kind of encounter when his outposts brought news that the enemy was piling down the road from the north. Hannibal had his back to the wall now waiting at Croton, which had been his base for the last years of the Italian War. An ancient Greek traveller, while emphasizing the advantages of Tarentum's siting, tells us something of this place:

> One may judge of the excellence of its situation from the prosperity attained by the people of Croton; who, though only possessing roadsteads suitable for the summer, and enjoying therefore but a short season of mercantile activity, still have acquired great wealth, entirely owing, it seems, to the favourable situation of their town and harbour, which yet cannot be compared with those of Tarentum.[1]

To anyone who has explored the coast, this small town is discovered sitting prettily on its headland with distinctive star-shaped castle and overlooked by clay brown cliffs. It had been a much greater place in ancient times. Founded by Achaeans in 710 it was particularly famous as the base of Pythagoras who shipped up there around 530 having travelled the world, forced out of Samos by a people who made just too many demands on his precious time. The likes of Milo, the celebrity wrestler, was a disciple of the great thinker, but success brought resentment and eventually the organizations of Pythagoras' followers were supressed and the man himself driven out to Tarentum and Metapontum where he starved himself to death, leaving a tomb claimed to have been seen half a millennia later by Cicero.[2] Croton was also famed for its physicians, with one such reported by Herodotus as treating the Persian king, Darius the Great.[3] More than two centuries before Hannibal, warriors from there had encompassed the downfall of Sybaris and later had headed a league of cities significant enough to both take on Dionysius I of Syracuse and keep local Italian peoples in check. But more recently it had suffered. It is suggested that before the Pyrrhus War people had marvelled at the twelve miles of Croton's walls stretching almost twice as far as Rome's Servian defences, with a concomitantly considerable population, but in that conflict the population had been cut in half with the River Esaro that once had flowed through inhabited areas now hardly reaching peopled neighbourhoods at all.

There is even a claim that only 2,000 people remained living in the town including 'boys and the aged' but this must be an exaggeration.[4]

Any revival in the city's fortune had not been facilitated by the conflict precipitated by the arrival of Carthaginian armies. The Bruttians, despite espousing the newcomer's cause, had been frustrated by their ally's refusal to allow them to pillage the cities on the coast. These locals had joined up largely to have a go at plundering these Greeks they had envied and disliked for centuries but soon realized that Hannibal wanted these places as friends and allies, not wrecked out husks with the people despoiled and the infrastructure devastated. The Bruttians, who joined up to assail both Locri and Rhegium soon after the Carthaginians arrived, found that at the first place Hannibal absolutely barred them from looting the town when it surrendered and in the latter Roman reinforcements coming from Sicily ensured that neither they nor the Punic forces were able to take it over. But with Croton they determined it would be different, as a force of 15,000 local warriors were 'enrolled and equipped' and marched, this time without their allies, against the harbour town intent on not being baulked of their prey.

In the target city there were divisions amongst the population, the not untypical split between local aristocrats who wanted to cleave to Rome and others who hoped for the kind of change siding with the Carthaginians might bring. In fact the latter led by a man called Aristomachus had already gone a good way to taking control, with many of the wealthier folk establishing a defended bolthole in the citadel. This refuge was pretty secure with cliffs on the sea side and steep well-walled slopes around the rest. Indeed even the cliffs were topped with tower stitched defences, the locals having been stung into building action after an army from Syracuse stealthily entered that way, a couple of centuries before when it was still unguarded. When the Bruttium army arrived they learnt of all this and more from a deserter who also explained that because the walls were so long and encompassed many deserted neighbourhoods, they were poorly manned and anyway most of the sentries belonging as they did to Aristomachus' party were not likely to put up much resistance. And this, as it turned out, was the case with the advancing army being let in without a fight, though undoubtedly with the expectation on the part of the citizens that they were acting on behalf of their Carthaginian friends.

Yet despite taking control of the town the Bruttians and their Crotonian supporters found their efforts to capture the citadel thwarted. These Italians were not hot on siege warfare and were forced to ask Hanno and his Carthaginian engineers for help, but found him on his arrival less interested in taking the citadel, than in sorting out a solution that would include many of the Bruttians settling in the town in an effort to restore the depleted population. But only Aristomachus was buying this while most of the inhabitants, of whichever party, were deeply concerned they might be swamped by any intrusion of country hicks, bringing with them their own laws and customs. Finally matters were resolved when the Locrians took a hand and backed by Hannibal persuaded the group holed up in the citadel and some of the commons to slip out, board ships in the port and migrate to their town, an evacuation that allowed the Bruttians, who probably facilitated the departure, to take over an almost deserted town that held firm to the Punic cause for the rest of the war.

That had been back in 215, but Hannibal was there now, in his own backyard waiting behind the defences of Croton, which despite the city being much reduced still stretched over the higher land around, currently not occupied by the modern habitations that cluster round the small harbour. But though he had a considerable fortress to defend the Carthaginian general sitting in his headquarters in 204 had no intention of staying behind its walls. As soon as he became aware of the enemy's movement he laid up in wait on their route. When Sempronius and his army approached the town they crossed the modern River Passovecchio sending up clouds of marine birds as they passed with the sea on their left, entering country open and flat enough, but still with ample folds in the ground and wooded cover to allow an ambush. The Romans were hit hard while in marching column and were never able to deploy properly into line as Hannibal's men smashed into them. So the invaders remained at a disadvantage throughout the whole combat, which was sufficiently bloody with Sempronius losing 1,200 men in the scrimmage. The consul tried for a pull-away to form a battle line but was never able to do so, with the enemy pressing his rear all the way. And unable to control his soldiers in action, it was not long before he felt his only option was to fall back to the defended camp the men had constructed the day before. Hannibal followed, but despite the momentum engendered by success decided it would not be to his men's advantage to involve them in trench warfare around the palisades confronting them.

The Romans, with little choice, decided to wait behind their defences until an opportunity occurred to make contact with the other army under Licinius Crassus. This arose when the Carthaginians pulled back after the defenders showed they would not come out from behind their wooden walls and fight. When night fell Sempronius, ordering his men to keep total silence, led them creeping in the dark, out of their encampment and towards a rendezvous point he had contrived to convey to his subordinate. These friends had been encamped some way away but on hearing of the consul's defeat on the first day moved quickly to join him. And if we believe the histories, Sempronius, once reinforced, determined to have another crack at Hannibal, deciding to stake all in a single throw against the best player in the world. The consul, at the head of two armies now and with recovered confidence, deployed for battle with an enemy who themselves, well pleased with recent success, were apparently happy to put things to the hazard of combat once more. This encounter unlike the earlier fight is claimed as a set piece affair, with both sides arranging their forces in the open, unconstrained either by cramped terrain or being in marching column. Any fighting presumably must have taken place in the coastal plain to the north of Croton as anywhere else the country is too rugged for two large armies to easily come to blows. Sempronius took the position at the front with the two legions he had raised, while Licinius Crassus' men were held back in reserve. Apart from this no details are vouched safe apart from that a decisive Roman victory was achieved, with Hannibal loosing eleven military standards, 4,000 men killed and 300 captured, losses that forced even this resourceful commander to withdraw and find safety behind the walls of Croton.

This last considerable campaign in southern Italy encapsulates so many of the difficulties with using Livy as a detailed source. It is the old story of a defeat for Roman arms followed directly on its heels by a compensating victory that does not really tally with what comes after. This pattern is plain on many occasions, the two most obvious examples being the third day's fighting at Canusium in 209, constructed to compensate for the Roman defeat on the previous day; and during the war in Spain when, after the destruction of the two Scipios' armies, a young knight called Marcius rallied the survivors and it is claimed with just these scraps of decimated legions turned the tables on two victorious Carthaginian armies. On this occasion the only evidence suggesting that anything was really achieved by Sempronius in 204 is the report that, having vowed to build the Temple to Fortuna in return for victory over Hannibal, ten years later he did indeed consecrate one in the north of Rome on the Quirinal Hill. It might be argued that surely he would not have made such a public display if it was common knowledge that he had been defeated in Bruttium those years before, but as so often it is the aftermath that calls into question the veracity of these accounts of significant victory after earlier defeat. The consul's behaviour after the battle clearly shows a reluctance to further tangle head-on with the enemy. Why, if the Carthaginians had been so well thrashed and lost so many men, did the Romans not push on and chase them back to Croton and try to take the place? There certainly was absolutely no suggestion that this was even contemplated and indeed all we are told is that the two Roman armies, far from pressing a dishevelled and wounded enemy, themselves withdrew back the way they had come.

Nor is much sure about what the consul and his colleagues did in the rest of the campaigning season either. There are claims of real success, that if they could not take Croton at least they got back some other cities in the region. Clampetia on the Tyrrhenian coast is reported as being stormed as well as the inland Bruttium towns of Consentia and Pandosia. But even these achievements are difficult to credit completely as others have it that it had been Licinius Crassus the year before who had brought over seven towns in Bruttium that included Consentia.[5] It is not really possible to know in which year these events occurred, or even if different places came over at different times or to what extent these represented much of a military success anyway. It seems very possible that the plague and famine in 205 had been the deciding factor. These towns had been solid for Hannibal for years and Rome-haters for generations and it is difficult to imagine them countenancing any change of allegiance with the Roman armies still so tentative in their dealings with Hannibal. But devastated by disease and without anything but roots and grass to eat they would certainly have considered giving in to an enemy, who even if known to be intractably vengeful still at least would, once they had surrendered, be in a position to bring in desperately needed corn from Campania, Sicily or Sardinia. Slavery might seem attractive when the alternative was certain starvation.

Whatever the exact details the feeling here is not at all of triumphant Roman armies pushing hard down the Peninsula and evicting an enemy who over a decade before had shattered their old hegemony. All that seems to have been happening at this time was that as the Carthaginians withdrew from certain of their remaining strongholds in Bruttium to make their redoubt around Croton more defensible, or in preparation for evacuation, the Romans were able to snap up these abandoned places. Nor is the confusion about the details lessened by what is claimed for the following year. This involved Gaius Servilius Geminus, a man whose great claim to fame was that in 202 he was the last dictator, brought in to supervise elections, until the time of Sulla in the first century when the defunct practice was resurrected to impose a real bloodbath tyranny. One of the consuls for the year 203, he was given Bruttium as his province, and it is not only asserted that he came to blows with the Carthaginian army but also to have captured some of the same Bruttium towns that were chalked up as successes for Sempronius the year before.

This lack of significant offensive military activity in the last year of the Italian War suggests that the Romans remained just as wary as they had always been of approaching Hannibal directly. And in fact though the Peninsula did see its fair share of fighting in 203 it mainly occurred far away at the other end. There in the north much had happened after a Carthaginian army had made its move from out of the fastness of Liguria. The man in charge of this incursion was another brother of Hannibal called Mago, who had arrived on the scene in the summer of 205. He was about five years younger than Hannibal and so even more the product of an Iberian upbringing and is the one sibling not mentioned as accompanying his father Hamilcar when that man died in a skirmish not far from modern Alicante on the banks of a Spanish river. Hardly surprising as he was only 15 at the time, but by the time the Battle of Trebbia was fought he was old enough to have an impact and it was he who rose in ambush out of the river marshes to flail into the back of the enemy formations with his 2,200 strong force of infantry and cavalry. He was also the key man commanding the rearguard when the Carthaginian column trailed south through the Arno marshes to triumph over Flaminius at Lake Trasimene. At Cannae this young commander stood with Hannibal himself in the centre, holding together the withdrawing Gauls and Spaniards and creating the mouth of the tactical bag that the Romans walked into, without breaking step, to their destruction.

It was also this Barca who returned to Carthage to tip, in the most dramatic fashion, the bag of gold rings taken from the equates and senators who had died in the battle, in front of the city's ruling council. There is a famous account of this incident where the valiant young warrior showed off the spoils won by his brother's army and called for this success to be reinforced with all that Carthage could muster. But he is contradicted by a political rival named Hanno who, taunted by a Barcid supporter, makes the point that if Hannibal had had the success he claimed in Italy he clearly did not need assistance and that if he had not, it would be dangerous to throw resources at a war that might well turn out badly. This dialogue in the end had little effect on an administration that was always going to be behind the party that had brought such success, though what occurred next did point out a problem that would remain to dog Hannibal through all the years of the Italian War. The intention behind Mago's return home had been to win military and financial support for his brother and initially it looked like this would materialize. But finally the 12,000 infantry, 1,500 cavalry and twenty elephants Mago was given were redirected to Spain after news arrived of his other brother Hasdrubal's bloody defeat at Dertosa. Once returned to Iberia this youngest Barcid brother played an active role, taking part in defeating the two Scipios in 211. But then with the rest of an ill coordinated high command he had allowed the younger Scipio to take Carthago Nova in 209 and then defeat the Carthaginian armies in detail.

In these years he had been particularly active in the south-west, around Gades or recruiting between the Tagus and the Douro rivers, though certainly present in 206 at the disaster at Ilipa, that put the finishing touches to the Roman efforts to dig the Carthaginians out of the Peninsula. He afterwards led a failed assault on Carthago Nova, before crucifying some magistrates from Gades who showed an inclination to make terms with Scipio. But unable to defend even this last base on the mainland he betook himself to the Balearic Islands, places that had long been under Punic influence. There he recruited more men to carry out the instructions he had received from home while still at Gades to take an army to northern Italy. After wintering in Minorca Hannibal's youngest brother materialized off the coast of Liguria, with a fleet of thirty warships and many more transports. Aboard these was an expeditionary force of 14,000 men, comprising 12,000 foot and 2,000 horse. The descent was unexpected and without any resistance to speak of he took over Genoa as a handy base, before moving west towards country where the mountains dropped directly down to the sea and he expected to find locals happy to join in a war against Rome. The people he hoped to enrol were the Ingauni, Ligurian hunters, herdsmen and foresters, hard men living very close to subsistence and inclined to brigandage, piracy and lucrative mercenary employment when it was available. To get an in with the local leadership Mago was first required to give backing in fighting some rivals called the Epanterii Montani, an intervention that worked, recruiting went well and 'his strength grew daily'.

The time this took allowed the new threat to become known at Rome where it caused a sensation; that another son of Barca had shipped up in the Peninsula intent on wreckage. It seemed they would never see the last of this family and now word came that this latest arrival had just been significantly reinforced by a Carthaginian leadership worried about the war moving to Africa and hoping to throw such a scare into their enemy that they would insist on the legions being kept back for their own protection. But if this intimidation largely failed against a community who had recently seen off another Barca brother on the Metaurus, it at least ensured a robust response. The proconsul in Etruria was ordered to take some slave volunteers to Ariminum, while a praetor was briefed to dispatch two city legions north to Arretum if he thought they were needed to block Mago's advance. Seven legions in all were deployed on this front with Livius, the conqueror of Hasdrubal, still charged with defending against any threat coming down from the north.

While his adversary drew up a defensive cordon, the next year looked to be one of useful gains for Mago. It had become clear there were people in northern Italy who wanted to take the opportunity of his arrival to get out from under the baleful hegemony of the Roman Republic; what is described as the whole of Etruria being eager to find a liberator and large numbers of local bigwigs made contact personally, or through agents with the Carthaginian camp. But if these revealing moves indicated there were potential friends within the borders of Roman Italy, just outside opportunities were even greater. In a riot of plaid cloth and gold torcs, at Gallic tribal councils in the Po Valley, war leaders and their councillors gathered to try and decide what was in the best interests of their peoples. They needed to agree how they should respond to the presence of the man who had just arrived in their bailiwick. They knew him to be not only a great Carthaginian officer, Hannibal's brother, but one who even since his arrival had not only recruited successfully amongst the Ligurians but had also just received considerable reinforcements from Carthage: 6,000 infantry, 800 cavalry, seven elephants and plenty of money indicated a commitment from home that could not help but impress. With such backing he was beginning to look like a good bet. But if these tribes of Cisalpine Gauls were natural warriors spoiling for a fight they still wanted to end up on the winning side and the experience of a generation gave them pause.

These men were as competitive and warlike as their Roman or Carthaginian equivalents, but not suicidal and they had received brutally instructive lessons from their central Italian enemy over the last decades. There had been bloody defeats in 225 at Telamon and at Clastidium in 222 and if in Hannibal's war they had prospered then came the Metaurus fight. Brutal

Roman retaliation and the reimposition of Latin colonies in the Po Valley had been most of the story of the recent past. Also there was a large Roman army just over the border in Etruria and another already crossed into their country. So feeling they could not openly take his side they refused to give official help to Mago, despite that most privately sympathized with his cause. This attitude was not what he had hoped for, the support proffered was limited, but he set about making the most of what was available. Recruiting agents were secretly dispatched to visit Gallic settlements where they knew plenty of the young men would join up, particularly when they became aware their leaders, though remaining officially neutral, were furnishing Mago with supplies. The Ligurian chiefs left, promising to raise more fighting men in two months. For them it was different: in their hilltop fastness they had felt less of Roman retribution, so signed up willingly and in numbers to line up alongside the Iberians and Africans who had arrived in their country. Two years after, Zama, a Carthaginian officer left behind after either Hasdrubal's or Mago's incursion, was still finding local support to fight the Romans despite his home city having had a conquest peace forced upon her. The response to Mago's recruiting sergeants amongst both peoples, though it could have been worse, still meant the numbers enlisted under his banners were not quite sufficient to justify any advance much beyond the Po Valley.

But it was a ripple elsewhere that perhaps suggests Roman concern about the northern threat was at least proportionate. Etruria was restless again and the problem needed to be nipped in the bud. The Romans called out the big guns as one of the consuls for 204, Marcus Cornelius Cethegus, led judicial inquiries into all the local elites that arraigned and condemned anybody with whom there was even a sniff of involvement with the Carthaginians, a tough line that meant that others not actually investigated fled into exile of their own accord. This man was kin of Scipio and had had a considerable career so far, a noted orator he had also commanded armies in Apulia before his election in 204, while also holding high positions as Pontifex Maximus and censor. The following year he would be even more active.

For two years Ariminum and Arretum had been the bases from where the jumpy Romans watched what this latest Barcid was up to. The high command had been deeply worried by the news coming in that the Gauls were joining this man whose name still carried a spell despite the failure of the last son of Hamilcar who had passed that way. Livius the victor at Metaurus had been coordinating the northern armies in the last years, keeping things tight but he had not been overly aggressive, despite his having by now something like eight legions under hand. But now some new commanders came into play. In summer 203 the presence of Cethegus, now proconsul, and a praetor called Varus brought a change. These two felt they had plenty going for them and determined to activate this front on the northern marches of Italy. With two good consular armies ready to go, the problems in Etruria seeming sorted out and Mago himself showing little ambition to push south to join his brother in the two years he had been in the Peninsula, they sensed opportunity.

We do not know for sure whether it was these two experienced, capable and enterprising Romans or Mago who actually precipitated the battle, but the proconsul and the praetor had certainly concentrated a large force to take the field. Upwards of 40,000 men, when four legions and the allies are counted. They were on the front foot at last pushing into enemy territory looking for a decisive solution to a war that had previously settled into three years of largely digging in and looking at the other side. The battle was fought in high summer probably near Mediolanum, modern Milan, the capital of the Insubrian Gauls, in a region that throughout history would be a cockpit of southern Europe. The Roman army encountering the enemy in this rolling country, hot and dry at that time of year, deployed from their march with two commanders each taking charge of a wing. When they saw that their foe was up for the contest the soldiers under Varus advanced first to the attack while his colleague kept his men in reserve.

Details are much hazier as to how Mago lined up his warriors, but the national units would have kept together, the Ligurians and the Celts in their war bands providing the bulk of what was probably two lines of troops, though these recent recruits would have been built around the core of Africans and Spaniards he had brought with him or had joined as reinforcements from home. But these probably would not have totalled more than 10,000 heavy infantry. The rest of the 18,000 would have been lights, many of them from the Balearic Islands, who now would have been ranged along his front line ready to skirmish with the Velites and allied lights, opening the battle for the enemy. Their numbers would have been swelled considerably by the thousands of Ligurians, who mostly fought as javelin men, with small shields and sword or dagger for protection. As for Mago's cavalry, the 2,000 who had arrived with him had been bulked up by recruits from home in 204 and would now have been supplemented by a few Ligurians but many more Gallic bluebloods with a long tradition of fighting from horseback.

The light infantry on both sides exchanged missile fire, allowing time for the main lines to come up and deploy. Going at once into attack formation Varus' Roman and allied first rank maniples went forward with a shout. These comprised the youthful Hastati supported as required by the Principes in the second line, all throwing their pilums before coming hand–to–hand, with swords stabbing and shields pressing to both protect their bodies and to unbalance the enemy in front of them. But Mago had not been wasting his time during the years he had been recruiting in Liguria and Cisalpine Gaul. At least two years of training and preparation meant most of the troops he was fielding were not some mob of flighty barbarians, ready to run if their first wild charge did not win the day. So despite the numbers and quality of the Romans and their allies, they did not find it easy to penetrate the Carthaginian line after they struck it. They also almost certainly suffered heavily at the hands of Mago's Balearic slingers, these expert men would have caused casualties amongst the advancing enemy, as we are told their pellets could, from men pausing while withdrawing out of harm's way, if well sped, penetrate helmets and even cuirasses.

With no decision achieved but with both sides taking casualties in the process, sweating and bloodied men from each army took breath as the two Roman commanders rode over from their respective wings to consult on a way forward. Their corporate leadership seems to have functioned well and between them they decided they needed to throw in the cavalry to have a chance of disrupting the enemy line. So Varus, seconded by his own son Marcus, well known as a young but able officer, took their place at the head of the army's horsemen. It is not clear if these troops were divided between the wings or held in one reserve, but probably the former, the notion being that by driving off the enemy cavalry wings, they would both unnerve the infantry in the centre and gain the opportunity to take them in the flank.

The cavaliers waiting with their horses were ordered to mount and array themselves for a charge. Wasting no time, and cheered on by their footslogging comrades, the troopers rushed against an enemy who was almost certainly outnumbered in its mounted arm. But if he did not have sufficient horse to face this new assault Mago had something else that might make the difference. One of the things we know about his army was that it included seven elephants that had been shipped in as reinforcements from home the year before. He clearly had these animals well in hand, thoroughly trained and with good handlers as on this occasion there is no sense of the beasts being as dangerous to their own side as to the enemy. The Carthaginian commander deployed them as soon as he perceived the enemy cavalry about to attack and when they spread out each with their protective foot guards of light infantry to face the advancing troopers it had the desired effect. The enemy horses were terrified by the sight, smell and sound of their bellowing and the attackers just could not get their mounts to even get close to the fearsome beasts. So while they were kept at bay unable to use lance or sword, they found themselves pelted with darts by the enemy's nimble Numidians.

With the mounted combat going against them, matters once again fell to the Roman infantry, but even here things did not turn out well in the beginning. The legions involved are mentioned by number, the twelfth were thrown in first and fought well, but soon had taken so many casualties that only an exceptional sense of duty kept them from collapsing. Indeed they were only rescued when another unit, the thirteenth, stepped forward to take the strain. These men had clearly been kept in reserve, but whether this was behind the first line or was brought over from the other wing that had not yet been involved, is not known. Wherever they came from again we learn Mago had kept sufficient of his strength available to be able to respond when these men swelled his enemy's ranks. He confronted them with a band of Gauls kept spare and who now charged forward to face these fresh combatants. Once the wild ferocious charge of these bare-chested men, with long narrow shields and slashing swords was held, they were of little further use though at least for a time their efforts blunted the progress of the onrushing thirteenth whose men were shaken by the sight of these tall muscular warriors with their hair held in dramatic spikes by applications of lime.

The picture now is of a battlefield with much of the order gone, with legions mixed up fighting together and most of the units of Mago's army committed. Infantry, horse and even elephants were jumbled together, all in varying states of terror, trying to ensure their own survival as much as win the confrontation, while the generals vainly tried to impose some purpose and direction on events. The telling action apparently occurred when a Roman officer rallied the Hastati of the eleventh legion and determined to lead these young men against the elephants who had turned from the cavalry to attack the main battle line. These animals had bunched together impacting like a clenched fist, busting in among the legionary lines, but now the young men of the eleventh, with plenty of javelins to hand, advanced close to the towering beasts and flung at them with great effect. The elephants were stopped in their tracks and turned, bellowing in pain at the wounds they had received from the volleys of pila. Four even dropped to their knees and finally collapsed from the loss of blood. Our source takes his cue from an earlier account that was convinced that it was when they fell that the tipping point came. With the trumpeting beasts no longer a significant threat or obstruction the Roman and allied cavalry were able to make the difference, dispersing the Numidians and threatening the flanks of Mago's battle line. Still it was no immediate rout, the Carthaginian officers were just able to keep their men in hand, organizing an 'orderly and regular withdrawal', their commander, standing with the standards and his best men, holding the ground as a rearguard, allowing his weary, haggard but still unbeaten followers to get out of the maelstrom alive and in order.

The Romans were themselves almost exhausted but still were not going to stand by while the invaders slipped away. Sufficient units were fresh enough to advance and hurl their javelins at the Carthaginian officers distinctive in their gaudy outfits and gilded armour. The effect was not decisive until one of the missiles struck Mago in the thigh and the Carthaginian commander slid from the back of his horse. Now the battle did turn into something like a collapse with the downed general needing to be carried bleeding and dangerously wounded in the wake of his men back to their camp. Not long into the afternoon the whole affair was over and while the Romans held the field it had not been decisive and no great attempt at pursuit was made. Most of Mago's army was still intact, if roughed up not a little, and tactically the battle had been little more than a tie. The partiality of our source also should make us query the casualty figures; if Mago's losses really did reach 5,000, the severity of the fighting might suggest that Roman losses may well have exceeded the 2,300 admitted. Particularly as two tribunes, twenty-two senior knights and several centurions are recorded as fatalities.

But broken and disabled, Mago's condition ensured that the whole Carthaginian campaign was left in a pretty parlous condition. They had little option but to slip away from their defended encampment in the dead of the night. It was a hard road, out of the Po Valley through the valleys of the high Apennines, with their general carried in a litter, as the army made its way back to their old base amongst their Ingauni allies, on the coast of Liguria. A difficult enough journey with their leader injured, as well as the other men who had also been hurt in the encounter. Though there was one consolation; it was soon clear the Romans had no appetite for the chase, leaving the defeated army alone as it approached the foothills of the great mountain spine of Italy and then descended the southern watershed. Once having reached the coast they might have anticipated weeks, if not months, of recuperation, with time for wounds to mend; and so new recruits, arms, equipment and remounts could be acquired. But in fact they found little rest was to be had as they encountered visitors waiting with dramatic news. The ships the officers and men coming down the hills had seen, bobbing at anchor in the waves along the shore, had brought important orders from Carthage. Envoys were waiting with intelligence that would completely turn around their operation. By establishing themselves in northern Italy they had achieved much, if nothing else it had taken upwards of 80,000 enemy soldiers to keep them contained, but now there were other imperatives. Mago was informed that the homeland was under direct and dire threat from Scipio's army of invasion and that it was an absolute necessity that he bring his soldiers back to Africa. These men from Carthage would also have informed the general that his elder brother Hannibal had been recalled too, for the final confrontation with the invaders.

The army that embarked would have been considerably smaller than the one Mago had just led into battle. Far from all the Ligurians or Gauls would have found the trip an attractive proposition and they would have anyway certainly realized they would soon be required to defend hearth and home from a vengeful Rome. The suggestion is that at the Battle of Zama, fought in the following year, the 12,000 troops, Celts, Ligurians, Balearic and Moorish soldiers in Hannibal's front line were mostly these same men who had just shipped back from northern Italy, though if they had reached Africa to fight at least one more time, one who did not was Mago himself. He had died as his fleet passed Sardinia, the sea voyage being too much for the weakened constitution of the wounded man.

This dramatic campaigning season had seen action down south as well as in the far north of the Peninsula, though what had happened there was both much less clear and considerably less remarkable. Gaius Servilius Geminus, consul for the year with Gnaeus Servilius Caepio, had been given orders to pin Hannibal, to try and prevent him returning to Africa. As for others involved in facing this enemy, Sempronius stayed in Bruttium keeping command of Licinius Crassus' troops, while that famously good-looking and articulate officer returned to Rome. The offensive these men contrived claimed some success, with apparently Consentia, Aufugum, Bergae, Baesidiae, Ocriculum, Lymphaeum, Argentanum, and Clampetia – all places in Bruttium – coming over to Rome with the Carthaginians making no attempt at their defence. But even our ancient gentleman from

Padua does not make much of what happened in this ultimate year. Indeed when he mentions a battle around Croton in which Hannibal is supposed to have been defeated losing 5,000 men, he makes it clear that he believes this to have been nothing more than fabrication.

> The story of that battle is not clear. Valerius Antias says five thousand of the enemy were slain – a victory on such a scale as to have been either shamelessly fabricated or else carelessly passed over.[6]

If Geminus really did attack the Carthaginians he completely failed to make any impact in terms of disrupting the preparations to repatriate the army and general who were looking very much like the last chance of succour for the great Punic city in Africa. Hannibal's officers were able to build the transports needed from scratch from plentiful local timber cut from the tree-covered hills of Bruttium and his commissariat was untroubled as provisions were accumulated sufficient to undertake the considerable logistical task of getting the army back home. Things that would have been scarcely possible if they had been bloodily defeated and Hannibal under pressure from a rampant and victorious enemy commander.

Certainly nothing the Romans may have accomplished stopped Hannibal tidying up the redoubt in the defensible hills of Bruttium around Croton that he had constructed in the last few years. This streamlining was certainly necessary, as he must have been expecting his recall at any time after the accounts of how dire affairs in Africa had become. The details are murky, but we know from Appian that he had been active, reducing the extent of his defensive ring, both to buttress its strength and ensure when his departure was required it could be done with as little risk as possible. Inevitably even in Bruttium when news of Scipio's victories in Africa became common knowledge there were people looking to their future when the Romans took back control. So with Petelia just north of Croton he worried about the loyalty of the inhabitants and turned the place over to his Bruttium soldiers, while removing several thousand locals who were known to be loyal to the Carthaginian cause, back to Croton. He may have adopted the same policy with other places too, Thurii being mentioned, though this place surely must have been held by Rome well before this time.

In the last year Hannibal would have been receiving news from home with some bewilderment as to whether his mother city had determined on fighting to the end or was preparing to submit with a slight anticipation of Roman mercy. Defeats in 203 had initially seemed to knock the stuffing out of the Punic leadership, particularly when their ally, King Syphax of Numidia, was again defeated and this time captured by Rome's local client ruler Masinissa, seeming to finally end any hope of significant succour for Carthage from these formidable warriors of the North African interior. In the light of this envoys were sent on the road to Rome to hear what they might expect from being on the wrong end of a victor's peace. Then everything changed; a Roman supply fleet en route to Scipio in Africa had floundered in foul weather, some grounding on the western beaches of Cape Bon, opposite Carthage and fell neatly into their hands, or were blown onto the island of Aegimurus, where fifty ships were sent to collect the windfall. The citizens, finding themselves thus provided by providence with military equipment to replace what they had lost in the fired camps outside Utica, began to consider continued resistance as against submitting to terms that included sending wheat to feed the invading army from city granaries already badly depleted by blockade. That Hannibal himself might be riding to the rescue may have been a factor in the stiffening line too. The impact of his name was considerable and Barcid supporters were undoubtedly crucial in the change of policy, but it was not just them. Even those who feared Hannibal as a political rival, or blamed him for starting the war in Spain in the first place, knew of his value on the battlefield and however many defeats they had suffered and however many African places had fallen by force or treachery to the Romans, it took little of an upturn to make a majority believe that with the great general at their head they could still fight it out for an honourable peace.

There is real contention over the details of what actually occurred in the final weeks as it became clear that Hannibal was bound to be recalled to fight in defence of his homeland. There are some pretty horrible accusations around what took place when he left the scene of his greatest triumphs and recent decline. It is suggested that an admiral called Hasdrubal arrived to bustle the great man along, only to find him in resentful mood. The last hope of Carthage preparing to leave Italy is reported as far from happy. Hannibal felt that his people had failed him in the past, that the grandees who ran the city had seldom pulled out the stops to get succour to him when he needed it. Only once that we know of had considerable reinforcements, including Numidians and elephants, been dispatched. The resources of North Africa had always seemed to be diverted to Spain or Sicily or even Sardinia, rather than being directed to reinforce success after Cannae, or when Capua or

Tarentum joined Hannibal's cause. But now Carthage itself was threatened he was remembered and expected to return and save his compatriots from disaster they had brought down on themselves. That this attitude is very human does not mean it is not difficult. The evidence, such as it is, suggests that if not actually in control of high Punic strategy over the years, Hannibal and the Barcids had still been the dominant voice at the war councils in the city; that it had been his family and faction undoubtedly in consultation with the general who had signed up to the policy that directed Carthaginian resources in the war. If this had not been the case it is difficult to understand why so much of their treasure had been poured into the campaign in Iberia, which had always been a family power base since Hamilcar Barca arrived there over a generation before. Nor should it be forgotten that the key players on the crucial Sicilian front are specified as Hannibal's men, Hippocrates and Epicenes, who took over control at Syracuse and were born of a Carthaginian mother and came from Hannibal's camp in Italy direct to the island to carry out their general's orders and at the very end of the war there, a man called Mutines who had been 'trained under Hannibal in the whole science of war' was sent to try and resurrect the Carthaginian cause. And if personal rancour and infighting had meant this talented man had ended changing sides this did not take away that his arrival had occurred under the directing hand of the great general.

It is recorded that, justified or not, in this mood he determined to leave a desert behind him. That he ordered the naval commander to drive the citizens from their homes and turn the places over to the troops for plunder:

> he sent Hasdrubal, the admiral, about, on pretence of inspecting the garrisons. The latter, as he entered each city, ordered the inhabitants to take what things they and their slaves could carry, and move away. Then he plundered the rest. Some of them, learning of these proceedings before Hasdrubal came, attacked the garrisons, overcoming them in some places and being overcome by them in others. Indiscriminate slaughter, accompanied by the violation of wives and the abduction of virgins, and all the horrors that usually take place when cities are captured, ensued.[7]

That he took what he could of value from the cities he controlled is probable, particularly as he would need funds to not only pay his men but to rally support back home, still there is no reason to believe that he had turned on erstwhile friends, 'Despising the cities still allied to him now as foreigners.'

This is just blackening the name of a feared enemy, as is the testament of even more brutal treatment claimed to have been meted out to his own soldiers. That Hannibal himself rounded up those of his Italian soldiers who were not prepared to embark for Africa on the excuse of rewarding them and, using the men who would accompany him, surrounded and either shot to death or enslaved these reluctant warriors, an atrocity supported by Livy who located the massacre in the Temple of Juno, where he described the victims as being butchered after seeking sanctuary there. Nobody actually mentions the numbers killed but, if anything took place at all, certainly very few can have been involved. There just seems to be no sense in it and the explanation that the victims might have been good soldiers who Rome could make use of, is not credible. They would have been seen as traitors and if not actively punished in the harshest manner, would certainly not have been trusted in action against the enemy. Much more sensible for Hannibal would have to been to keep the soldiers he left behind onside and encourage them to make what resistance they might against whoever led an invading army of occupation into Bruttium. And indeed, that he did leave garrisons in key places indicated this was just what was intended. To kill men who could have defended themselves and their homes against a shared foe was madness and such an act would have been bound to have had an awful effect on the morale of those who followed him to Africa. To have ordered these soldiers to massacre their old comrades as their last act on Italian soil could only make these veterans he depended upon contemplate how in another circumstance he might treat them if he could do this to men who had fought hard for him in recent campaigns. It is no purpose here to whitewash this ancient warlord whose career was almost bound of its nature to include considerable brutality, if not atrocity, but still these particular indictments hardly stand up to scrutiny.

Whatever the behaviour of the Carthaginian commander in these his last days in Italy, in terms of what he could do in 203 the options were few. Not a man to tilt at windmills Hannibal knew his time in Italy had run its course and if he was to do anything for himself, his men, and his motherland, it would have to be done in Africa. That he left is not in doubt, slipping out of Croton's small harbour late in June, where a few fishing boats and leisure craft now bob on the blue water. A curious and deeply trepidatious crowd would have seen the evacuees cast off to wait for a wind to Africa, and soon Hannibal and his men would have seen the temple complex on Cape Colonne as they passed, before the transports rode the open waters to Africa. Taking him, to the music of water rushing by the bow, away from a country where he had dwelt for nearly sixteen years but would never return. Amongst the men pacing the deck would have been Sosylus and Silenus, tame historians and propagandists, who perhaps perceived more than most the poignancy of their putative, latter-day Hercules-Melqart departing the Peninsula, this time without having freed the inhabitants from a tyranny located on the banks of the Tiber. The roots of Carthaginian power in the Italian Peninsula had failed to cling in its rich volcanic soil, despite Hannibal's extraordinary tenure in the heartland of his enemies. This Punic transplantation had lasted nothing like the hundreds of years of involvement in Sicily or even its one generation of imperialism in Iberia. On this occasion the incumbent power had been just too resilient, despite the fact it had had to face one of the most consistently successful commanders that any ancient state could boast.

It was an old world in a new condition that greeted Hannibal's men jumping down onto the beach or pressing down the gangplank onto the quay at Lemta, six or so miles south of modern Monastir in Tunisia. The armada that made landfall at this Phoenician trading post, that would soon wax rich on the olive oil trade, was carrying a very different set of men than those who had arrived in Italy so long before. Desperate but determined, the bulk of the army Hannibal brought to save his homeland was now made up of Italians who had been fighting for him for years. Probably even most of the cavalrymen, men distressed to leave their mounts behind because of the lack of room and who had seen them slaughtered alongside thousands of pack animals so they would not fall into Roman hands, were from the Peninsula too, outnumbering the few Numidian Iberians and Gauls still under arms. He certainly tried hard to get those of his veterans he could, horse and foot, to come to Africa with him. Though many would not have needed 'lavish promises' because they would have known if they had stayed in Italy they would have been hunted down once the Romans took over. These men had originally joined partly out of patriotism, to fend off the imposition of a hated Roman dominion and part for pay and plunder under an ever victorious leader and with them were a good number of Roman deserters, either full citizens, Latins or allies who knew they could expect nothing except a gruesome death if they had stayed in Italy and come within reach of Roman vengeance.

Experience at places like Capua and Tarentum had shown what the price of joining Hannibal would almost certainly be, so for many soldiers when the time came the choice had been to go with Hannibal or stay and die. The option just to go back to the family farm was not there, as inevitably in their home communities there would be personal enemies who would turn them into the Roman authorities or just informers eager to gain a bit of local kudos with their new rulers. Brigandage might have been a possibility for a while but such a life would almost always end with being hunted down, and getting lost in the crowd in another city would be very difficult too. Identification and control may not have been what it is in modern times, but it would have been sufficient to catch most who tried this, in a period when any stranger whose past was not known was bound to be considered suspect. At least those who followed Hannibal could hope that victory against Scipio might mean the opportunity to return in triumph back to Italy, or perhaps to find a new home in Africa, and at worst they might at least find a glorious death.

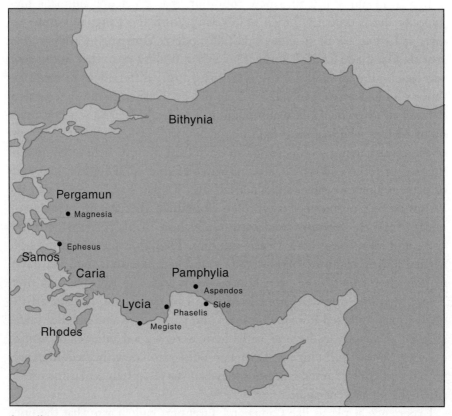

Anatolia.

Epilogue

'Let us ease,' said he, 'the Romans of their continual dread and care, who think it long and tedious to await the death of a hated old man. Yet Titus will not bear away a glorious victory, nor one worthy of those ancestors who sent to caution Pyrrhus, an enemy, and a conqueror too, against the poison prepared for him by traitors.'

Plutarch, *Flamininus*

Hannibal had been 28 or 29 years of age when he commenced his war against Rome and 45 when he led an army to a last-ditch fight at Zama in what turned out to be his first defeat in significant battle, a disaster brought on when he had to face a veteran Roman army with a significant edge in terms of cavalry. These were provided by Scipio's ally Masinissa, the young king of the eastern Numidians called the Massylii, who had overcome his rival Syphax, king of the Masaesyli in the west, himself taken prisoner and very soon dying in captivity at the town of Tibur near Rome. If, in this encounter, Hannibal's eighty elephants had done little good, chivvied down the lanes expressly opened up in the legions' ranks or felled by massed missile fire, the infantry fight could have gone either way with his Italian army veterans making a splendid contest of it. Until the Roman cavalry supported by their Numidian auxiliaries returned, after seeing off the few thousand Carthaginian horse that had been scraped together, which decisively tipped the scales by their falling on the exposed rear of the enemy. A good proportion of the army that represented the last military fling of the great Punic city fell on that day and, after this disaster, their ability and their will to resist was exhausted. So they had little choice but to accept a peace that allowed them little more than survival, certainly with no chance of ever again rising to anything beyond a minor regional power.

But twelve years later, now at the age of 57, Hannibal was in command again. The grey-bearded general was treading the boards of a great warship, now in waters far to the east of those that lapped Cape Bon, Sicily or Magna

Graecia. He was part of a major naval effort by Antiochus the Great, the Seleucid monarch, to defend his Asian dominions from an expanding Rome that had not looked back since their climactic victory in Africa. At the time there was a considerable Seleucid fleet under an officer called Polyxenidas based at Ephesus, but they had already been roughed up in a confused sea fight at Samos by a combined Roman and Rhodian force that remained well placed to stymie any further Seleucid endeavours to bar the Hellespont crossing to Asia against the Roman armies moving towards them.[1] In the light of this, Antiochus had ordered his Syrian, Cilician and Phoenician squadrons to sail west to reinforce the man on the spot. But the move was expected and Rome's Rhodian allies prepared to counter it. Fifteen vessels under an admiral called Eudamus were rushed south down the coast past Caria, Lycia and Pamphylia to contest their enemy's passage and once in place they were joined by a further seventeen warships from Rhodes under another officer called Pamphilidas. They were now in sufficient force to first drive off an enemy investing Daedala near Peraea before moving on, as even more ships joined when Megiste, an island just offshore from modern Kas in Lycia, was reached. So it was in real strength that the confederates arrived at Phaselis, perfectly placed, on the eastern shore where Anatolia bulges south, to control the sea lanes from the east. Eudamus initially planned to lie in wait there for the closing enemy fleet, but midsummer heat and a pestilential stench made him reconsider and with men dropping with sickness all around, he upped anchor to push along the coast towards the mouth of the Eurymedon River.

Once there they had the first concrete news of the enemy, as friends from Aspendos informed them the opposition had already arrived off the coast at Side town. The Seleucid armament raised in Antiochus' eastern Mediterranean holdings, many no doubt hailing from Tyre, the home of Hannibal's own ancestors, was impressive, comprising thirty-seven large warships. The biggest were four sixers and three sevens and the rest of the decked ships were probably quadremes, with on top ten triremes in support. But they had not had an easy time of it, having had to fight against a heavy Etesian wind from the north-west, common at that time. The commander-in-chief was Apollonius, a great noble of the court, but with him was Hannibal the Carthaginian in charge of one squadron and these two, once arrived, had good reason for confidence as they were appraised of the fact that they outgunned a foe whose biggest vessels were thirty-two quadremes backed by only four triremes. The Rhodians though did have a thoroughly deserved reputation as formidable maritime fighters.

The day before the battle, scouts sent on ahead alerted Eudamus that the enemy was virtually on them and anchored just beyond the headland of Side. Though it was not until dawn on the following day that the sailors in both fleets pushed their vessels off from the beaches they were drawn up on and into the steady swell of the sea. With their sails and masts dumped on shore and left with a few men to guard them, the Seleucid officers and their followers now spotted the enemy passing round the head of the Side Peninsula and fanning out seawards to give themselves the kind of sea room the Rhodians knew well how to make use of. Now both sides could see the other's formation in the crystal morning air, under a sun rising in a cloudless clear sky. The right of the Syrian line, led by Apollonius, showy in his gorgeous armour, was able to take its mark from the walls of Side, a town standing on a short peninsula running out from a coast now crowded with high-rise holiday hotels. On the other flank, the vessels spreading out into the open sea on the left of the Seleucid line were under the command of the great Carthaginian, taking on a maritime role that he would come to specialize in over the next few years. His fleet seem to have had the jump on their opponents, 'they already had their ships in line', while the coalition forces were still in a long column of route, surprised at the speed with which the enemy had come on them. Eudamus, at the head of his fleet, tried hard to guarantee that this did not turn out too much to his disadvantage and attempting to ensure his ships got sufficient room on the right to deploy properly in line, he signalled five of them, close to him, to move forward of the others. Putting himself at their head he pushed straight into the firing line, to confront Hannibal's vessels, close enough now with their beaks creaming the waters towards him.

In the midsummer sun with their commander-in-chief buying them time, Chariclitus in command of the rear squadron and Pamphilidas in the centre, were able to turn into the open sea and array themselves in line, the former on the left and the latter on his right.

But the excellence of their vessels and their own practised seamanship took away all fear from the Rhodians in a moment. Each ship in turn steered towards the open sea and so allowed room on the land side for the one which followed it,[2]

Though jockeying for position, Chariclitus found things did not begin well, as his ships lacked sufficient space between the land on their left and the squadron on the right, so even the brave and brilliant efforts of Eudamus failed to completely ensure against some initial disorder amongst his formations. Referring to the left wing of the confederate fleet we hear, 'they were still in confusion when the fighting began on the right with Hannibal.'

But the Rhodians were top sailors and while others might have blanched at the numbers against them, the crews of five vessels that had accompanied their commander-in-chief kept cool. With plenty of open sea they tore into the abundant enemies in their front.

> whenever any of them closed with an enemy vessel with its beak foremost, it either tore a hole in its prow or sheared off its oars, or else, where it found a clear way through the line, it passed it and attacked its stern.[3]

While these few intrepid captains tried to compensate for their lack of number with high expertise, those facing the right of the Seleucid line had finally sorted themselves out into decent order after initially finding themselves congested between the shore and their centre. Their adversaries found it difficult to cope when fighting became general on that side and the contest turned from difficult to almost disastrous when one of the smaller Rhodian vessels headed straight for a Seleucid seven. The towering battleship, 140ft in length and 18ft in beam decked over and crowded with not just plenty of marines but light artillery too, tried to take evasive action but its agile attacker was too quick. The Rhodian struck at its prey's most vulnerable point and one blow was enough to put it out of action and well on the way to sinking. This episode seemed to knock the stuffing out of the crews of the ships nearby and soon we hear the whole of the right side of the Seleucid line was contemplating flight.

But with Hannibal's squadron it had been very different. It is clear, despite the expertise of the enemy on his front, his extra numbers, the size of his battleships and the initial disorder and exposure of the enemy's lead ships was not about to be easily overcome. Hannibal as far as we know had little experience of war at sea but it was clear his leadership skills had not been in the least blunted. Manoeuvring his squadron to concentrate on Eudamus and his lonely five vessels he 'would have hemmed him in' and destroyed them if not for events elsewhere. The Rhodian admiral in trouble, now gave the signal that called the ships of a scattered fleet to his side and luckily for him plenty were there to respond. Hannibal was not going to be able to reap the benefits of his success as the enemy ships on the left, close to the shore, had now driven off the vessels facing them so when their pilots recognized their commander's distress signal the steersmen pushed hard on their oars and the crews made all speed to the rescue of their beleaguered comrades.

Seeing these reinforcements ploughing towards them with their oars flashing in and out of the water like great wings Hannibal's captains were suddenly thrown into confusion. Despite having held the upper hand so far, having fought well and successfully against the enemy in front of them, they now found new adversaries coming down on their front and flank, foemen with all the skills to make use of the advantage. The enemy came in, ramming where they could or approaching close to board their targets and they were not long in turning the fight. Soon one then another of the ships in Hannibal's squadron turned to get away, even these ancient dreadnoughts could show a turn of pace when they pleased and in the end they had some good fortune as well. Many of the chasing crews were still suffering the effects of the illness that had struck near Phaselis and so had not the strength to keep up an effective pursuit. In fact they were soon so exhausted the men had to halt to recoup their strength with some food and while they were thus occupied the Seleucids managed to tow their damaged, holed and crippled ships away, a considerable task with 'not much more than twenty getting away uninjured'.

The Seleucid captains generally had seemed to be well underway when Eudamus tried again to push a pursuit. He organized his own undamaged ships to get moving despite he himself not being able to carry on, his flagship having been rammed by a number of the enemy and taking on water. But Pamphilidas and Chariclitus took up the gage chasing the defeated fleet they could see 'for a considerable time', until Hannibal and the Seleucid rump approached a windbound shore where it would have been dangerous for even adept Rhodians to keep up the pursuit. So the hunt ended with the main trophy the victors had to show being the seven that had been struck and crippled early on in the fight. A great ship that was to be dragged back to safety, first to Phaselis and afterwards home to Rhodes itself was to delight a local crowd who always enjoyed glorying in the achievements of the island's matelots. Though even this only slightly mollified the feeling of some, who felt the opportunity to entrap so many more of their enemies had been let slip. Hannibal had certainly not been part of a victory but at least where he had personally commanded he had done well enough and the evidence was that he was far from downcast by the outcome and still eager to make his mark, hoping to get his squadron to the main theatre around Ephesus until he found out he could not pass Lycia because Eudamus had left twenty ships based at Patara and Megiste, while he himself went north with seven of his largest vessels to join the Romans at Samos. In the grand scheme of things this affray did not figure as that important compared with the fighting that had gone before or would come after, but the fact of the great Hannibal acting as admiral for the king of Asia is fascinating, as indeed is so much of the whole of his life after Zama, stuff that would have taxed the imagination of almost any adventure novelist to invent.

Before leading his Phoenician battlecruisers into this affray in Pamphylian waters, Hannibal had in fact been a fixture at the court of Antiochus the Great for quite some time. The motive power behind these developments came about because of a combination of local rivals at Carthage and enemies at Rome, who had never been happy that Hannibal had not been handed over for execution as part of the peace Scipio won in 201. Only five years later in 196 Hannibal came out of retirement, as one of that years' 'suffets', and using his still potent authority undertook reforms of public finance that cut hard at the corrupt practices of the local elite, resulting in a significant increase in revenue, sufficient in fact to mean the city would soon be in a position to pay off its war indemnity in full. On top of this he pioneered a policy which would ensure that membership of the powerful 'tribunal of the Hundred and Four' could only be held for one year and never in two consecutive years. While winning further kudos with many, particularly amongst the commons, this activity made him bitter enemies amongst the moneyed classes, men who knew the levers to pull to make life impossible for someone who was making it difficult for them. These grandees let it be known at Rome that Hannibal was involved in treasonous correspondence with Antiochus the Great and when, as a result, ambassadors were sent from Rome to Carthage, he anticipated a demand for his extradition by fleeing, leaving his domestic enemies frustrated when the two ships they dispatched after him came back empty-handed. Though these petty men still had the satisfaction of destroying his house and confiscating his property, while ingratiating themselves with Rome by declaring that city's old enemy an outlaw.

The man who had scrambled out of Africa fearing vengeful diktats from the Roman Senate had headed straight for the headquarters of a ruler he must have known was looking very likely to lock horns with his old Italian enemy. The suggestion that he had long been in contact with the court at Antioch is probably just our partial sources but it is difficult to be sure. Hannibal certainly was a thorough man and must have known the likelihood of requiring a friendly refuge might well arise, so perhaps he had put out feelers. So this military celebrity, having stopped first at Tyre, before being entertained by Antiochus' son at Daphne near Antioch, arrived at Ephesus entering a new political world when still only middle-aged and with all the talents any new employer might ask for. But what impact he had at the centre is difficult to be certain of, he might have had the knack of manipulating folk from every station but the king he now had to deal with had just made a name for himself by conquering most of inner Asia and had an ego concomitant with this achievement. To expect Antiochus the Great to take his military line from this stranger from far away, who had anyway finally been defeated in war, was perhaps always a stretch.

Still we know he was there in Antiochus' council as that king started out to try and deal with Romans who were entering an Aegean world so long the stomping ground of the successors of Alexander the Great. He was certainly present at Demetrias in Thessaly as the Aetolians, who had persuaded the king to venture over the seas to Greece, crowded the court. There is an account that during this time Hannibal harangued his host to take the war to the Romans. That while leaving some of his men in Greece and Asia he should send most of his armament, the best of his fleets and armies to invade Italy with Hannibal himself at their head. It makes a great story but whether true or not it did not gel with the approach of the man who it was directed at. The feeling is that Antiochus was really just chancing his arm in Greece now Philip V of Macedon had been knocked out of the game and the Romans had removed their garrisons from the Peninsula. He was seeing what hay he could make rather than being intent on some life and death struggle with a western power that was hardly more than just beginning to swim into his ken. Not a mindset that was accessible to Hannibal as a 'Cassandra' cautioning that whatever Antiochus intended, any war with Rome would be a fought *à outrance*. He found the king's attitude difficult on more than one occasion, even suggesting impiously on his losing an opportunity due to unpropitious entrails; 'You defer to a piece of meat, and not a man of sense.'

Antiochus on this occasion was disinclined even to throw much of an army into Greece, never mind fight Rome on the Adriatic, or venture to Italy itself, despite the reputation of the Carthaginian who recommended it.

The king's hope was to make progress in Greece for as little investment as possible. So it was with just 10,000 men, a few elephants and allies that he first encountered the Roman army at the historic hot gates of Thermopylae and came off very badly indeed. Even when the war migrated east to Asia, though recognizing his talent and experience, Antiochus just could not take on board what Hannibal was saying about his new enemy. He found it impossible to credit that the Republic, so far to the west, could really be a danger to the heart of his empire and by the time he understood, it was almost too late. The Carthaginian exile was present in camp at the climactic Battle of Magnesia back from his maritime adventures in Pamphylia, and it is almost impossible not to wonder what might have happened there in early 190 if the king had given Hannibal his head to command the army. 'What ifs' can be silly but this could be atypical. The Carthaginian commander might have made the difference; he had after all done great things with multifarious, multinational forces before. All his victories had been won with just such armies recruited from all corners of the Mediterranean, and if the core of Antiochus' army, the phalanx, was cumbersome it was also strong and solid. Equally the Seleucids fielded plenty of that good cavalry that Hannibal knew how to use so well. And if Scipio Africanus was present in the opposing camp he was not in official command and the Roman army on this occasion did not possess those numerous squadrons of Numidian horse so vital when the two had last met at Zama. Success for Antiochus on this Anatolian field of blood might have had a real impact too, at least significantly postponing Roman intrusion east of the Hellespont, perhaps allowing the Seleucids to suppress or at least curb the power of Eumenes II of Pergamum and even the Rhodians, who were both so crucial in drawing the Italians into this arena and such key auxiliaries in the contest itself.

But the chance, that admittedly would probably only have delayed the intrusion of Roman power in Asia not halted it, was not taken and a defeated Antiochus had to bow to the new power in the east and accept a peace in which he was shorn of all his country up to the Taurus Mountains. And this king of a Syrian rump, and those places that might stay loyal in Babylonia and the upper satrapies, was no longer going to be relied upon to offer a safe haven for the man who, though recently active in his navy, in the face of a vengeful Rome demanding the Carthaginian be handed over. Indeed Hannibal must have worried that if he remained within the great king's control he might be utilized as a bargaining pawn. So the better to be safe, the exile took his leave of Syrian service to look for securer harbours elsewhere.

He took himself off to Crete, an island of contending, but crucially, doggedly independent city states. There he chose Gortyn as his base, but how long he stayed is unknown. In fact little is heard of either the Cretan years or indeed the whole later picaresque though there is a nice story about what happened when he was leaving this exile's billet. The islanders might be determinedly independent and less inclined than most to buckle to Roman pressure but they were suckers for the glint of other people's gold and Hannibal knew it. He had to keep his ready money about him, to be able to move at a moment's notice, and this was bound to get about and make him a target for sticky fingers. To escape the attentions of his larcenous hosts, he deposited what seemed to be his valuable gold and silver articles in the local Temple to Diana while actually putting his treasure in some worthless looking brazen statues that he kept in the open in his house. So while the Cretans kept an eye on the temple he easily got his wealth away when he had to leave this latest bolthole.

The chronology of his wanderings is problematic and the itinerary opaque, there is even a story that he went upcountry as far as Armenia and when there, designed the cities of Artaxata, nestling beneath Mount Ararat on the Araxes River and Arxata, the situation of which is not definitely known, in the service of King Artaxias who had just established himself as independent from the Seleucid Empire.[4] And more than this, it seems he occupied himself with the fine arts too, not only writing Greek literature but also a history addressed to the Rhodians about the conquest of the Galatians in Anatolia conducted by a Roman called Cnaeus Manlius Vulso.[5] But the finale sojourn in this catalogue of wanderings was in Bithynia. In this country where Asia meets Europe, the local dynast Prusias I stood in need of an innovative military man. Nepos even claims he tried to get this king to attack the Romans in Italy too, but this is foolishness and it was in a local brouhaha that the petty king wanted guidance. In the year before his death Hannibal took a hand in his host's local spat with Pergamum and Prusias got good value out of his visitor who remained tricky as ever; it was needed as the Bithynians who had been getting the worst of the war and having been defeated on land decided to challenge their enemy at sea.

When the navies met in battle the squadron under Hannibal was somewhat smaller than that of his enemy. So to even the odds he ordered poisonous snakes to be collected and put in earthenware containers.[6] At an officer's council he then outlined his plan that they concentrate on attacking the flagship of the enemy King Eumenes while just holding the rest of the enemy ships at bay. It was against these others he expected the serpents to be effective while his best vessels would win the battle by killing or capturing the king. Nor was this the complete extent of his cunning, he also determined to use a ploy to make absolutely sure which ship the enemy commander was on. To do this before the fleets came together, he sent a messenger under a herald's protection, claiming he could only hand it to the king and so it was taken to his flagship, thus learning exactly which one it was. The whole enterprise was almost a complete success, except that Eumenes was able to get away to the protection of his army on the shore, where from behind the shields of his guard he saw his more numerous fleet worsted and driven back on the coast because they could not both handle their vessels and fight when these were crawling with venomous serpents. Not that even this was the end of his usefulness as there are strong hints that the adept man also trounced the Pergamine land forces on at least one occasion.

But if Hannibal's new employer found much to be happy about, half a world away developments ensured there was to be no easy retirement after these efforts, this old soldier was not going to be allowed to fade away. There is a debate as to how he once again came within the sights of unforgiving men on the banks of the Tiber. Though it is accepted that the denouement was engineered by Titus Quinctius Flamininus, some see a coincidence that Flamininus, when consul, accidentally learnt from Bithynian envoys who had arrived in Rome, that Hannibal was holed up in their homeland. Once it was common knowledge the reaction was predictable: 'The conscript fathers, who thought that they would never be free from plots as long as Hannibal was alive.' So in 183 this same man as part of an embassy took ship to Prusias' kingdom.

Not many years before this Flamininus had been a golden boy making his name, young and proud of his winning ways that certainly seemed to work with many Greeks. His search for popularity was such that in the triumph he was given for his victory against Philip V he paraded Romans enslaved in Hannibal's war and liberated by the Achaeans to please him. But his activities were not just public relations and unlike many of his peers he does not seem to have been an inveterate warmonger, from the start offering Philip V peace, if he would leave the Greeks free. And if this overture ended with marching his army against the Macedonians, after the Battle of Cynoscephalae when the war was won, he showed himself genuinely prepared to take note of the wishes of the locals in fashioning a Greek settlement. Even persuading the commissioners sent by the Senate to resolve the question of Greece to withdraw Roman garrisons from the famous 'fetters' at Demetrias, Chalcis and Acro-Corinth that held the country in thrall. He ended being loved for it by the locals and after an excursion round Greece was hailed at the Isthmian games to such an extent that Plutarch, to entertain the gullible, suggested the shouts of approval were so loud they knocked crows out of the clear summer air.[7] Equally he emancipated places in Asia Minor from Macedonian control and interceded to protect the Aetolians and Chalcidians when they were being battered by a different Roman general.

Despite this ample record of glorious success he still felt the need to cap his career by chasing down Hannibal, and on arriving in Bithynia made it clear to a reluctant local ruler that the Romans had the muscle and they would be prepared to use it if he did not give the exile up; 'and although Prusias made many fervent intercessions in behalf of a man who was a suppliant and a familiar friend, would not relent.'[8] It turned out the king of Bithynia was even less well placed to consider what he owed Hannibal than Antiochus had been, when the Romans came calling. The great king of Syria still had sufficient clout and would have been far enough away that he could have afforded to allow the Carthaginian space to slip away even if this did leave him in some bad odour with the Italian power. It would not have meant risking his life and throne but the same could not be said of Hannibal's current host. His country just across the Bosporus from Europe was far too proximate to Roman power to take any risks and Prusias' own resources would hardly have allowed even the weakest resistance against any assault from the western power. The king had little option but to arrange the arrest of the man who had served him so well, not just on the battlefield either; his town planning skills had been called on during his stay, designing a new town while he was resident in the kingdom, 'and now as to the remaining places on this coast. On the road from Cios into the interior is Prusa, in Bithynia, founded by Hannibal at the foot of Olympus, at a distance of twenty-five miles from Nicæa, Lake Ascanius lying between them.'[9]

The soldier, sailor and architect though had been careful, the house the king had given him had been modified so there were seven underground passages for making a quick getaway, but this time it would not be enough. The Roman ambassadors had heard of his precautions and made their own arrangements, so Hannibal's servitors, looking out of the residence, had to inform their master that the exits were guarded by armed men clearly intent on taking him prisoner. The presence of the king's retainers meant the hunted man had no way out. But years on the run had made him anticipate just such an eventuality and he took the poison he always kept to hand. Now the old man, with not a little conceit that, still in his mid sixties and with his ravaging of Italy long years in the past, his name sent shivers up and down Roman spines, decided on self-destruction. As only to be expected in such a dramatic termination the details vary from the probable use of poison to a more gory picture of a servant strangling his master with his cloak or even that he 'drank bulls' blood too in imitation of Themistocles and Midas'.[10] And of course there are the tales, so familiar with the demise of any great figure, of a misinterpreted oracle, where it is suggested that Zeus Ammon had given assurance that Hannibal would die and be buried on Libyan soil, with the kick being that the place in Bithynia where he succumbed was known by the locals as Libyssa.[11]

Coincidentally even in fatality Scipio could not disentangle himself from his great antagonist. This dimension of these two military greats encountering had been developed in Hannibal's time at Antiochus' court when they were claimed as conversing at Ephesus, while Africanus was part of a delegation sent to the Asian power. This is when we get an anecdote that shows both the Carthaginian able to put his point across, while equally being capable of caressing the ego of his interlocutor. On being asked who the greatest general ever was he disappointed Scipio by putting Alexander, Pyrrhus and himself before the Roman, only tossing him a crumb of comfort by saying that if he, Hannibal, had beaten Scipio, he would have placed himself at the head of the pack. These two are twinned so habitually despite confronting each other on the battlefield so infrequently when others like Fabius, Nero, Marcellus, Flaccus or Gracchus faced the great man far more often over the years. It is the drama that is irresistible of each making reputations on different fronts before finally coming head-to-head like Napoleon and Wellington or Lee and Grant. And as with these, the more talented and impressive figure finally succumbed to a lesser nemesis. Finally the two were joined in death as Scipio expired in the same year as Hannibal, at 52 years of age, after failing to respond well after Zama to a homecoming that included years of vilification by the likes of Cato the Elder for anything from peculation to an un-Roman fancy for all things Greek.

Another had gone long before; Fabius had died even before he could hear of the triumph at Zama, but perhaps for him it was a sweet release not having to see Scipio return in triumph. He would no doubt have looked on smugly from the afterlife when his own funeral was funded by small donations from the ordinary citizens who regarded this long-lived grandee as a real father of his people, a show of home town appreciation for a man for whom flashy victories on Libyan battlefields were as much a cause for worry as celebration. Others who had played really significant parts in the epic war in Italy had also, as far as we know, predeceased the opposing generals who clashed in Africa. Fulvius Flaccus probably died old, even before Fabius and Nero, though of a younger generation is hardly heard of after his censorship in 204. These men who had been part of the Hannibal epic had struggled against their great opponent in the hope that their reputations would ring down the ages. Fabius, Marcellus and Flaccus had reached the apogee of the consulship, four or even more times, matching men from a century before when it was reported that the likes of Quintus Fabius Maximus Rullianus and Publius Decius Mus had also attained that kind of number of consulships. Matching them in repute was Scipio who, if he did not notch up so many occupations of the greatest magistracy, outshone the rest by not only finally defeating Hannibal but also being part of a family affair that orchestrated the overthrow of Antiochus the Great.

Hannibal, who had been the context of all these lives, had failed in the great enterprise of his existence. Some have seen a failure of nerve after so brave a beginning that he should have gone for the jugular, attacked Rome itself after the first great victories, but this would surely never have been achievable. No quips placed in the mouth of the general, Maharbal, that Hannibal knew how to win a victory but not how to use it, should make us think this was ever an option. However many scars he inflicted on the republican body politic it is just impossible to imagine how he would have captured the city of Rome itself. All the great places that fell to the Carthaginians did so because a considerable faction within wanted them to win and such was never the case in the capital of the Republic. However angry the populace became over the incompetence and corruption of their rulers or the outrageous profiteering by war contractors, who sent out ships rotten enough they were bound to sink so they might pick up the insurance and then used violence to disrupt any attempt to prosecute them. However high the demands for blood and gold and however raucous were popular voices in the streets of Rome crying that the consuls and senators were extending the conflict to serve their own interests, for glory and even to crush the people by their exactions, still there was never a constituency that would listen to the idea of admitting Hannibal within the Servian walls. And to assault such a well-defended and populous city was never on; particularly by a general who depended so on his cavalry, men who could have little part in an escalade over guarded ramparts. Equally, to blockade the place into surrender, without a fleet to close the river route was again asking the impossible and anyway any such attempt would have given time for the legionaries and allies posted in many tens of thousands around Italy to return and crush the besieging forces.

Nor was this his strategy. From the start, Hannibal had come to Italy with the highly intelligent policy of winning over Rome's friends and allies. But he found an enemy who had somehow fallen on an extraordinary capacity to keep her supporters steadfast and close in a way that is really quite exceptional in the history of the world before that time. That meant despite years of awful war-weariness, having lost blood enough and more, Rome still kept most of her close friends tight. The Republic's USP in the marketplace of ancient imperialism was incorporation. The Romans might be compared by some to the Spartans, something that would not have made them at all unhappy, but whatever the other similarities, what they did not do was to make 'helots' of the peoples they conquered. Instead over the previous centuries the Romans had stumbled upon contrivances that enabled a kind of secure expansion that had not been available to any other empire before them. Theirs was no state based on national cohesion with sufficient power and military muscle to swiftly dominate those around them like the many and various empires that dominated west Asia, Mesopotamia and Iran for centuries. Nor a league of cities dominated by a metropolis as had occasionally risen in Greece and amongst the Etruscans. Rome rose slowly and steadily and sent roots so deep that it endured for a period of time that would have astounded the inhabitants of any of those other great states. And the secret had been and would remain the ability to incorporate into the body politic the extraordinary variety of peoples, tribes and organizations that she brought within her power, who she had usually bested in war often in the most brutal fashion. The procedure was complicated and differed over time and place but the essence was that she allowed the overpowered both to become kinds of Romans but also to retain an attachment to their original community, to be a citizen of their home town but also to be part of the Republic on the Tiber.

A range of constitutional arrangements, a 'complicated mosaic of statuses' that almost allowed people to be citizens of two places at once, that satisfied many of the aspirations of the neighbours and enemies who over many centuries she pulled into her orbit, first in Latium and then spreading out from there.[12] The process had been fundamental even from legendary times when the Sabines were amalgamated when Romulus was in charge and whose leaders would spawn great families in the Roman political firmament. But while these enjoyed complete incorporation, others remained happy with Latin rights, which if it meant they could not vote, did permit a form of social and commercial integration that gave them the wealth and status they looked for. Not that this should be seen through rose-tinted glasses; it did not make Romans some kind of internationalists. They were as chauvinistic as anybody. Life in central Italy remained dramatically Hobbesian, nasty, brutish and short, and the people as unpleasant, selfish and small-minded as in most societies. In any era, ancient or modern, a Thatcher could call out the worst in people much more easily than a Mandela can call out the best as was well shown in the wake of Cannae. Then the need to refill the Senate after so many of its members had fallen meant two dictators were appointed to solve the problem. But when a proposal was made that replacements should be chosen from the aristocracy of the Latin towns, the reaction of most was to call on the shade of an earlier xenophobe who declared that if any such turned up in the Senate house he would personally gut them on the spot.

Nor were the feelings of these friends and allies themselves uncomplicated, it was not always with unalloyed joy that they received the benefit of Roman citizenship. After all, for most people, even in Latium, exercising the vote would have meant walking for what might be days for the privilege of registering a vote in favour of some man they had never seen or heard of and certainly never knew. So this democratic delight might have been considerably less attractive than the ability to have a voice in the selection of a local man to carry out home town responsibilities that really mattered. Though there were definite handicaps for those denied the franchise, full citizens pleading their cases at court were inevitably taken more seriously by a leadership that might need their support to win election to high office. Interestingly the garrison of Casilinum that fought so well, if ultimately unsuccessfully against Hannibal in 216, was made up largely of men from the town of Praeneste and afterwards not only was their leader honoured with a statue in breastplate and toga, symbolizing his civic and military distinction, but while the people accepted an exemption from military service for five years and increased pay for their soldiers, when they were offered Roman citizenship they refused it.

But citizenship, full or Latin rites, entitlement to intermarry and carry out commerce, all made these people something very different from foreigners, from strangers. Allowing them to join a people whose army might lead them in conquests, where if they spilt their blood they could also win treasure in abundance and the impecunious might find themselves allotted wide open acres taken from the enemy for their trouble. To share in the income stream of loot and booty by participating in booming Roman military success was certainly a motivation, though it was clearly not a complete explanation, after all those allies who did transfer allegiance to Hannibal had experienced many of these benefits too. But amongst these confederates who bled profusely on behalf of Rome but gained riches in return, were those who had clearly hated that they retained little real freedom of action; that the pact they had made with a master who had bettered them after long fought wars allowed nothing more than nominal autonomy. And with some folk, often with glorious pasts to remember, this led to sufficient resentment that when the chance came they were prepared to throw over their old hegemon in the hope of prospering even more in a new world.

Yet if hindsight is 20/20, it is surely unreasonable to have expected Hannibal in Spain or his supporters in Carthage to have understood quite how tight the relationship was in central Italy between the Romans and the Latins, Volsci, Marci and the rest. And anyway that their armies might acquire a necklace of the three great pearl cities: Capua, Tarentum and Syracuse as well as the adherence of peoples in Samnium, Apulia, Lucania and elsewhere would have seemed worth doing, even if they would never be able to get any of those hard diamonds of the central belt. This achievement alone might well have seemed, to those looking in from outside, sufficient to clip the Republic's wings and reintroduce something like the balance in the middle Mediterranean that had been in place before the First Punic War. They could not reasonably have been expected to be so prescient that they would know for sure that the bonfire Hannibal was trying to light was just not quite dry enough. Perhaps it might have been a hundred years earlier when the Samnites, Etruscans and Gauls were already howling in eager confederacy in a last failed attempt to muzzle Rome and her strongholds in Apulia, Campania, Samnium and Lucania were either not yet established or were very new built. If the Carthaginians had arrived then, all might have been possible or perhaps even later, when, in the run-up to the Social War, friends and allies had become bitter and resentful against a people who had not ensured that the process of incorporation advanced in a sufficiently inclusive manner.

But arriving as he did in the middle when the gamble, if not impossible, was still a very long shot indeed, the question remains that, once up against the juggernaut of a fully mobilized Roman Republic how long did Hannibal continue to hope his strategy could succeed ? Did he really expect the arrival of Hasdrubal, and after him Mago, to make the difference of victory or defeat and what was he trying to do in his last years in Italy? What were his long term plans while he bristled in Bruttium, able to deal with all that the enemy might throw at him, yet with little prospect of breaking out of his southern redoubt? Finally why did he not return to Carthage earlier, soon after Scipio had invaded, when, with the undepleted resources of the African homeland, with a powerful Numidian ally Syphax on hand, he might have achieved so much more? We just do not have the evidence to answer these sorts of inquiries, fascinating though they are.

In terms of Carthaginian grand strategy, from the start it needs to be asked: what could have been the alternative to the strategy implemented by Hannibal? If he had waited to fight in Spain, the Romans would have sent troops to engage him there while they built up an army strong enough to invade Africa and take Carthage itself. Indeed this was exactly what they had already begun to put in train when the Carthaginian army arrived in Italy in 218. He really took the only viable option outside of capitulation or completely surrendering the initiative to his enemy and what is remarkable is not that he failed, but that he achieved so much against the odds. And in doing so involved Rome in a war that, if she was victorious, still promoted seismic changes in the people and the polity that so blithely entered into a conflict brought on by hurrying to the help of a city, who was not even a formal ally and where, according to an earlier treaty, Hannibal was well within his rights to interfere.

The resultant war had turned out extraordinary, awful and splendid and during it the people of Rome had shown the measure of their greatness. It was an age of heroes when men like Marcus Sergius, the great grandfather of the Catiline whose conspiracy would provide the background for Cicero's finest hour, who:

In his second campaign Sergius lost his right hand. In two campaigns he was wounded twenty-three times, with the result that he had no use in either hand or either foot: only his spirit remained intact. Although disabled, Sergius served in many subsequent campaigns. He was twice captured by Hannibal – no ordinary foe – from whom twice he escaped, although kept in chains and shackles every day for twenty months. He fought four times with only his left hand, while two horses he was riding were stabbed beneath him.[13]

And it was not just these individual votaries of extraordinary sacrifice, it is equally no coincidence that Machiavelli in his paean of praise to ancient armies in the *Art of War* finds many of his exemplars from the Hannibal wars. If the Romans had not quite drawn on glabrous infants to feed the war they certainly drained the manpower pool from teenagers to grizzled old men and the time was looked back on as one of glory. This was the equivalent of the USA's greatest generation who fought the Second World War, a completely justifiable defensive war when it is claimed both societies showed the very best of themselves. There is no concern here of later generations who inevitably indulged in soul-searching about Rome's entitlement to invade and conquer the rest of the Mediterranean world and could finally end with Tacitus putting in the mouth of a British chieftain called Calgacus, that Rome 'they make a wilderness, they call it peace'.[14]

The stakes had been incredibly high and it is possible to claim the changes the experience had brought to the nature of the state, saw one Rome pass away and a truly imperial one take its place, that would change the whole world around it in an extraordinarily short space of time. Certainly increasing interaction with places outside of Italy was anyway bound to have bred change, but the period that made this world shift truly inevitably had been the generation when Hannibal was at the gates. City states and great kingdoms across the Mediterranean soon would fall and be subsumed and a conquered cosmos be created that was so much more the womb of western civilization than was the experiment that took place at Athens two centuries before, despite the echoes of that earlier world being transmitted by a power that from the start accepted its indebtedness to the great Greek example.

The achievement of facing Hannibal on home soil was for the Romans their finest hour. The measure of a people that had withstood extraordinary ordeals, that had faced exhaustion and trauma but never considered coming to terms, never mind capitulating. And if this had brought pain and terror across the classes in a manner that they had hardly ever experienced before, it had also brought kudos and reputation, a very definition of 'virtus' for those who had gone through the awful time. Yet if the poison that had entered the system when Aeneas left Dido cursing his progeny before stabbing herself on a funeral pyre, had finally been washed out, some had not seen this as unalloyed joy. There were those who perceived the complete defeat of Carthage as sowing the seeds of the end of Rome's greatness, when she finally found there were no more opponents worthy of her steel, degeneration that had begun when there were no longer any significant enemies as whetstones to keep the Republic's virility honed; all leading to imperial success in later years that somehow spoilt the people and almost demanded the sort of nostalgia that envisaged contemporaries as completely incapable of holding a candle to those who had seen off Hannibal. A suggestion of moral failure that also assumed ancient mores had been tainted by foreign ways. That the values of the small farmer – diligence, hard work and respect for authority – all had been lost. And though this was the tedious cry of every age that would even have been possible to make from the first victories over Veii or local Latin rivals, after all these places produced spoils, still it was again events in the Second Punic War that had given a new dimension. It was not just the wealth but the artworks of Syracuse and Tarentum as well, when they were dumped wholesale into the streets of the capital for some would represent a turning point; when Rome would be seduced by the very refinements of those they had conquered and so begin to lose her Romanness.

Yet for the aristos who made their names, the equites who made their fortunes, or the husbandmen who won the war, the old well lauded traditions were always a function largely of memory rather than written rules and so eminently open to argument. But one thing was clear; the Roman leadership that fought the Great Italian War, whatever its profound egoism and selfishness, still had had sufficient self-control, shared values and ingrained restraints that it had been possible to sustain the Republic despite the stresses it came under. No one, whatever the military power that came into their hands, felt a sufficient imperative to seize permanent control of the state; to become the greatest among peers certainly, to gain an incomparable reputation in the history of the Republic, to try for that was a given, but there was no sign yet of any desire to stamp on the traditional ways that demanded power would be shed at the appropriate time and that all within the senatorial class should be allowed their go at the greatest prizes. But things would change and in the end it would not be foreign arms that brought the Republic down but internal tensions. Class and party strife combined with overweening personal ambition would finally make a broken polity and open the road for the roll call of Sulla, Pompey and Caesar that would end in the Empire of Augustus.

Notes and References

Introduction

1. Previously during the Samnite wars and other conflicts of the fourth and fifth centuries there had been instances of men claiming to have won the consulship four and five times.
2. Livy, *History of Rome* 23.24.
3. ibid.
4. Cassius Dio, *Epitome by Zonaras* 9. 3.
5. Suetonius, 'On the Life of the Caesars' 2. 23.
6. Walter Scheidel, 'Roman population size: the logic of the debate'.
7. Polybius, *The Histories* 2.24.
8. DS Levene, *Livy on the Hannibalic War*.
9. Polybius, *The Histories* 9. 26.
10. Polyaenus, *Stratagems* 6. 28.
11. Frontinus, *Stratagems* 3.10.

Chapter 1

1. Richard Miles, *Carthage must be Destroyed*.
2. Plutarch, *Fabius*.
3. Livy, *The History of Rome* 24. 3.

Chapter 2

1. Quintus Fabius Maximus Gurges was consul in 292 BC and campaigned with his father as a legate to win a triumph against the Samnites where his father, himself a consul five times before, rode beside his son's chariot.
2. He could do this as his lictors still had their axes because they were outside the city in the Campus Martius, so he had the power to execute even a citizen with no right of appeal.
3. Plutarch, *Fabius*.
4. Livy, *History of Rome* 14.45.
5. ibid. 14.46.
6. ibid. 14 47.
7. Strabo, *Geography* 6.3.1.
8. Polybius, *The Histories* 8. 28.
9. ibid. 8.32.
10. Appian, *War Against Hannibal*. 33.
11. Livy, *History of Rome* 15.11.

Chapter 3

1. This had occurred very occasionally in Livy's earlier books on the Samnite wars and numbers are also mentioned during the division of army between Fabius and Minucius in 217 and in 216 when Marcellus sent troops from Ostia.
2. Paul Erdkamp, 'Late-Annalistic Battle Scenes in Livy'.
3. TA Dodge, *Hannibal*.
4. TA Dodge, *Hannibal*.

Chapter 4

1. Polyaenus, *Stratagems* Book 6.38.
2. Pliny The Elder, *Natural History* 10.16.
3. Polyaenus, *Stratagems* Book 6.38.

Chapter 5

1. Livy, *The History of Rome* 16.5.
2. Polybius, *The Histories* 9.25.
3. Livy, *History of Rome* 16.9.
4. Polybius, *The Histories* 9.6.
5. ibid. 9.6.
6. Livy, *The History of Rome* 16.11.
7. ibid. 16.22.

Chapter 6

1. Pliny the Elder, *Natural History* 3.16.
2. Appian, *Hannibal's War* pp. 45–47.
3. Livy, *History of Rome* 26.39.
4. Alexander Zhmodikov, 'Roman Republican Heavy Infantrymen in Battle (IV–II Centuries BC.)'.
5. Frontinus, *Stratagems* 2.2.6.

Chapter 7

1. Plutarch, *Pyrrhus*.
2. Plutarch, *Marcellus*.
3. ibid.
4. ibid.
5. Livy, *History of Rome* 27.12.
6. Cicero, *On Duties*.
7. Cassius Dio, *Epitome by Zonaras* 16.9.8.

Chapter 8

1. Plutarch, *Marcellus*.
2. Polybius, *The Histories* 10.32.

Chapter 9

1. Livy, *History of Rome* 27.40.
2. Cassius Dio, *Epitome by Zonaras* Book 16.9.
3. Livy, *History of Rome* 27.41.

4. ibid. 31.10–11.
5. ibid. 17.46.
6. ibid. 27.47.
7. Polybius, *The Histories* 11.1.
8. Livy, *History of Rome* 28.11.
9. Plutarch, *Fabius*.

Chapter 10
1. Polybius, *The Histories* 3.59.
2. Cicero, *On Friendship*.
3. Polybius, *The Histories* 33.
4. Livy, *History of Rome* 28.46.
5. ibid. 28.46.
6. David F Epstein, *Personal Enmity in Roman Politics 218–43 BC*.

Chapter 11
1. Strabo, *Geography* 6.1.
2. Cicero, *On the Ends of Good and Evil*.
3. Herodotus, *The Histories* 3.131.
4. Livy, *History of Rome* 13.30.
5. Appian, *War against Hannibal* 56.
6. Livy, *History of Rome* 30.19.
7. Appian, *War against Hannibal* 58.

Epilogue
1. Appian, *Syrian Wars* 27.
2. Livy, *History of Rome* 37.24.
3. ibid.
4. Strabo, *Geography* 11.14.
5. Nepos, *Lives of Eminent Commanders* 23.13.
6. ibid, 23.10–11.
7. Plutarch, *Flamininus*.
8. ibid.
9. Pliny, *Natural History* 5.43.
10. Plutarch, *Flamininus*.
11. Pausanias, 8.11'10–11.
12. Mary Beard, *SPQR*.
13. Pliny the Elder, *Natural History* 7.
14. Tacitus, *Agricola* 30.

Bibliography

Ancient Sources

Appian, *War against Hannibal, Syrian war, Punic wars*
Cassius Dio, *The history of Rome*
Cicero, Collected works
Cornelios Nepos, *Lives of Eminent Commanders*
Diodorus Siculus, *Universal History*
Eutropius, *Abridgement of Roman History*
Frontinus, *Stratagems*
Livy, *The History of Rome*
Paulus Orosius, *History Against the Pagans*
Pausanias, *Description of Greece*
Plautus, *Miles Gloriosus*
Pliny the Elder, *Natural History*
Plutarch, *Parallel Lives and Moralia*
Polybius, *The Histories*
Polyaenus, *Stratagems*
Silius Italicus, *Punica*
Strabo, *The Geography*

Modern Works

Africa, Thomas W, *The One-Eyed Man against Rome: An Exercise in Euhemerism* Historia: Zeitschrift für Alte Geschichte (December, 1970).

Austin, NJE and NB Rankov, *Exploratio* (Routledge, 1995).

Badian, E, 'The Family and Early Career of T. Quinctius Flamininus' *The Journal of Roman Studies* Vol. 61 (1971).

Bagnall, Nigel, *The Punic Wars: Rome, Carthage and the Struggle for the Mediterranean* Pimlico (New Ed edition, 7 January 1999).

Bath, Tony, *Hannibal's Campaigns* (Patrick Stephens, Cambridge, 1981).

Bauman, RA, 'The Abrogation of "Imperium": Some Cases and a Principle', *Rheinisches Museum für Philologie Neue Folge* 111. Bd., H. 1 (1968), pp. 37–50.

Beard, Mary, *S.P.Q.R: A History of Ancient Rome* (Profile books, 1 April 2016).

Born, Lester K, 'Tanks and Roman Warfare', *The Classical Journal* Vol. 23, No. 8 (May, 1928).

Broodbank, Cyprian, *The Making of the Middle Sea* (Thames and Hudson, 2013).

Caven, Brian, *Dionysius I* (Yale University Press, 1990).

Caven, Brian, *The Punic Wars* (Marboro Books, New edition June, 1994).

Champion, Jeff, *The Tyrants of Syracuse* (Pen & Sword, 2012).

Charles, Michael B and Peter Rhodan, 'Magister Elephantorvm: A Reappraisal of Hannibal's Use of Elephants', *The Classical World* Vol. 100, No. 4 (Summer, 2007) pp. 363–389.

Connolly, Peter, *Greece and Rome at War* (Macdonald Phoebus Ltd, 1981).

Cook, SA, (Editor), FE Adcock, *The Cambridge Ancient History: Volume 8, Rome and Mediterranean: Rome and the Mediterranean, 218–133 BC* v. 8 Hardcover (Cambridge University Press, 1st edition, 2 January, 1930).

Coox, Alvin D, 'Son of Barca', *The Classical Journal* Vol. 43, No. 5 (February, 1948).

Cottrell, Leonard, *Hannibal enemy of Rome* (Da Capo Press, 1961.

Cowan, Ross, *For the Glory of Rome* (Greenhill Books, 2007).

Crake, JEA, 'Roman Politics from 215 to 209 BC', *Phoenix* Vol. 17, No. 2 (Summer, 1963).

Davies, RW, *The Supply of Animals to the Roman Army and the Remount System*, Latomus T. 28, Fasc. 2 (April–June, 1969).

Develin, Robert, *Prorogation of Imperium before the Hannibalic War*, Latomus T. 34, Fasc. 3 (July–September, 1975).

Dittman, Marion, 'The Development of Historiography among the Romans', *The Classical Journal* Vol. 30, No. 5 (February, 1935).

Dodge, Theodore Ayrault, *Hannibal* (Greenhill Books, London, 1994, first published 1891).

Donaldson, GH, 'Modern Idiom in an Ancient Context: Another Look at the Strategy of the Second Punic War', *Greece & Rome*, Second Series, Vol. 9, No. 2 (October, 1962).

Drogula, Fred K, 'Imperium, Potestas, and the Pomerium in the Roman Republic', *Historia: Zeitschrift für Alte Geschichte* Bd. 56, H. 4 (2007).

Epstein, David F, *Personal Enmity in Roman Politics 218–43 BC*, (Croom Helm, August, 1987).

Erdkamp, Paul, 'The Corn Supply of the Roman Armies during the Third and Second Centuries BC', *Historia: Zeitschrift für Alte Geschichte* Bd. 44, H. 2 (2nd Qtr., 1995).

Erdkamp, Paul, 'Late-Annalistic Battle Scenes in Livy' (Books 21–44), *Mnemosyne* Fourth Series, Vol. 59, Fasc. 4 (2006), pp. 525–563.

Fitton Brown, AD, 'After Cannae', *Historia: Zeitschrift für Alte Geschichte* Bd. 8, H. 3 (July, 1959).

Frank, Tenney, 'Roman Historiography before Caesar', *The American Historical Review* Vol. 32, No. 2 (January, 1927).

Glover, RF, 'The Tactical Handling of the Elephant', *Greece & Rome* Vol. 17, No. 49 (January, 1948).

Goldsworthy, Adrian, *The Fall of Carthage: The Punic Wars 265–146 BC* (Weidenfeld & Nicolson, 2003).

Goldsworthy, Adrian, *In the Name of Rome* (Weidenfeld & Nicolson, 2003).

Gowers, William and HH Scullard, 'Hannibal's Elephants Again', *The Numismatic Chronicle and Journal of the Royal Numismatic Society* Sixth Series, Vol. 10, No. 39/40 (1950).

Green Peter, *Alexander to Actium* (University of California Press, 1990).

Head, Duncan, *Armies of the Macedonian and Punic Wars 359–146 BC* (Wargames Research Group Publication, 1982).

Holland, Tom, *Rubicon* (Abacus, New Ed edition, 10 June, 2004).

Hoyos, Dexter, 'Maharbal's Bon Mot: Authenticity and Survival', *The Classical Quarterly* New Series, Vol. 50, No. 2 (2000).

Hoyos, BD, 'Hannibal: What Kind of Genius?', *Greece & Rome* Second Series, Vol. 30, No. 2 (October, 1983).

Jaeger, Mary, 'Livy, Hannibal's Monument, and the Temple of Juno at Croton', *Transactions of the American Philological Association* (1974–) Vol. 136, No. 2 (Autumn, 2006).

Lancel, Serge, *Hannibal* (Wiley-Blackwell, New Ed edition, 5 October, 1999).

Lamb, Harold, *Hannibal* (Robert Hale Ltd, 1959).

Latte, Kurt, 'The Origin of the Roman Quaestorship', *Transactions and Proceedings of the American Philological Association* Vol. 67, (1936).

Lazenby, JF, *Hannibal's War* (Aris & Phillips, 1978).

Lendon, JE, *Soldiers and Ghosts* (Yale University Press, 2005).

Levene, DS, *Livy on the Hannibalic War* (Oxford, 2010).

McCall, Jeremiah, *The Cavalry of the Roman Republic*, (London, 2001).

Messer, William Stuart, 'Mutiny in the Roman Army, The Republic', *Classical Philology* Vol. 15, No. 2 (April, 1920), pp. 158–175.

Miles, Richard, *Carthage Must Be Destroyed: The Rise and Fall of an Ancient Civilization* (Penguin, 24 February 2011).

Moeller, Walter O, 'Once More the One-Eyed Man against Rome', *Historia: Zeitschrift für Alte Geschichte* Bd. 24, H. 3 (3rd Qtr., 1975).

Montagu, John Drogo, *Greek and Roman Warfare*, (Greenhills Books, 2006).

Muecke, Frances, 'Hannibal at the 'Fields of Fire': A 'Wasteful Excursion'?', Silius Italicus, *Punica 12, Materiali e discussioni per l'analisi dei testi classici* No. 58 (2007), pp. 113–157.

Oakley, SP, 'Single Combat in the Roman Republic', *The Classical Quarterly New Series* Vol. 35, No. 2 (1985).

Paget, RF, 'The Ancient Ports of Cumae', *The Journal of Roman Studies* Vol. 58, Parts 1 and 2 (1968).

Peddie, John, *Hannibal's War* (Sutton Publishing, 1997).

Penrose, Jane, editor, *Rome and her Enemies* (Osprey Publishing, 2005).

Piper, Deryck J, 'Latins and the Roman Citizenship in Roman Colonies: Livy' 34, 42,5–6; *Revisited, Historia: Zeitschrift für Alte Geschichte* Bd. 36, H. 1 (1st Qtr., 1987).

Rankin, David, *Celts and the Classical World* (Routledge, London and New York, 1987).

Reid, JS, 'Problems of the Second Punic War', *The Journal of Roman Studies* Vol. 3, Part 2, (1913).

Ridley, RT, 'Was Scipio Africanus at Cannae?' *Latomus* T. 34, Fasc. 1 (January–March, 1975).

Rosenstein, Nathan, 'Marriage and Manpower in the Hannibalic War: "Assidui", "Proletarii" and Livy' 24.18.7–8, *Historia: Zeitschrift für Alte Geschichte* Bd. 51, H. 2 (2nd Qtr., 2002).

Rosenstein, Nathan, 'War, Failure, and Aristocratic Competition', *Classical Philology* Vol. 85, No. 4 (October, 1990), pp. 255–265.

Sabin, Philip, *Lost Battles* (Hambledon Continuum, 2007).

Scullard, HH, *A History of the Roman World 753–146 BC* (Routledge, first published 1935).

Scullard, HH, *Scipio Africanus: Soldier and Politician (Aspects of Greek and Roman Life)* (First edition, Thames & Hudson Ltd, 23 February 1970).

Sidnell, Philip, *Warhorse* (Hambledon Continuum, 2006).

Sumner, GV, 'The Legion and the Centuriate Organization', *The Journal of Roman Studies* Vol. 60, (1970).

Sumner, GV, 'Elections at Rome in 217 BC', *Phoenix* Vol. 29, (1975).

Vishnia, Rachel Feig, 'The Shadow Army: The Lixae and the Roman Legions', *Zeitschrift für Papyrologie und Epigraphik* Bd. 139, (2002).

Walbank, Frank, *A Historical Commentary on Polybius* (Oxford, 1979).

Yalichev, Serge, *Mercenaries of the Ancient World*, (Constable, London, 1997).

Zhmodikov, Alexander, 'Roman Republican Heavy Infantrymen in Battle (IV–II Centuries BC)', *Historia: Zeitschrift für Alte Geschichte* Bd. 49, H. 1 (1st Qtr., 2000).

Index